MW00779053

GREAT LAKES
SHIPWRECKS &
LIGHTHOUSES

True Stories of Courage & Bravery

WES OLESZEWSKI

Avery Color Studios, Inc.
Gwinn, Michigan

©2005 Avery Color Studios, Inc.

ISBN 1-892384-31-0

Library of Congress Control Number: 2004115509

First Edition 2005

Published by
Avery Color Studios, Inc.
Gwinn, Michigan 49841

Cover photos:
The *E.M. Ford*, Huron Cement photo
The Point Iroquois Lighthouse, Whitefish Bay, Michigan

Publishers note: Originally published as *Keepers of Valor* in 2000. Revised and updated by the author in 2005, as *Great Lakes Shipwrecks & Lighthouses*.

To my cousin Susan,

We all grew up together, same subdivision, same streets, same playground, same pools, same bikes, same school, same classrooms and same teachers. To this day, Susan recalls the way that our fourth grade teacher tormented me without end because I refused to read the "Dick and Jane" dribble that was presented for our consumption and the fuss that was made because "Wes wouldn't read". In that recollection, she wishes that she could take all of the eight books that I have written to date, and "stick 'em in that teacher's face."

To you, Susan, this book is lovingly dedicated, and provided for you to shove toward anyone that you find deserving.

TABLE OF CONTENTS

PREFACE

"Pan pan, pan pan, this is the United States Coast Guard group Tawas with a broadcast to all vessels..." the voice crackles across VHF marine channel 16, "...a vessel is reported afire between Charity Island and Sand Point, all vessels in that area are requested to keep a lookout and inform the nearest Coast Guard Station of any vessel in distress..." In the keeping of the constant vigilance across Lake Huron the crew of Tawas Station has been alerted to only the suspicion of a boat in distress. If needed the station's crew can man the 44-foot motor lifeboat, or MLB and charge out onto the lake. At more than 170 miles-per-hour an HH-65 Dolphin helicopter can be rushed to the scene and lower a rescue basket or drop rescue divers into the water. The whole operation being coordinated by VHF radio on channels 16, 21, and 22. Looking across the horizon a billow of dense black smoke is visible in the distance. This time, however, the smoke turns out to be a fire on the Michigan mainland and no vessel is involved. No lives are in peril so once again the Coast Guard machine shifts into the standby mode silently maintaining its vigil across the waters. Out on Tawas Point, the building that was the original Ottawa Point Lifesaving Station from 1876 sets idle and in fear of the next vandal. BMC Smith, the Tawas Station commander does all that he can to protect the building, but it is a losing fight. The budgets are far too low and the manpower too scarce, while the attitude of the public is too ignorant, to preserve this place of historical significance. Fear is that the vandals will soon claim this structure in a senseless act of destruction in spite of the Tawas Point crew's vigilance. Meanwhile, at the Tawas Point Lighthouse, a Coast Guardsman patiently stands in the doorway to the light as a line of eager tourists clad in lighthouse-embossed garments wait their turn to visit the light. He warns each of the lighthouse buffs of watching their heads as they enter the door, and then watches as they experience the light firsthand. The job of lighthouse keeper is a bit different in 1998 than it was in 1898 and indeed the job of lifesaving is different for the United States Coast Guard than it was for the United States Life Saving Service. All around the Great Lakes the story is much the same for the modern storm warriors. Their existence is tedium peppered with terror. In doing the job of the Coast Guard its members often act in the finest traditions of the old United States Life-Saving Service and they usually do not even realize it. You see, the United States Coast Guard is the direct descendent of the United States Life Saving Service and the United States Lighthouse Board. Their tradition of bravery and vigilance against the vengeful Great Lakes dates all of the way back to the mid 1850s.

In an era when the job of the Coast Guard crews has often been relegated to the attending of pleasure-boaters who continually insist upon running out of gas, sailing into weather beyond their capability and idly chatting across the emergency airwaves of channel 16, many of the modern-day Coast Guard personnel may feel a great detachment from their predecessors in the Life Saving Service and Lighthouse Board. When asked, "What do you know of the old lifesavers?" most Coast Guard folks reply that they recall little or nothing about the surfmen of the past, but that they really want to know more. Likewise, it is the same response when considering the lighthouse keepers. The modern-day Coast Guard personnel attached to tending the now automated lights sense a kinship, but are not intimately acquainted with those keepers with whom they share the bond. This response is due to the fact that all storm warriors feel the same calling. The need is to stand vigilant, to launch toward rescue and to do their duty.

Along the East Coast of the United States, shipwrecks had become so numerous from the mid-1700s to the mid-1800s that some coastal residents actually earned a living from the flotsam that would wash ashore after the wreck of a merchant vessel. These shipwreck scavengers were called "moon-cussers," the name having been derived from the fact that such people would cuss the moon when it shined brightly in the night, because on those nights a vessel was far less likely to wreck on their beach. Often, mariners wrecked very near the shore were left to perish aboard a crumbling ship because there was no way to reach across the breaking surf and bring them to safety. Their bodies would wash ashore while the moon-cussers waited to plunder the cargo and fixtures that would soon follow. Rarely was anyone brave enough to strike out in a boat and attempt a rescue, and even then there was no real method or training that would allow such attempts to succeed. More often, anyone who attempted a rescue became a part of the death toll. From the state of Maine to the sands of the Carolinas, the beaches of the East Coast were one long graveyard. In light of the toll that the seas were taking, State Representative William Newell of New Jersey had been pushing for a government-sponsored service that would give rescue to those in distress on the waters. His involvement led to Congress appropriating the sum of $10,000 toward the establishment of coastal lifeboat stations staffed by volunteer crews from the local communities. The object was not for the rescue of property, but for the saving of lives. No doubt the moon-cussers had little objection because now there would be fewer dead bodies in the way of their pickings.

As soon as the stations were in place, the numbers of shipwrecked persons being saved started to grow. On the Great Lakes in 1854, a large number of lifeboats were dispersed, but they were placed in the possession of bonded caretakers, and no provision for housing, staffing or record-keeping was made. Still, the intention remained for local citizens to volunteer in rescue efforts. There developed some problems in the volunteer crewing of the lifeboats. When a shipwreck occurred in the vicinity of a lifeboat station, often it took a considerable amount of time and effort to muster the lifeboat crew. Also, when the equipment was left unattended in protracted storage in wait of a wreck, it tended to deteriorate. Once the crew was mustered, they often pulled equipment to the beach that simply fell apart. What was needed was a series of stations that were fully-manned by disciplined crews who would maintain both equipment and constant vigilance, and in 1871 it happened. That year Congress invested $200,000 for the establishment of full-time lifesaving stations. Many of these new stations on the Upper Lakes were established in locations where lighthouses were already in existence. On Lake Huron in 1876, for example, the Life Saving Service established the first stations at Pointe aux Barques, Tawas Point, Sturgeon Point, and Thunder Bay Island, and all were located near the local lighthouse. Tactically, this was a very wise decision, as lighthouses are normally constructed in the most treacherous of locations and, thus, that is where a shipwreck is the most likely to occur. There was also the side benefit of establishing a station where a government installation was already in existence.

Word got out quickly that brave men were needed by the Life Saving Service who would be duty-sworn to place their lives between the lake and shipwrecked souls. To sign up meant that the individual would trade in his title of local citizen for that of "surfman" and that he was enlisted in a war against the mighty lake. At any time the lake may have to be faced and without regard to their personal safety, the surfmen would be called to their duty. The individuals of the service would keep and hold the honor of their calling based on their performance alone. Failure to do so would have the results of the most dire consequences. For all of this, the surfmen would be paid $40 per month but would gain no retirement or medical benefits and would have cash deducted for meals. In comparison, an assistant lighthouse keeper, such as Alexander Esler at the Pointe aux Barques Station, made $33.33 a month with no deductions. Also, any Great Lakes mariner could make more than $60 per month acting as nothing more than a deckhand and gain a full belly courtesy of the vessel owners. Crews that manned the new lifesaving stations were to be selected from the most hardy of the local population based on their mariner's skills and physical fitness. For the most part, just like their Coast Guard kin of the future, these were brave and honest fellows who had a passion for that rescue which may occur in the season ahead. Most of the surfmen were true storm warriors. Unfortunately, there were a few who were attracted by the image alone and others who were hired based on political or family connections. The low pay, strict discipline and duty, plus the poor motives that attracted some to the service, often resulted in dismissals and desertions. There were always others who were ready to answer the call. The service would survive and grow in spite of the hardships and because of its people.

Following its 1871 establishment, the United States Life Saving Service came to the Great Lakes in 1876. Stations were constructed at strategic points where it was believed that mariners may find themselves in distress. In all, 16 fully-staffed "lifesaving" stations were placed around the lakes and the same number of "lifeboat" stations were opened. "District 8" consisted of the shores of Lakes Ontario and Erie with stations established at Big Sandy Creek and Salmon Creek (both in eastern Mexico Bay), Oswego, Charlotte, Buffalo, Presque Isle, Fairport, Cleveland and Point Marblehead. The first stations in what was called "District 9" were placed on Lake Huron at Pointe aux Barques, Tawas Point (then called Ottawa Point), Sturgeon Point (between Oscoda and Alpena), Thunder Bay Island (off of Alpena) and Forty Mile Point (halfway between Alpena and Mackinaw City), and on Lake Superior at Vermilion Point (just west of Whitefish Point), then at a location exactly seven miles west of the Vermilion station at what became known as Crisp Point, at Two Heart River and at the Sucker River just west of Deer Park. Lake Michigan, at that time, had so much vessel traffic that it was considered as being a district all by itself. Stations in Lake Michigan's "District 10" were located at Beaver Island, North Manitou Island, Point Betsie (then called Point aux Bec Scies), Grand Point au Sable, Grand Haven, Saint Joseph, Chicago, Racine, Milwaukee, Sheboygan, and Two Rivers (then listed as Twin Rivers). An additional Lake Michigan station at Evanston was under construction in that first season. The stations were located in areas where it was thought that shipwrecks would most likely occur. In later years, more stations were added until the total number of stations stood at 64. The locations were actually quite well-considered as most shipwrecks in the years ahead did happen in the areas of the stations, and few were out of reach of the service.

Crews manned these stations from late March until late December keeping almost the same seasonal schedule as the lighthouse keepers. A watch was kept on the lake 24 hours a day, seven days a week, but unlike the lighthouse keepers, the surfman's watch was supplemented by on-foot beach patrols that extended from two to four miles out from the station in all kinds of weather, from dusk until dawn. On the Great Lakes, this duty went on from the opening of navigation in early April until the close of navigation in December. Station crews practiced their rescue techniques nearly every day in a regimented weekly schedule that included use of the surf boat and lifeboat and firing of lines across a mock ship's mast. Interestingly, the drills with the lifeboat involved rowing out into the lake and deliberately capsizing the craft. Then the surfmen had to right their lifeboat and continue rowing. A time limit of two minutes was said to be the limit for successfully completing the maneuver. Most crews could capsize and re-right in under 20 seconds, and some boasted times such as 11 seconds. A form of artificial respiration, then called "restoration of the apparently drowned," was also practiced each week. And there always were drills in the setting of the beach equipment. Stations, regardless of their remoteness, were kept in the most immaculate and orderly condition and crews wore uniforms embroidered with their ranking number on the left arm. The proud life-ring with crossed oar and boat hook initials "U.S.L.S.S." was on the right arm. From its beginnings the service was one of duty, valor, sacrifice and honor.

A long list of equipment was supplied to the stations, the most important of which was the station's surf boat, Lyle gun, breeches buoy and the Coston signals. Surf boats were sleek two-ended rowing boats that were self-bailing, meaning that when flooded, the water was able to flow back out through a system of one-way flappers as the boat crested the next wave. The boats were designed to slice through breaking waves and like it. The Lyle gun was a small cannon designed to shoot a projectile and line out to a stranded vessel where the shipwrecked crew could use it to haul in the breeches buoy. A breeches buoy is much like a large pair of shorts sewn into a life-ring and gets its name from the term "britches." Much the same as a hand-held flare, the Coston signal was used to warn or acknowledge mariners at a distance. Along with these tools, plus a vast assortment of other devices and equipment, the lifesavers proceeded to write one of the most thrilling and colorful chapters in Great Lakes maritime history. Then nearly the entire adventure was closed and forgotten.

Lifesavers on the lakes rescued or assisted 55,639 souls from the vengeance of the Great Lakes, and many of these events were spectacular feats of heroism. Their efforts and duties went far beyond the dramatic rescues, however. It was not uncommon for the surfmen to dash to the rescue of swimmers in trouble, pleasure boaters in grief and kids on rafts who ventured too far into the lake. Dock and house fires were extinguished, horses and cows rescued, and drunks given shelter all in the duty of the U.S.L.S.S. In 1899, one surfman even rescued and revived a worker from a Chicago sewer!

Lighthouses and the Lighthouse Board came to the Great Lakes long before the Life Saving Service. The first lighthouse on the Great Lakes was constructed around 1803 at Mississuga Point near the mouth of the Niagara River. Standing 45 feet tall and constructed of stone, the lighthouse was commissioned and erected by the Canadian Government. Colonel Isaac Brock, who was in command of Fort George, 4th Battalion, Royal Artillery at the time, was ordered to select one soldier from his troops to tend to this light. The man selected was Dominic Henry, who thus became the first lighthouse keeper on the Great Lakes. Sources indicate that he served with that light from 1804 to 1814.

From that point on, navigation on the Great Lakes would be expanding and so would the ranks of lighthouses and their keepers. A careful analysis of the records seems to show "spurts" of lighthouse activity and construction. Around 1822, a large number of lighthouses were established on the Lower Lakes, and between 1850 and 1859 a number of lights were established on the Upper Lakes. Additionally, there was an effort to "modernize" many lights in the late 1850s. Following the Civil War, commerce on the lakes began a series of "booms" in growth as did lakes navigation. For that reason there was another spurt in lighthouse activity, from 1866 to 1878. Thereafter, lighthouse establishment and improvement took on a more measured pace with lights being constructed and replaced at a more regular and even rate across all of the lakes. The final small spurt of activity came during the Depression years of the 1930s. It would seem odd that new lighthouses would be constructed and established in a time when lakes navigation was at its lowest volume in history, but the fact was that these Depression-era lights were a small part of a vast government program to use public works projects to bolster employment. The final spurt in lighthouse activity continues today, as the lighthouses are being abandoned by the Coast Guard and turned over as surplus property. In between all of this activity, the keepers of the lakes lights have gone from being British Red Coats to Lighthouse Board appointees, to Coast Guard duty personnel, to private owners and preservationists. Oddly, the lighthouses still retain their history, their stories and their ghosts. The lifesaving stations and their heritage, however, are all but lost.

Still, the modern storm warriors go on doing the best they can, often with slim budgets. Much like the days of the U.S.L.S.S., the bureaucrats in Washington, D.C. often place the Coast Guard at the bottom of the list of military spending when funds are disbursed, and at the top of the list when budgets are cut. The lifesaving stations and lighthouses are left to fend off the elements on a budget shoestring. Yet, the Coast Guard remains the one branch of the U.S. Government whose members are sworn to risk their lives in order to save your life. It is an interesting paradox that the politicians who are elected on the promises of making our lives better will find such little use for a division of the military sworn to rescue us from death.

ACKNOWLEDGEMENTS

It is always the name of the author that appears on the cover and binding of every book. Yet without many other people lending assistance and contributing facts, no single book of nonfiction could ever be successfully produced. Fortunately, the publishers are kind enough to allow each author the opportunity to give credit where it is due within the Acknowledgments section of the book. Since the assembly of a text such as this takes years—often individual chapters are started, stopped and restarted—it is likely that some of the people who have helped could be easily overlooked. I will say, however, that I have done my best to make sure that everyone is mentioned.

Persons who guard, manage, and tend to the lighthouses are essential in the making of a book like this. Such people are Ray and Martha Janderwski of the Pointe aux Barques Lighthouse, who were very helpful in the construction of chapters involving that site; Bernard Hellstorm, who offered much insight as to the needs of the abandoned lights, and Thomas Taylor, the Ponce De Leon Inlet Lighthouse historian was more than helpful with his inside tour and expert information on the restoration of lenses and nearly every other aspect of lighthouse preservation. Boatswains Mate Chief, E.R. Smith at the Tawas Point Light deserves thanks for his help and insight. Importantly, no book of Great Lakes lighthouses can be produced without the acknowledgment of one of the deans of lighthouse historians on the freshwater seas—Jack Edwards. One can learn more about the lights of the lakes by simply chatting on the phone with Jack than by accessing the accumulation of every text in the lighthouse section of any bookstore.

Historians of the Great Lakes in general also played a major role in the production of this book. Dave Swayze is always just a few computer keystrokes away, and often provides important information at the speed of light. Likewise, Richard Palmer can be counted upon to provide answers to anything that can be asked concerning Lake Ontario. The reclusive but highly respected Ralph Roberts is one of the best sources on the planet for needed history. Fellow lighthouse author and dean of shipwreck authors, Fred Stonehouse, is always there to share information. Research divers Roy Pickering and Cris Kohl did their best to help with making the details clear. Thanks must appropriately go to Rick Peuser and Rebecca Livingston of the National Archives, and Suzette Lopez and the staff of the Milwaukee Public Library. Special thanks are in order to Noel McFarland, David Scali, and Carla LaVigne of the Great Lakes Historical Society, for their quick response to my calls for help. Likewise, Charles Hoover, Sandy Schwan and Sherri Green of the Historical Society of Saginaw County were of great help. Kay and Joe VanDosen, caretakers of Point Iroquois

Lighthouse, deserve thanks, as well as Kristi Merren and Mary McWilliams, who also volunteer at Point Iroquois. Gretchen Duever of the Huron City Museum also deserves thanks, although she wasn't quite sure if I was a real author or just boasting.

There are also the staffs of the libraries who have tolerated my endless sessions at their microfilm machines. For all of the times I ran out of copy paper and toner I wish to thank the people of the Bay City Branch Library, Port Huron Public Library, Annapolis Public Library, and most of all the staff and director of the Nimitz Library at the U.S. Naval Academy. In particular, Mary Felton of the Hoyt Public Library's research room was helpful to this author.

In conclusion, there is my family to thank for putting up with my author's ways—my wife Teresa, my dad Walt, mom Sue, sisters Jeanine and Karen, and my brother Craig, as well as my in-laws, Andy, Akie, and Karen.

To all that I have mentioned, and to anyone who I may have missed, I offer my gratitude for your input and aid in the making of this book.

INTRODUCTION

What you are holding is a book of "factual historical narrative." In other words, this is a collection of absolutely true stories of real adventures, of real people and actual places on the Great Lakes. This is not a textbook, not a school book, not a technical report nor an encyclopedia. This book is also not written as a docudrama or a work of fiction. The text within these pages contains the sagas of some of the most obscure and thrilling events that can be told of the lighthouse keepers, lifesavers and lake mariners. It is presented for the reader's enjoyment and discovery. Some enjoy being teleported to another time and place by the reading of these stories. Others enjoy the detailed description of events of which they had not before been aware. Still others enjoy researching the events described in these tales, and a few enjoy picking apart my work bit by bit. It is all the same path of discovery and that is one purpose of this book.

Along this path of discovery you will find people who, in the face of what seemed like an insane lake, performed acts of courage that sometimes defy explanation. These individuals find valor within their souls and remain true to it, often with a frozen death hanging over them at every moment. They are the tenders of bravery and often have only that to use against what seems like a lake bent on vengeance. Sometimes the person wins, sometimes the lake wins, but the story is always inspirational. Then there are the people who, through nothing more than common decency and a willingness to help someone in need, became heroes without really knowing that they had done so. Lastly there are those who attempted to act as a hero, but were robbed by the lakes. Considering that we live in a time when a person needs to do little other than sink a basketball, toss a football, sing a song, play a likable character on our television, or make an empty political promise in front of the cameras in order to attain hero status. It is important to remember that those who are mentioned within this book performed actual acts of courage, they did real things of bravery and are thus true heroes. Researching their stories has been a refreshing toil for this author, refreshing indeed.

In the effort to reconstruct these events, this author has gone to great lengths to get the stories straight. The method used in creating this text is threefold. First, documented sources from the same era as the event in question are used and cross referenced to gain the chronology of the activity. Sourcing the events can be a time-consuming task, and is often filled with traps and puzzles. In the case of the burning of the steamer *Annie Young*, for example, the only existing record of the captain's account of the wreck was copied into microfilm with an angular fold running right down the text! That same microfilm was later badly scratched, thus adding to the obliteration of the words. Salvage of this information required transcribing all of the words, letter-by-letter and then filling in the missing spaces like a word puzzle in order to recover most of what the captain had to say.

On occasion, modern sources are used to gain data that relates to the events, but I find that reliance on modern sources can become a trap to avoid. Often, modern published accounts of events in Great Lakes maritime history are garnished with twisted information, myth, hearsay and just plain concoction. In one example of this, an account of the schooner *Ariadne's* dilemma, published in 1995, detailed the lifesavers using their beach gun to fire a line over the boat. However, the official records of the action taken by the lifesavers, as well as local newspaper reports of the event clearly show that the lifesavers never even removed the beach apparatus, which includes the gun, from the station. These official records, the *Annual Reports*, were not only a record of actions, but were also accounting documents used to demonstrate to Congress of the United States the need for the service and its supplies. The more the equipment was used, the better the next year's appropriation of funds would likely be. Every time a beach gun was fired in a rescue action, it was reported. The 1995 published inaccuracy was either the result of sloppy research, or simply the over-active imagination of that particular writer. In order to get around these types of inaccuracies, I prefer to go to original sources and work both forward and backward. It is important to you, the reader, and to the memory of the folks who worked the boats and stations who are documented in this text, that their stories be told as closely to the actual events as possible.

The second method used in writing these stories is an investigation of the event in question. I like to put aside opinion and lore and look at the events with the same type of mind-set that modern investigators from the National Transportation Safety Board would use. Often, human factors can lead to as many conclusions as can physics. Although it may seem nice to romance about mariners and the sea, to me that does not answer the many questions that surround these tales. We must start with a blank sheet and gather evidence from all areas, and then synthesize a "probable" cause. It is also too easy to say, "On this date and at this place this boat wrecked on the beach." At that point I end up asking "Why did it wreck on that beach?" Often the answer to that question leads us to a whole new dimension in the event as well as a score of new questions.

In the third aspect—that of construction of this text—I have put each story into a factual and descriptive narrative. Facts of shipwreck, lighthouse and lifesaving rescues are nice to have, but it is only when we look at them with a human element attached, that their true impact hits us. When the human aspect of each event is considered, and names and personalities are attached where they belong, we can really experience the vengeance of the lakes and the bravery of those who challenge them. In order to do that I must put you, the reader, at that event. I must turn the pages that you read into your own time machine, while attempting to avoid the trappings of the pop-culture's docudrama, and at the same time resisting the temptation to just make things up. I have found that the facts of a story are always more thrilling and dramatic than almost anything that a writer can concoct. Although the adage is true that "there are as many ways to tell a story as there are story tellers," the facts will never let you down.

As the author, I do not normally publish things that I can not find in writing from sources of the same time period of the event. In some cases, however, by interpolating between published facts it is possible to draw conclusions regarding probable movement of individuals and vessels. In those instances I have indicated clearly that what is being given to the reader at that point is only speculation. Not being one of those "lettered historians" who finds that a Ph.D. is a license to suck all of the fun out of history, I have synthesized some dialogue. Such discourse adds to the readability of the story. Not all of the dialogue, however, is synthetic as I have usually mixed it with quotes found in written accounts of the events. The reader may be assured that bits of dialogue are the only parts of the stories that are devised.

The effort to research the smallest detail is most of the fun in constructing these tales. My parents can testify to a spring evening while I visited their Michigan home on a research trip. After a long day in a local library, I sat poring over a stack of photocopies in a vain attempt to find the last loading dock of the schooner *Dolphin*. Frustrated, I decided that since I had everything ever written about this vessel's final passing, the name of the dock was apparently never recorded. My mom said, "You know, you could just pick a dock, and no one would ever know the difference." Aghast at such a suggestion I replied, "I'd know, and so would the six people who sailed her out of the Saginaw River 110 years ago." Perhaps such details seem trivial to most folks, but I feel that this job demands attention to such detail while keeping the reader's interest. History can be dry and no fun at all, but then you have to write it that way, and I simply can not.

Spellings of names can drive a researcher nuts. For example, in one event the spelling of the name of Sutherland McKay was also spelled "Southerland" in another source. I used the *United States Life Saving Service Annual Report's* spelling because I found the other source, in my opinion, to be less reliable. In the case of the schooner *Dolphin*, one crew member had his name reported as "Alfred" and "Albert." Through extensive digging, I discovered his sister quoted as calling him "Fred," so I went with that. Additionally, there are many occasions when a person's name is given only as initials; in those cases that is what you will read. I often say that when I visit the lakeshore, I look out across the waters and sands and visualize the wrecks and rescues of the past. When I get up each morning and look in the mirror, in my mind I see behind me the images of crowds of bygone mariners, waiting patiently for their stories to be told. For some reason I hold that responsibility, so the least I can do is try to get their names right and their details straight.

Confusion within original sources can also give a person fits when attempting to reassemble these types of events. And a foul-minded critic can even attack and attempt to discredit legitimate sources. For example, the *Annual Reports of the United States Life Saving Service* have been assaulted on at least one occasion. These documents, however, were official reports presented before the United States Congress. If they are not a legitimate source, what is? In the construction of this text, great use has been made of the reports, but in most cases, the facts were checked via other sources giving a multiple-sided view of the event. Being a person who deals in the most obscure of Great Lakes events, I sometimes find that a single source is all that points to a given aspect of a story, and that no other source exists. In that case the choice is to not write the whole story, or just present what is available. I choose to present the story. Additionally, we research historians of the Great Lakes are constantly correcting and assembling documentation on a daily basis. I am not always 100 percent correct, and admit it. Anyone who tells you that they are correct all of the time probably wants your vote, so the best that I can say is that I did my utmost to bring you these tales and make them as complete as I was able.

In the telling of these stories, I feel very much as if I have gotten to know people such as Lon Cross, Martha Hart, Joseph Sawyer, Thomas Cox , Abbot Way, Frank Hackett, Thomas Currie, Fred Perry, and many others. Perhaps by reading their stories, you will come to know these people too. It is important to keep in mind that these are all true stories, and the names that you read are those of real people who actually experienced the events as described. These are not fictional characters created by some Hollywood writing staff. The stories here are all authentic and all of the pain, frostbite, fire, bravery and sorrow actually happened. When next you visit the Great Lakes, it is my hope that you will take this book in hand, look out across their fresh water splendor and remember those who have had their stories recorded within these pages.

COURAGE AND REVENGE

Dispatched from Tri-City Airport on the outskirts of the town of Freeland, Michigan in the bone-dry summer heat of 1988, a tiny Cessna 150 buzzed like an insect and headed directly toward Saginaw Bay and the glistening expanse of Lake Huron. The mission was one of routine involving a course that would start in the pocket of the bay and follow the shore around the thumb of Michigan and down to the St. Clair County Airport near Port Huron. Aboard the two-seat Cessna were a pilot and an observer from the Michigan Department of Natural Resources, and their job was simply to survey and count the fishermen on the shores, docks and boats along their route. As the aircraft leveled at 1,000 feet above the lake the DNR observer went to work, busily clicking his counter and scribbling the totals on his clipboard. For the pilot the toil was substantially less exciting as all that there was to do from his seat was to maintain altitude and follow the coast. Often, the DNR surveyman, who was supposed to be counting, also wished to "steer," so the work could gain a greater degree of dullness for the aircraft's pilot. It is said that professional aviation is endless hours of boredom garnished with moments of pure terror. On this day, at least the first half of that adage was holding true. In fact for the pilot there was little more to do other than monitor the engine instruments and look out at the lakeshore below as Sand Point, Oak Point, Flat Rock Point, and Pointe aux Barques passed below. Shortly after passing the Port Austin Reef lighthouse, the diminutive aircraft turned south toward Port Huron, and the end of the first leg of the day's trip.

It was at that moment that something in the bolder-peppered shallows below caught the pilot's eye. For a moment he thought that he was looking at an odd outcropping of rocks, but an instant later it dawned upon him that what had just passed below was the outline of a long-forgotten shipwreck.

"Knock it off for a minute." he told the DNR man, "I've got the aircraft...," as he pulled the Cessna into a tight left bank somewhat beyond what the passenger was accustomed to.

"What!?" the observer queried in a near panic as the horizon ahead tilted toward 50 degrees, "What's wrong!?"

"Nothing," he was assured by the airman, "I just saw something down there."

Seconds later the little aircraft was circling atop the reef.

"There," the pilot indicated to his observer, "right down there, it's an old wooden shipwreck."

Beneath the circling airplane the transparent waters revealed two distinctive hull-shaped shadows. The water was less than a dozen feet deep and the clear image of a wooden ship's keel, ribs and planking could be seen. The apparition in the sands appeared to be well within a mile of shore, and vacation cabins were all around the area. Indeed, the area immediately below the distracted survey flight was the sight of a Great Lakes maritime disaster of the past. Certainly, the wreck could not have been there without someone knowing which one it is. In haste a navigational chart was broken out, and fixes were taken from local electronic navigation aids. The spot was the reef off of Burnt Cabin Point, about one-half of a mile off shore. Crystal waves rolled peacefully below, but in the aircraft above there came an overwhelming feeling, as if that very spot radiated a disturbing sensation, one of both courage and revenge long since past. Looking down from the aircraft it was easy to imagine the images of struggling mariners, intrepid lifesavers and an ice-coated vessel twisted in its death throes. Certainly, for the men in the aircraft, it was not difficult to picture all of the players in a shipwreck while looking down upon the scene. Yet the two airborne observers could not envision the extent of the tragic play that had actually been performed on the ice water stage below. It was the setting of a disastrous performance that has given curtain calls as recently as the 1960s.

"So..." the puzzled DNR observer pondered aloud, "I wonder how it got there?"

Oblivious to the aircraft circling overhead, the shattered timbers of the once-proud laker sulked silently beneath the clear sheet of Lake Huron. For more than a century they had rested on the bottom as the lake attempted to make them its own. Oddly, after 111 sailing seasons the hulk remained waiting for someone to discover its story. You see, in doing the research it was found that not a single resident of those local cabins, and not a single boater from the local marinas was aware that this old wreck was resting in the shallows off of Burnt Cabin Point. Over the decades, she has become one of the overlooked shipwrecks waiting for someone, anyone, to rediscover her story of woe—and you, the reader, will be among the first to do so. Like all tales of the lakes it is a story that extends far beyond that one individual wreck, and requires that we spin the clock back across the expanse of history. In doing so we must go to another time and place and meet persons who have long since passed on.

Lieutenant Thomas D. Walker's office at Number 16 Broadway, in the city of New York, seemed about as far away from the ice water fury of the Great Lakes in autumn as a person could get. Yet, Lieutenant Walker's position as Assistant Inspector of lifesaving stations was about to send him to one of the most treacherous spots on the fresh water seas. It was Friday, November 23, 1877, and having taken a foothold in the Great Lakes region just a year earlier, the U.S. Life Saving Service was currently in its infancy on the fresh water seas. Now an ugly charge of neglect of duty had been levied against the service, and Lieutenant Walker was being dispatched to investigate the matter. The letter centered on the inspector's desk directed him to proceed at once to Lifesaving Station Number 1, District Number 9, Pointe aux Barques, Lake Huron, in order to investigate all of the circumstances surrounding the loss of the schooner *Berlin*. Apparently, a group of local residents had charged that the keeper and crew of the Pointe aux Barques station had failed to respond properly to the vessel's distress, and this was a black mark that the newfound service could ill afford. Walker was to interview all persons involved in this matter and submit a written report directly to the Secretary of the United States Treasury, the honorable John Sherman. In short order Inspector Walker had packed his bags and boarded the first train headed west. He would get to the bottom of these charges, of that there would be no doubt!

On Monday, November 26, 1877, Inspector Walker stepped from the clouds of steam that hedged the railroad platform at the Detroit train station and was met by District 9 Superintendent Joseph Sawyer. A brief handshake was followed by a letter handed to the inspector by a stone-faced Superintendent Sawyer. On the carriage ride through the streets of Detroit toward his hotel, Walker studied the communication. Dated 12 November, 1877, the letter charged that on or about the hour of five a.m. on the ninth day of that same month an urgent telegram had been dispatched to the Pointe aux Barques station. It beseeched the keeper and crew to come immediately to a point four and one-half miles northwest of the station and to the aid of the crew of the stranded schooner *Berlin*. The letter went on to state that the weather was calm enough to launch a common yawl boat, but instead of launching at the station and rowing the "five miles" to the scene, the lifesavers ineptly hauled their surf boat overland and did not arrive until sunset of that same day. It also charged that the loss of life associated with the wreck was a direct result of the tardiness of the station crew. According to the communication, the entire event had been witnessed by Captain Peer, Captain Walters, Captain White, Oliver Bosely, James Hamilton, James Calhan and Eugene Foot, as well as those who signed the letter, R. Cooley, C.H. Cooley, F. Dhyse and

Frank Wilson. At first reading it appeared a most compelling condemnation of the crew at Station Number 1, but there was something about the letter, itself, that seemed to nag at Walker. That evening in his hotel room the letter seemed to haunt him and he read it time and again. There was something odd about the circumstances as described. Why would there occur a shipwreck in "calm" weather? Also, there seemed something strange about the two Cooley signatures. The inspector did not make any written record of his personal feelings, but we can imagine his dilemma. Perhaps it was just his deep hope that no lifesavers in his service could be that derelict in their duties, but still, Walker must have retained a nagging feeling that the circumstances in the complaint did not add up. Certainly, he would find the truth, and soon at that.

Early the following morning Walker and Superintendent Sawyer boarded a steamer bound for Port Hope, Michigan, just six and one-half miles south of the Pointe aux Barques Station. As the steamer plowed up the Detroit and St. Clair rivers the two travelers probably spent the hours discussing that infernal letter. Without attempting to influence the inspector, Sawyer would likely have vouched for Station Keeper E.C. McDonald. Sawyer knew the man as a competent and capable lifesaver who was unlikely to be so neglectful. On the trip up-bound, there was little else to do other than sit in the steamer's cabin and discuss the letter. By the time that the steamer reached open Lake Huron the sea had put on its nasty autumn face and greeted the boat without politeness. Rude gray waves slapped at the bow and spray hissed as it slung across the decks. This certainly would have brought to mind one of the irregularities in the letter. If the weather was so calm when the *Berlin* wrecked, as to allow the launching of a "common yawl-boat," as stated in the letter, why then did no one on the scene do exactly that? Additionally, if the conditions were so forgiving, why was the vessel lost and how did the loss of life take place? Then there were the two Cooley signatures— they simply looked too much alike, as if signed by the same hand. As the steamer neared Port Hope, the curiosity of the two administrators grew like the lights of the oncoming village.

On Wednesday morning a team of horses was rented and the six-mile journey to the Pointe aux Barques lighthouse and lifesaving station was started. Both the light and station are misnamed as neither is anywhere near Pointe aux Barques. In fact, the lighthouse and lifesaving station, in 1877, were located eight miles down the coast from Pointe aux Barques, itself, which is at the tip of Michigan's thumb. Pronounced "Point aw Bark" the name of the place when loosely translated from French means "Point of Boats," an appropriate name considering that it is the place where Lake Huron's vessel routes divide between Saginaw Bay and the lower lake. The road to the station was a rutted trail of half-frozen mud, and the late November wind blew from off of Lake Huron with a cold that was nearly as bitter as the accusations that Sawyer and Walker were on their way to investigate. Of one thing there was certainty, if Station Keeper McDonald was going to get a fair hearing from anyone, it would come from Sawyer. A veteran of the Union Navy in the Civil War, then Ensign Sawyer held claim to being one of the few survivors of the burning of the Mississippi Squadron vessels at Johnsonville, Tennessee. In later years Sawyer had become a part of the Life Saving Service at its beginning on the lakes in 1876. The service, its people and purpose quickly became a part of his soul and, as superintendent of the Tenth District, he spent countless days visiting and inspecting the stations in his district which included both Lakes Huron and Superior. The lifesavers themselves were men sworn to give their own lives in the effort to rescue mariners in distress. It was a calling of valor and bravery that meant living in the most remote of areas and working in the worst of climates. Each station keeper had been hand-picked by Sawyer and it was he who carried the burden of their performance as his own. Indeed Keeper McDonald would get a fair hearing, and he had better come out clean or Sawyer would surely have his head as well as his command. Men such as Sawyer and Walker were out to see to it that not a smudge could be brought against the U.S.L.S.S.

The Pointe Aux Barques Lighthouse. (Author's Photo)

Hours after Sawyer and Walker had started the bone-chilling trek to the Pointe aux Barques Station, the lighthouse tower became visible above the trees and shortly thereafter the trail leading to the light was found. Constructed in 1857 as a replacement for the original lighthouse of 1848, the brick tower stretched 89 feet above the lake. Atop the tower a third order Fresnel lens refracted the beam of light more than a dozen miles out into the distance. Even in modern times the access to the light seems remote as it cuts off from the two-lane blacktop road that is Michigan Route 25, so in 1877 the place was extremely isolated. As the team of horses snorted along the trail, a clearing in the trees was suddenly come upon and the expanse of Lake Huron loomed as its backdrop. A meager farm that belonged to Lightkeeper Andrew Shaw appeared to be the only other hint of civilization while all else was smothered by the surrounding forest. The thick smell of wood smoke hung heavy in the air and the crash of the autumn surf roared as if to deter all visitors. The stinging cold wind that had clawed at the two men all of the way along the road now seemed to blast at them as if to send them into a benumbed retreat from their investigation. At the base of the brick lighthouse were the quarters for the lightkeeper, and a short distance to the south was the cottage-like structure of Life Saving Station number 1. Approaching the station, Walker and Sawyer found the lookout at his post in the tower atop the building's roof peak, dutifully scanning the frigid distance in search of vessels in distress. A moment later they met Keeper McDonald and the inquest was promptly started. Telegraphic messages had been sent to Port Austin, Huron City and Grindstone City summoning all of the parties named within the letter to come forward and give testimony in the investigation, as those places would next be visited by Walker and Sawyer. At the station, all personnel, including the lightkeeper were put under oath and prepared to give their account as to the events surrounding the loss of the schooner *Berlin*. One after another Surfmen William Sayres, Dennis Deegan, Robert Morison, James Pottenger, as well as one whose name was recorded only as "surfman Martain" and two others, were made to raise their right hand and swear to tell the truth upon the Bible. Now the facts would be found. Nearly every person interviewed gave the same story of a stranded schooner and the daring effort to rob Lake Huron of helpless mariners.

Early in the first week of November, 1877, the 213-ton schooner *Berlin* had taken aboard the final rocks of her limestone cargo. The stone dock at Marblehead, Ohio, was the place where the schooner's moorings had held her for the duration of the loading process. Giving the orders to let go the line and set the sails, Captain A.M. Johnson, at age 60 was a senior mariner and would supervise the departure. There is no record as to when, exactly, the *Berlin* moved from the dock, such was not kept in this era, but the likelihood is that she was out on or about the sixth of November. After a brief sail up to the mouth of the Detroit River, her canvas power would have been replaced by a chartered tug for the 25-mile trip up the river to Lake St. Clair. Such tows were commonplace and often a string of a half-dozen or more sailing vessels would be shuttled in long, tandem tows. Use of sails in the river, especially when attempting to pass upbound against the extremely strong current, was awkward and at times impossible, so the tug shuttle business boomed in the days of the schooner. After another abbreviated wind-powered 16-mile passage across Lake St. Clair, the *Berlin* came upon the lower mouth of the St. Clair River and most probably another tow, this time far longer than the previous haul. Some 40 miles of twisting indigo water and a powerful current needed to be overcome before Lake Huron would be found.

Upon reaching Lake Huron and being released to her own, the *Berlin* made haste in her upbound pursuit. The port city of Saginaw, Michigan, was the destination and Captain Johnson wished not to waste a moment. Fair weather had lingered all the way up and he knew too well that in November that asset would run out quickly and without warning. He was correct. As the second Thursday of that month grew late, a northeast gale developed. The evening turned a sackcloth black, and a cold rain that chilled every man to the bone came in sheets. Waves grew and began boarding the schooner in black hills of water bearded with white foam. All around Lake Huron roared in another of its autumn tantrums, the likes of which made every man aboard the schooner feel as insignificant as an insect. Along with four able-bodied seamen, Captain Johnson had his 22-year-old son, Richard, aboard learning the ways of the lakes, and tonight he was about to be shown Lake Huron's ultimate lesson.

First tasting the water of the Great Lakes in 1854, the *Berlin* weighed in at 213 tons register. The Ruggles yard at Milan, Ohio was the place of the vessel's birth, and her three masts towered among those of the finest sailing boats of the day. By 1877, however, the once proud wind-grabber had seen her best days. Captain Johnson purchased the *Berlin*, and shortly after pressed her into service hauling anything that could be put aboard. As she took on her cargo at Marblehead, the insurance underwriters could only see fit to grace her with an insurance rating of B2. To Johnson, the fact that his vessel had seen better days meant very little—the *Berlin* had always been a "workin' boat" and this cargo was supposed to be just another step on her way to a slim profit for the season. As the *Berlin* progressed up Lake Huron amidst the howling storm, all of those years began to show. Groaning in protest to each wave the schooner's timbers strained. These were the sounds of the big lake taking advantage of a helpless laker and her crew.

Being well aware that the two-dozen-year-old *Berlin* would not take much more of Lake Huron's punishment, Johnson was eager to run her around the tip of Michigan's thumb. Once into Saginaw Bay, the lee provided by the thumb itself would shelter his boat from the gale. After

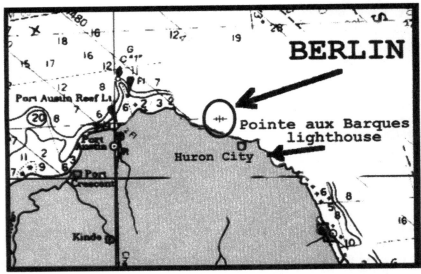

Map of Berlin's *wreck site.*

passing the Pointe aux Barques Light, the good captain calculated his time closely, and at a little past six o'clock that evening he made his haul to the west and Saginaw Bay. It was a fateful turning of the *Berlin's* helm, one that would leave her image on the bottom to be rediscovered 11 decades later. There were few lights ashore and it is probable that any of those would have been obscured by the storm. Navigational charts of the lakes in 1877 were so poor as to be of no use at all, and Johnson could only gamble that he had the *Berlin* far enough north of the thumb to miss the shoals whose location were more a matter of lore than survey. In betting his instincts against the lake, Johnson had won on countless occasions but, at seven o'clock on Thursday evening November 8, 1877, Lake Huron extracted its due and the keel of the *Berlin* slammed into the outer rocks of the twin shoals off Burnt Cabin Point.

In calm weather the water over the Burnt Cabin Reef is, in places, less than four feet in depth. In a northeast gale bare rock would be exposed in many areas and the deeply laden schooner with the wind on her heels did not have a chance of passing over. A heartbeat after her oak keel shattered on the boulders, Lake Huron pounced upon the *Berlin*. Pivoting on her grounded bottom, the stricken laker was blown around putting her beam to the wind. The first of an endless series of breakers exploded against her side as she rolled and began to grind against the boulder studded bottom. All around the frigid wind howled and the soaked clothing that the men were wearing froze stiff with an ice water starch. The winds and seas quickly found the schooner's lamps and shortly there was not a hint of light to be found. It is difficult to describe the blackness of a storm-shrouded night in an isolated spot. With the dense clouds overhead obscuring the moon and stars and not a man-made light to be found, the world distorts in a pool of inky blackness. None of the crew could see what was going on below, but the sounds were that of the vessel breaking up. At times there was every indication that the boat was about to crumble and drop them to their doom in the bitter cold surf. What no one on the schooner could know, however, was that the wreck was being worked toward the beach by the wind and seas. There was nothing that the crew could do other than wait for daylight and attempt to get high enough on the boat to stay out of the waves which began to sweep the decks. Shortly before dawn, some of the crew took to the standing rigging in an effort to get out of the seas that were gaining on the vessel and swirling knee-deep across the deck. Climbing into the rigging would get a person out of the water, but would expose him to the stinging wind. Captain Johnson instructed his son to climb up and no matter what, not to let go. It was a trade-off of absolute desperation.

Daylight slowly won the fight with the darkness and the illumination revealed the *Berlin's* true plight. The power of the seas had shoved the wreck to within one-half of a mile of the beach, but had also beaten her hull down so that only her bow and foremast remained above the water. Wailing in a frozen madness, the wind blasted from the open lake and attacked the luckless mariners with an arctic cold that began to become unbearable. Shortly after daylight it became evident that one of the crew had simply had his life sapped away, and now was just hanging dead in the rigging. A short time later, Lake Huron came for Captain Johnson as it reached up with a single frigid wave and swept him from the *Berlin* before the terror-filled eyes of his son. Watching his father being clutched by the lake and pulled to his doom was just more than the younger Johnson could take. His sorrow and shock did what Lake Huron could not, and loosened his grip on the frozen rigging. As if slapped by a ghostly hand the captain's son was blown from the rigging and plunged into the churning ice water. Lake Huron, however, was not finished with young Johnson. No sooner had the lake drowned the poor lad than it gave back his lifeless body, depositing it in the web of wreckage that lay afloat of the leeward side of the shattered schooner. There the corpse bobbed and rocked with each wave as if to beckon the remaining crew in the direction of their fate.

Unfortunately for the *Berlin's* people, the wreck site was about two miles outside of the beach patrol area of the Pointe aux Barques Lifesaving Station, and up around the curving shoreline well out of sight of the lookout tower. As a result the surfmen at the station had no idea that the wreck had occurred on Burnt Cabin Shoal. At daylight, however, the residents of Grindstone City, less than a mile from the *Berlin*, discovered the hulk. Captain A.G. Peer and George Robertson were on the beach and discovered the boat just before 10 o'clock in the morning. They knew at once that the schooner was fast going to pieces. Without hesitation the two local residents made a hasty trot to James Green's telegraph office. Dropping his work, Green was immediately set to the task of tapping out a message to Lifesaving Station number 1 at Pointe aux Barques. At the speed of light, Captain McDonald received the message and mustered his storm-soldiers to their action stations. The thought to launch the station's surf boat was quickly dispensed with because the sea was running from the north-north-east and the winds continued to blow a gale. The pull to the *Berlin* would have been against the winds and seas all of the way. Although the straight-line distance to the vessel from the station was only four and one-half miles, the actual distance required to row the surf boat safely out onto the lake, then around the scalloped shoreline and back in toward the wreck, would have been much closer to eight miles. Considering the prevailing conditions, Keeper McDonald wisely concluded it faster to transport the station's rescue equipment overland. As the station crew prepared the apparatus, one of the surfmen was sent to procure a team of horses from the barn of Lightkeeper Shaw for the purpose of hauling the beach-cart and surf boat cart up to Grindstone City by way of the road. A second team of horses was obtained from the Dixon farm, about three miles from the station, and as soon as all was in readiness the surfmen set out for Burnt Cabin Point with as much speed as possible. The road headed up to the point was just as bad as that leading up to the station, and was little more than a wagon-rutted, muddy trail. Progress in the direction of the wreck was painfully slow, the narrow wagon wheels being constantly swallowed in the mud as the teams of horses snorted puffs of steam and pulled with all of their brawn. For the better part of four hours the crew of Station Number 1 struggled in the cold and mud while the remainder of the gale screamed in the trees overhead. Feeling as if they were mired in a surfman's nightmare the crew pressed on at a pace of just over two miles an hour.

At three o'clock in the afternoon the site of the wreck was finally reached and the nearly exhausted lifesavers were reinvigorated by a charge of fresh adrenaline. There, out across an endless succession of breakers, was what remained of the *Berlin's* bow section. All of her masts were gone and the waves were exploding over her as if to sweep her from existence right in front of the surfmen. With the cadence of hundreds of hours of drill, the life-savers took their positions and hustled the surf boat into the infuriated lake. Using every ounce of strength that each man could find, they pulled as a team at the oars of the surf boat. This was it—not a practice, not a drill, not a response to some stray vessel seeking a tug—this was a shipwreck and the crew of Station Number 1 would reach the *Berlin* or die trying.

Plowing up the face of the first breakers the surf boat felt as if it were standing on end. Spray shot into the air and rained down across the surfmen as Lake Huron roared all around in thunderous protest. Over the noise of the crashing waves Keeper McDonald shouted encouragement to his oarsmen while he grappled with the tiller. But his words to the boys were not needed because each was pulling at his oar knowing that the life of suffering mariners depended on each stroke. From the beach the residents of Grindstone City watched in breathless fascination as the lifesavers punched through one whitecap after another until the surf boat was just a bobbing dot in the distance between the wreck and the shore. The questions murmured around the crowd centered on speculation over which vessel this was, how many people were aboard and most importantly, was there anyone left alive?

Using what little lee the shattered bow provided, McDonald ordered the oars shipped and the surfmen grappled onto the wreck of the *Berlin*. There they found two benumbed mariners clinging to the wreck with what little life remained within their souls. From this ice-coated perch the sailors were pried and dropped into the surf boat like frozen sacks of potatoes. The only other human form to be found was the body of Captain Johnston's son. It too was recovered and the surf boat then headed for the shore. The passage to shore was a bit less difficult than the pull out to the wreck, but the surf boat was still tossed about like a chip on the breakers. Tossing in the bottom of the tiny surf boat, the two rescued sailors bounced and bumped in a frostbitten stupor. To them it was unclear if they were being carried to safety by a team of surfmen or carried away by the grim reaper's lifeboat. In less that one-half hour the lifesavers managed to complete the round trip to the *Berlin* and back to the beach. As they skidded their waterborne ambulance stylishly onto the stony beach at the crest of a single wave, the surf-warriors bounded over the rails and whisked their stunned passengers onto dry land. Wrapping the poor souls in warm blankets and rubbing their limbs to regain circulation of their chilled blood were the first steps. Additionally, one of the surfmen was sent dashing to a nearby store to obtain a bottle of brandy, the trademark elixir of the lifesavers which was used as a stimulant. As both of the castaways took their treatment and began to recover their senses, the men of Station Number 1 stood nearby beaming in cold-soaked pride. This had been their second response to a shipwreck, their first call to duty against the mighty lake in the infamous month of November, a true test of their training. In passing those tests, the boys of the Pointe aux Barques Station had pulled two helpless souls from the death-grip of Lake Huron. They had saved two lives, and that was a reward greater than any other. As the *Berlin's* survivors steadily regained their wits, the surfmen patted one another on the back and beamed with pride.

Their celebration was suddenly cut short as a messenger shouldered his way through the crowd with the urgent news that the schooner *Triumph* was high and dry ashore just a half-mile farther west up the coast from the *Berlin*. In a snap the storm-warriors again prepared for action. As swiftly as their frozen hands would permit, the crew gathered and organized their rescue equipment in preparation for another storming of the surf-picketed gates of Lake Huron. While two surfmen continued to look after the *Berlin's* survivors, the rest went about loading the surf boat back onto the cart for the trip to the new wreck. Just as the surf boat was secured, another messenger came huffing up and delivered the news that the *Triumph's* crew had gotten ashore on their own. Such was not convincing enough to satisfy an aggressive lifesaver like Keeper McDonald. Ordering his men to continue to look after the two survivors, McDonald commandeered a nearby horse and leaping upon it he galloped up the beach splashing surf and sand. He would go to the *Triumph* and make certain that no lives were at risk. As the crowd of local residents looked on the lifesavers of Station Number 1 demonstrated that not a chance would be taken in the execution of their sworn duty. It was a scene that would make any youngster want to grow up to be a lifesaver.

One after another all of those sworn gave testimony which painted the same picture, that of a dedicated station crew doing their duty to the utmost of their ability. During their visit to Port Austin and Port Hope, anyone who had any knowledge of the events surrounding the *Berlin* wreck was interrogated by Walker and Sawyer, and the stories were the same, all described the fearless effort used by McDonald's crew in the rescue effort. In fact, the statements were so close in detail from both the station crew and the civilians that Inspector Walker deemed it necessary only to commit one of them to writing for official submission to the Secretary of the Treasury. When it came down to the interview of the men who had actually signed the accusation, Frank Wilson and Frederick

The original 1876 Pointe Aux Barques Life Saving Station. (Author's Photo)

18

Dhyse, they were said to be out in the woods at a lumber camp and quite unreachable, leaving only the Cooleys to answer questions. Additionally, the persons who had their names attached to the document added another piece to the puzzle. Eugene Foote, James Hamilton, James Calhan and Captain White could not be found, although an emissary was sent to their known haunts. Oliver Bosely, and A.G. Peer, both of whom had their names mentioned in the letter, gave the same account of the event as the lifesavers. This left only the two Cooleys. When found, the elder Cooley claimed that he had never signed the letter, but later recanted slightly saying that he had given his son, C.H. Cooley, permission to forge his signature onto the document. Clearly, Keeper McDonald and the crew of Station Number 1 were beyond reproach in this matter. But why, then, was the letter written and sent? Inspector Walker was not satisfied, and pressed the Cooleys for the instigator of the charges. They were far less than cooperative but a name did pop up—Frank Walters. As a matter of fact, every person questioned about the letter itself stated, without exception, that "Captain" Walters had instigated the writing of the letter. In fact, C.H. Cooley stated that the letter had been composed at the Walters home, but Walters himself had cleverly avoided signing the document.

In a matter of days Walker and Sawyer had gathered as much firsthand knowledge as was needed to find the truth. Both men returned to the Pointe aux Barques Station to inform Keeper McDonald and his men of the preliminary findings, and the results that would appear in the official report. Sliding up to the dining room table, Inspector Walker, Superintendent Sawyer, Keeper McDonald and those of the crew not on duty, gathered in a wilderness-style formality. As the logs in the wood-stove popped and hissed in the background, the report of the investigation was outlined by Walker. It was his conclusion that Frank Walters had instigated the fabrication of the misleading charges so as to make life difficult for the station crew. Walters had then persuaded Dhyse and Wilson to sign onto the document knowing full well that both men would shortly be isolated for the winter at a distant lumber-camp. It was also to be concluded that he induced the younger Cooley, who the locals described as being of questionable character, into signing both Cooley signatures onto the letter. The result was very clear, Keeper McDonald and his crew had acted properly during the whole ordeal and the charges were found to be completely untrue. After a few brief questions and handshakes, the two administrators departed for their homes. From the lookout tower on the roof of the station's boathouse, the surfman on duty lowered his binoculars long enough to watch Sawyer and Walker pass through the bare-branched forest on their way back to Port Hope. He, like all of the station crew, could ask and answer the question that is forever lost to us in the passage of time. That was, just what was it that Frank Walters had against the crew of Station Number 1?

Using pure conjecture we can point to at least one possibility that may give us a clue to the treachery of Frank Walters. On October 11, 1877, the station crew responded to their first shipwreck. This was the wreck of the Canadian brig *Abeona* which found the rocks just one mile west of Port Austin. She was packed with a cargo of lumber which spilled out and went adrift. The crew of Station Number 1 rescued all four of the boat's crew and recovered $200 worth of her $400 lumber cargo. The rest of the cargo would surely have been scattered ashore where the local residents would easily gather it. Perhaps the lifesavers in their effort to rescue the property of the *Abeona's* owners somehow crossed paths with local beachcombers, and just maybe one of those was Frank Walters.

Without regard to such speculation, the record of the crew of Station Number 1 was now as clean as the lake water off Pointe aux Barques. During the autumn of 1877 the lifesavers of the station had plucked six souls from Lake Huron's death grip. In the first week of December the station closed with the end of the year's navigation season, and all of the crew looked forward to their future in the lifesaving service with a renewed sense of pride and expectation. In the near future, however, Lake Huron would exact a terrible toll on nearly every one of the lifesavers in this story.

It was at dawn on the stormy morning of April 23, 1879 and the Pointe aux Barques Station was then under the command of Keeper Jerome Kiha. (Just what had become of Keeper McDonald, as of this writing, is unknown—although the records show a massive shake-up in station keepers in 1878, with some being relieved of duty and others moved. It is likely that McDonald was either moved or removed in the purge of 1878.) Before daylight, Lake Huron took hold of the scow-schooner *J.H. Magruder*, and proceeded to maul her in an evil manner. But, the lake did not want the *Magruder*, as her prize. The Pointe aux Barques Station crew had robbed the freshwater sea of nearly 100 victims since 1876, and now Lake Huron would have its revenge on the daring mortals, and the *Magruder* would be the bait.

Just before nine o'clock on that ugly spring morning, Samuel McFarland was tending to his small farm a short distance from the lifesaving station when the sound of screeching seagulls drew his attention down toward the lake. After a short distraction, McFarland elected to ignore the cries of the birds and get back to his chores, but a moment later his dogs bolted toward the beach and the annoyed farmer decided to follow and find out just what was going on down there. As he looked out across the breaking surf, McFarland saw an overturned surf boat bobbing about 200 feet from shore. At that point the beach is nothing more than a protracted stretch of rounded boulders that lead up to a bluff shore rising to a height of about 15 feet. Figuring that some mariner may be in distress, McFarland made a dash toward the lifesaving station with the intention of alerting the crew. When the breathless farmer reached the station, however, he found it vacant with the doors to the boathouse propped open. For a long moment he pondered the situation until a shocking realization snapped him back to reality. What he had spotted from the beach was the surf boat belonging to the station! In a second mad dash, McFarland found the door of the lightkeeper's residence and pounded frantically upon it. A heartbeat later Lightkeeper Shaw flung open the door to be confronted by the flustered farmer who conveyed his message in very few words.

As fast as their feet would carry them the lightkeeper and farmer set off in the direction of the capsized surf boat. If it was, indeed, the station's boat it meant only one thing—that the occupants were out thrashing in the frigid seas, and in the month of April the lake is as cold as it can get without being a sheet of ice. A person in the water can survive only a matter of minutes. Arriving at the scene both men saw the station boat already washed ashore, and 30 feet away a horrid figure stood wobbling on the slick boulders. With one hand clutching the root of a fallen tree and the other using a lath stick as a pitiful cane the man's face was a purplish color and swollen like that of a corpse. His eyes glared straight ahead as if McFarland and Shaw were not there, and an eerie foam flowed from his nose and mouth as he attempted to walk but moved not an inch. Looking upon the monstrous image, the farmer and lightkeeper at first thought that they were in the presence of a ghost of a ghastly drowning, then they realized that this was not an apparition at all, but a survivor.

Stepping closer to the stricken man, McFarland and Shaw reached out to lend support to the trembling refugee of Lake Huron. At that moment they discovered that the walking deadman was Station Keeper Jerome Kiah. Taking Kiah between them they attempted to walk him back to the station. Each step was a painful ordeal for all three men, and as they moved along Keeper Kiah began to mumble.

"Poor boys," he whispered through swollen lips, "they're all gone."

One agonizing step after another led the three men toward the lifesaving station. Suddenly Kiah stiffened out both legs, threw his head back and convulsed violently. McFarland and Shaw were certain at that instant that they were holding onto a dead man, but a moment later the benumbed keeper recovered from his fit and again began to make an effort at walking. As they arrived at the station, the keeper's wet clothing was removed and he was wrapped in dry blankets and put to bed. While Kiah drifted in his bed, and was spared a few hours of grief by his unconsciousness, Lake Huron proceeded to deposit the fruits of her vengeance at the very doorstep of the Pointe aux Barques Lifesaving Station. The bodies of all of the lifesaving crew were spit from the lake and put upon the rocks within a quarter of a mile of the station; the only man on earth who knew what had happened to the surfmen lay inside the station nearly dead.

So what did happen to the crew of the Pointe aux Barques Station? The answer is amazingly simple—they were just doing their duty. Shortly before sunrise Surfman James Nantau was standing watch in the lookout tower when he spied a vessel southeast of the station flying her flag at half-mast, upside down, and having a red lamp in her main rigging in a signal of distress. Immediately the whole station was alerted and prepared the surf boat for launch. As the crew manned the boat, Surfman Dennis Deegan came running from his beach patrol. He too had spotted the distressed vessel from McGuier's Point a mile and a half north of the station, and had run all of the way back to the station to report it. When he reached the station, Deegan, who was a member of the same crew that had rescued the survivors of the *Berlin*, was given a cup of the hot coffee that was being passed among the crew in preparation for their pull across the angry lake. Also taking the hot beverage were Robert Morison, James Pottenger and William Sayres, all of whom had taken part in the *Berlin* saga a year and a half earlier. Surfman Walter Petherbridge, like James Nantau, was beginning his first season at the station. Once all of the crew had gulped down their coffee ration, they launched the surf boat down the ramp to the lake and took to the oars with Keeper Kiah at the steering oar. It was just before eight o'clock in the morning and no one ashore witnessed the crew's departure. The wind blew from due east and the waves were running northeast. Calculating the nearby reefs and shallows, Kiah directed his boat so as to most effectively clear the breaking surf. His zigzag course worked perfectly and the surf boat transcended the whitecaps with grace. The spirits of the surfmen soared and they began congratulating one another on the fine job as their arms pulled at the oars with renewed energy. Kiah then headed the surf boat directly for the imperiled schooner in the distance. It was then that Lake Huron chose to extract its revenge on the Pointe aux Barques lifesavers.

Running nearly due east, the surf boat was taking the seas from the northeast on her port quarter and Kiah would head his bow in that direction each time a big wave came calling in order to take it on the bow. The seas were bigger than he had expected, but no larger than others that he had been in before. Soon the surf boat had pulled to within a quarter of a mile of the stricken schooner, and just about a mile out into the lake, when a giant breaking wave came roaring toward them from out of nowhere. There was no time for Kiah or his crew to turn the surf boat as the sea seemed to simply rise up and crash toward them. In an instant a cascade of arctic cold water swallowed them whole and then left them floundering. Immediately, the keeper gave the order to the crew to begin bailing, but it was pointless because the surf boat was filled to her rails. A moment later the bantam surf boat rolled over and spilled the lifesavers into the stinging cold bath of Lake Huron. As they had been trained, the surfmen took hold of their boat and righted her, but the trough of the seas had her now and

Inside the Pointe Aux Barques Life Saving Station, now a museum, a photo of Keeper Jerome Kiah is proudly displayed. (Author's Photo)

was not willing to let go. Again the surf boat was rolled by the lake, and again the surfmen righted her. This was a chore that took nearly superhuman strength and coordination. The crew would take hold of the righting lines strung along the sides of the boat and using their weight and feet, turn the surf boat rightside up. All of this was done while bobbing chest-deep in the frigid lake, supported only by a cork lifebelt. It was a drill that the crews all practiced weekly, but now they were in a heaving sea and dunked in water that had been a sheet of ice a dozen days earlier. Putting their training to work the crew righted their craft, but no sooner did they turn her over than the seas capsized them again. Once more the crew pulled their surf boat onto an upright keel, just in time to have it rolled upside down for a third time. What had happened was that the surf boat had been lodged in the sea trough at exactly the proper angle to the wind to make her an easy victim for capsizing. No matter how many times the surfmen righted the boat, as long as it was filled with water, the very next wave would roll it over. After a few of these dunkings in the ice water of Lake Huron, the strength of the lifesavers was quickly sapped. After three-quarters of an hour the lake had won the fight. Now all of the crew were left holding onto the lifelines of the overturned surf boat and drifting in the waves, too benumbed to do anything more.

Lake Huron had beaten the lifesavers, but that was not enough. Now the lake started to take the surfmen one at a time. Pottenger went first, the strength being drained from his body he bowed his head into the water and simply let go, drifting away. From the distressed schooner *J.H. Magruder*, which was now riding at anchor, her crew stood helplessly by and watched the lake take the surfmen. Keeper Kiah did his best to keep his crew alive. They tried time and time again to crawl atop the overturned hull and escape the bitter water, but the waves would wash them off each time. The keeper urged his men to think of their families and hold on until they washed ashore, but it was no use. One by one the lake plucked them away. Surfman Deegan was the last to let go, leaving Kiah alone with Lake Huron. Eventually the surf boat drifted back across the reef and into calmer waters where the lone survivor managed to drag himself onto the rolling hull. As he floated atop the capsized surf boat, Kiah passed in and out of consciousness. In the times when he was conscious, the benumbed station keeper pounded his limbs against the boat in an attempt to regain his circulation. Being too frozen to move he screamed with what little strength he had remaining. At the top of his lungs he shouted toward the gray sky above in the hope that he might attract some kind of attention of those ashore. His cries went unheard and the lake finally dumped both him and the surf boat on the rocks near the McFarland farm. By noon that day Kiah recovered to the point where he was back on his feet, and the lake was giving up the bodies of his crew one at a time just as she had taken them. One after another the lifeless surfmen found the beach and were properly collected by the local residents.

Once again Superintendent Joseph Sawyer paid a stoic visit to the Pointe aux Barques Station. The lighthouse still loomed in the clearing and the wood smoke hung among the trees as it had on that November day in 1877, but this time there was no crew to question, the poor boys were all gone. The schooner *Magruder* that the surfmen had given their lives attempting to reach, managed to free herself later that tragic day and escaped to shelter at Harbor Beach (then known as Sand Beach). Lake Huron would allow her to survive until September 18, 1895 when it would wreck her on Sturgeon Point. The immediate problem for the superintendent was the station at Pointe aux Barques itself. Sawyer went about writing his report and restaffing the station. Keeper Kiah was in bad shape, both mentally and physically. The shock of having "his boys" taken by the lake while he floated helplessly within arms reach became a continuing nightmare. We can only imagine his feelings of guilt and anguish each time he looked out across the expanse of the enormous lake. His job, his calling, his duty, had been to go out in the face of the lake's vengeance. But now it seemed as if Lake Huron had not only duped him into a costly mistake, but robbed him of his crew and his valor. Any such thoughts would have been completely wrong. Kiah had performed his duty bravely and correctly, but found that one constant fact which so many humans are too arrogant or naive to realize—man can never overcome nature. The lake was only the instrument of Providence in Kiah's life and his anguish was the price paid

Pointe aux Barques' lifesavers prepare to go about their weekly boat drill. Notice the "drogue" attached to the stern just forward of the rudder. This was thrown into the water, it acted as an underwater parachute and applied drag astern to keep the boat headed toward shore and through the breaking waves. Although these are not the same lifesavers who were lost in the 1879 tragedy, they carry out the exact missions as those lifesavers that were lost before them. (Superior View Photo)

for doing his duty. What we know now is that Huron would soon become the tool of Divine Providence in Kiah's life once again.

As fate would have it, Superintendent Sawyer, himself, would not escape the ire of Lake Huron. On October 20, 1879, less than six months after the Pointe aux Barques Station crew were lost, Sawyer departed from a routine inspection of Station Number 8 at Forty-Mile Point at the northern end of Michigan's Lower Peninsula. Both Sawyer along with the station's keeper, George McFeaben, and Surfman Joseph Valentine, set out in the station's small 32-foot sailboat *Arrow* in an effort to shuttle the superintendent to Rogers City. It was a distance of just 16 miles to the south and once there Sawyer would catch a steamer to the Soo where he would arrange passage to the Vermilion Point Station on Lake Superior. The stop was simply another routine inspection that was all a part of the superintendent's job. When the three men were just a few miles north of their destination, a sudden and violent squall came ripping from off the land and struck the little sailboat, setting her on her beam-ends and sinking her in minutes. In a twinkling, the three lifesavers found themselves thrashing around in the icy lake with a half-mile swim between themselves and dry land. A swim of such distance on upper Lake Huron in late summer can be a chilling endeavor; in late October it is normally fatal. All three men surfaced and made their way to the tip of the *Arrow's* mast which, after she had settled on the bottom, was sticking above the surface. Climbing upon the spar like drenched kittens, the shivering lifesavers found that they could see the lumber dock at Rogers City and could also see the men working there. They shouted and waved their hats, but no one ashore took notice. They finally concluded that at least one of them would have to swim for it—or all of them would perish on the mast. Kicking off his boots and removing his overcoat and undercoat, Surfman Valentine jumped into the water and stroked away toward the beach with confidence. He made 50 yards before his hands became so numb that they cramped into fists and he was forced to struggle back to the spar. Keeper Feaben helped renew Valentine's circulation. Again Valentine set out in a swim for the beach, this time he made only 20 yards before the cold forced his return. Now Keeper Feaben stripped off all of his own clothing and jumped into the water in an effort to make the swim but made only a dozen yards before he too had to return. Finally Superintendent Sawyer removed his clothing and made an effort at swimming ashore. He only managed to swim a short distance before he was forced to turn back. Unlike the others, however, Sawyer did not return to roost on the mast. When he got to within 50 feet of the mast he suddenly stopped swimming and simply sunk like a stone. He was not seen again and his body was never recovered.

Only Surfman Valentine survived the ordeal. Picked up by a boat from shore, he went on to become a station keeper himself. Keeper Feaben let go of the mast and dropped into the lake shortly after Sawyer drowned.

The keeper's body was given up by the lake 23 days later. Upon Sawyer's death, Jerome Kiah, the only survivor of the Pointe aux Barques tragedy, was appointed superintendent, a job that he remained at for three and a half decades. For some unknown reason Lake Huron seemed to favor Kiah. It plucked away his command and then facilitated his promotion to a post that he would keep until the U.S. Life Saving Service was merged with the Revenue Cutter Service in 1915 becoming the U.S. Coast Guard. At that time Kiah was allowed a pension and retired with the honor of a lifetime of service and the hidden trace of guilt of a lone survivor.

In one final twist to this story, a modern mariner found himself in the same painful dilemma as Jerome Kiah in nearly the exact same location, but 87 years later. On the gale-ripped night of November 29, 1966, the 600-foot oreboat *Daniel J. Morrell* broke in half just over two dozen miles north of Pointe aux Barques. When the boat went down it left behind its life raft with four crewmen aboard, 36 hours later only one of them, Dennis Hale, remained alive. The best account of Hale's ordeal can be found in Dwight Boyer's outstanding book *Ships and Men of the Great Lakes*, while several other authors have taken stabs at the tale. Just before his rescue by a Coast Guard helicopter, Hale's raft ran aground in the shallows within a mile of the spot where Keeper Kiah's overturned surf boat had found the shore. Hale knew he was close to land, but was so frozen that he was unable to move. Shouting at the top of his voice he was in hope of attracting attention, his voice emptied into the distance just as Jerome Kiah's had in 1879. Having been without food and water since his boat went down, Hale had previously been dipping the lanyard on the handle of a broken flare gun into the lake and drinking from the runoff, now his body was absolutely paralyzed with frostbitten pain and he took to nibbling at the ice on his peacoat, which had been his only cover while on the raft. (It is important to note here that accounts of Hale's ordeal universally state that he sheltered himself beneath the bodies of his dead shipmates. This author has spoken to Hale and he has stated that such claims, although good for storytelling, are untrue.) As soon as he began to nibble on his icy garment, the ghostly figure of a man appeared on the raft. With deep-set eyes and long white mustache, the stranger was a commanding figure. He told Hale not to eat the ice, then vanished. A little later the castaway again began to nibble at the ice and once more the apparition warned Hale, shaking his finger on a cragged hand that the tormented crewman remembers to this day, "Do not eat the ice," because it would lower the body temperature and he would die. A short time later a Coast Guard helicopter hovered down and pulled Dennis Hale from the grip of Lake Huron.

By the time of that awful event in 1966 most of the lifesaving stations had been abandoned and the service, as it had been known prior to 1915, was long forgotten. The Pointe aux Barques Station was deemed "inactive" in the 1937 fiscal year ending 60 years of operation. It is interesting, however, to ponder that if the station had been in operation in 1966 in the same manner as it was in 1879, the lookout would have surely spotted Hale's raft, and the surfmen would have launched their boat and rushed out onto the lake to save his life. Perhaps one of them did exactly that, in the form of a white apparition who knew a great deal more about hypothermia than Dennis Hale did.

Today, anyone can make the pilgrimage to Huron City where the structure of the Pointe aux Barques Station has been relocated as part of a preservation of historic buildings of the Huron City Museum. As state road M-25 cuts across the very tip of the thumb between Port Austin and Grindstone City, the large white signs lead the way to the contemporary home of the original Pointe aux Barques Station. Visitors can see firsthand the building from where the crew departed to rescue a distressed *J.H. Magruder*, but never returned. From the first day of July to the Labor Day holiday the buildings are opened for tours until about half past four in the afternoon. All of the apparatus used by the service are on display within the boathouse portion of the building, including two of the station's Lyle guns, projectiles and faking boxes. A large picture of Keeper Kiah hangs in the living quarters as if still supervising the station. Standing outside the boathouse doors it is easy to imagine them about to swing open as the surfmen dash to the rescue of another vessel in distress. Then, driving less than a mile to the southeast on M-25 and turning off on Huron City Road, you will find yourself on the same track taken by Sawyer and Walker as you come upon the gleaming white lighthouse. At the base of the light, in the quarters once occupied by Keeper Shaw, a museum is now located with shipwreck artifacts of all kinds on display. Leaving the building you find Lake Huron spread out in front of you in all of her indigo glory. Visitors need only to walk about 100 yards to the east where the public access ramp to the lake has been constructed. This is the exact spot where the Pointe aux Barques Station once stood, and the jut of land that supported the launching ways for the station's boats still exists. On a hot summer day it is hard to picture the lake at its icy worst, so it is important to keep in mind that nearly everyone who perished in this story did so in the frigid water within 3,000 feet of shore.

To visit the Pointe aux Barques Lighthouse and lifestation is to see one of the sites where brave men challenged the lake, yet did not always win. When you go to this place take a walk along the bluffs of the rocky beachfront. Remember that it is here that the storm warriors made their living in life and death battles with Lake Huron. And the rocks of the beach are where the lake deposited the results of its vengeance. Keep in mind also, that somewhere in this same area lurks the apparition that performed the duty of a Pointe aux Barques lifesaver. Just who he is we will never know. After all, many a soul has reason to haunt this shore.

BUT, EDITH MORGAN WAS THE FIRST

When the United States Life Saving Service was established on the Great Lakes in 1876, there were a number of qualifications that candidates being considered for the position of Surfman had to meet. These individuals were to be selected from the best of the mariners who were local to each lifesaving station. The station keeper was assigned the job of selection, and the persons under consideration had to have skills in all areas of nautical toil. Additionally, they had to be persons of good character, have no ties to any salvage interest, and had to be of the highest courage. Then there was one unspoken qualification—they also had to be male.

Exclusion of females from the Life Saving Service does not say that the service, itself, was discriminatory. In fact, the Pea Island Station in North Carolina was totally staffed by a black crew of lifesavers. Of course, no white lifesavers were staffed at that station. So, although segregated, the service was somewhat liberal for its time. Even with that bent, the service did not allow females to conscript as lifesavers. The fact that this exclusion now should be upsetting to the reader says much more about the filters through which we view history than it does about the Life Saving Service itself. It is important to put the era of the mid-1800s into proper perspective in order to understand the story that is about to be presented. Recall that females in the United States were not even given the right to vote until the ratification of the 19th Amendment to the Constitution on August 18, 1920. So, although the preceding paragraph may make the modern feminist grind her teeth, the fact is that the era mentioned was a man's world, and would remain that way for decades to come. Then again, that is not the way that Edith Morgan saw the world.

Exclusion of ladies from many types of jobs in the mid-1800s was not just the custom of males in society, many females of the day were outspoken about a lady's "proper" place. For example, by the late 1870s many ladies of the lakes were taking jobs on lakeboats as cooks. The jobs in the galley were plentiful and female cooks "worked for less," meaning that they were given less pay than their male counterparts. The trend soon turned into a fad and ladies all over the Great Lakes region found an escape from their boot-button society ashore. This movement of ladies into jobs in vessel galleys did not escape the focus of their peers. A good example of this was printed in the *Chicago Inter-Ocean* in the spring of 1883, and a short time later reprinted in the *Port Huron Daily Times*. The letter to the *Inter-Ocean* was apparently published unsigned and credited as being submitted by "the wife of a captain living in Chicago." It read:

> Several years ago you brought happiness to many homes along the lakes by driving female cooks off the lakes. Now I want to post you. Captains are sneaking in these women again. They destroy all discipline on shipboard and the assertion by captains to owners that they are cheaper than men cooks and save to the vessels, is all false. Then in a storm men cooks can take hold and help, while a woman is only in the way, or worse, for she often unnerves the crew by her alarm. Besides all this the mate wants to love the woman cook as well as the captain does and there is often trouble between these two commanding officers. A great grain fleet is about leaving Chicago for below, and I want you to drive the women off these vessels. My husband's schooner is among the rest.

Such was the atmosphere concerning a woman's "place" in the maritime world of the Great Lakes in the mid-1800s. In reading this publication, many of the ladies of the lakes would likely fume with an anger that a modern feminist might find intimidating. The part that described a woman's role in a storm was particularly maddening, especially to a woman such as Edith Morgan. She knew well that her valor was well certified, and no storm that could blow across the lakes would back her down. Not even if that storm wind came from a winter gale or a prudish captain's wife in Chicago. If Edith had read that letter to the *Inter-Ocean*, she would have likely created a storm of her own. All of that rubbish about not being able to take hold and help, and getting in the way—surely a woman such as Edith would have found those words more insulting than the implication of stray "love." Edith knew of the scorn of such parlor-bound hens such as the letter's author, and she knew that her own ability was beyond anything that such people could understand. You see, it did not matter that the Life Saving Service would not employ women. Edith Morgan was more than qualified to stand among the service's best, and she could prove it.

The lifesaving station at Grand Point Au Sable on Lake Michigan's coast was one of the first stations opened on the Great Lakes. Although Thomas Welch is listed as the initial station keeper, Captain Sanford W. Morgan was one of its earliest keepers, and Edith was the keeper's daughter. Due to the remoteness of some stations, families of station keepers, and sometimes families of the surfmen, were allowed to live on station grounds. Keepers often resided at the station, itself, in an attached dwelling. Surfmen who were married were permitted to have a small cottage on station grounds. It was found that having family members on the station grounds provided an element of stability in a profession that called for continuous duty for eight months of the year, 24 hours a day. Surfmen were far less likely to become quickly fed up with the low pay and nonstop duty if their wife and family were living within shouting distance. So, when Keeper Morgan took charge of his station at Grand Point Au Sable, he brought his family along. Besides Edith were her two brothers, James and Frank, the latter of which is described simply as "...a little boy." Thus it was that Edith Morgan found herself on the Lake Michigan shore, residing among the storm-warriors.

Grand Point Au Sable, which is known today as Big Sable Point, is located about six miles north of Ludington, Michigan, and although the shore is an often-visited state park today, it was far different in Edith Morgan's time. The lifesaving station itself was planted near the beach about five miles north of Ludington, with the closest structure being the lighthouse located a mile farther north along the shore. Although the life-saving station was somewhat removed from the city of Ludington, it was not nearly as isolated as many other stations in the service, and the trail between the station and the town was well traveled. Ludington was an active seaport in the late 1870s and it would be a simple matter for one of the local residents to buy a passage aboard a steamer and travel to the big city of Chicago. Any of the goods and services that most of the larger communities on the Great Lakes could offer could likely be had in Ludington as well. For the Morgan family, duty at the Grand Point Au Sable Station must have been far more desirable than it would have been at many of the other stations on Lake Michigan.

There is little doubt that Edith watched each day as the station crew went about their daily duties and drills, and she desired to be among them. She was sure that she could handle an oar or a line just as well as any of the men. Each time the surf boat was launched in the weekly drill, capsized and then righted, she looked on wishing that she were aboard, swiftly scrambling to maneuver the boat. To someone like Edith this did not appear to be a wet, cold, and dangerous undertaking. It appeared to almost be fun. Even the nightly beach patrol would have been a welcome diversion from the restraints of a "lady's world" which held Edith as tightly as a cork lifebelt. On occasion, it was the habit of the lifesavers to practice with their breeches buoy and allow local ladies the thrill of a demonstration ride aboard the device. We can only wonder how often the breeches buoy of the Grand Point Au Sable Station contained the keeper's daughter, but it is the author's guess that she was in the device as often as possible. Still, when she returned to solid ground, there were always the corset strings that kept her in "her place" once her ride in the breeches buoy was finished. Indeed, Edith was a person confined by the norms of her day, yet fate would soon demolish all of those barriers.

It was a stormy Saturday, the 23rd day of March, 1878, and the gray clouds above Lake Michigan were reaching down as if seeking a soul or two to pluck from earth. Winds came howling from the north and the waves beat upon the shore like thunder. Navigation on the lakes had opened early that season; in fact, it was one of the earliest openings ever. The first vessel to pass through the Straits of Mackinac did so on March 14, and that was the earliest such passage since 1854. This early beginning of the shipping season did not mean that all of the elements for safe navigation were in place. Many of the lighthouses would not be manned and illuminated until early or mid-April, and none of the lifesaving stations would be manned and activated until the first day of that same month. Any mariners who ventured out onto the lakes prior to that time would do so at their own peril. At the Grand Point Au Sable Station, there was no crew of surfmen, and the facility was buttoned up for what remained of the winter. Through those dark, gloomy winter months the lake had tossed ice up on the beach and spit every form of flotsam imaginable in with the ice cakes. The shore in front of the station had become an impassable tangle of the winter's refuse—driftwood of all sorts and sizes was mixed with a jumble of anything else that the lake could toss up. From the first day of the previous December, the Grand Point Au Sable Station's only occupants had been Keeper Morgan and his family. With the closing of the 1877 navigation season, the station was transformed from a government facility into a winter residence of sorts. Keeper Morgan knew too well, however, that the season of duty was not far off and as the stormy Saturday raged it only served to remind him of the work ahead. That deplorable day would do two things that no individual person could achieve. The storm would force the premature activation of the Grand Point Au Sable Station and it would place Edith Morgan in the role of lifesaver.

Records are sparse as to what occurred that day, but what is recorded is that somewhere just north of the point a small sloop was being pounded out on the lake. The unnamed sloop apparently was manned by two individuals who were reckless enough to sail out onto Lake Michigan in the month of March. To most persons familiar with the lakes, such an undertaking would be worse than careless, it was near to being suicidal. Although the lake may appear free of ice, the temperature of the water at that time of the year is right at the freezing point. A human body immersed in water that cold would have a life expectancy of only minutes if they remained in the water, and only a few hours if they are soaked and then managed to get out of the water. Also, the gales of early spring are often as bad as their autumn counterparts, and tend to spring up much faster. Just such a storm was now blowing, and had caught the little sloop in its grip. In short order the sloop was capsized and its two occupants were tossed into the ice water. It was simply by luck that the overturned sloop, with its occupants clinging atop the hull, was spotted by a member of the Morgan family as the boat drifted past the station. Records say that the capsized sloop was three miles out onto the lake, so someone in the family must have been keeping a keen watch on the waters. Odds are that they had observed the sloop prior to its turning turtle, and perhaps were even discussing the foolish fellows out on the lake when the boat suddenly went over.

Keeper Morgan now was presented with a dilemma of enormous proportions. He knew that those who had been capsized in that cold water may have only minutes to survive, but the only persons with him in the station were his two sons, one of whom was just a small boy, and his daughter Edith. The surf boat and its launching ways had been designed to use a crew of eight full-grown men, and the present members of his family simply did not represent enough muscle power to deploy the boat, or man its oars. If he sent to town for help, the people out on the lake may expire before he could reach them. To make matters worse, the end of the launching ramp from which the surf boat must deploy was a jumble of driftwood, ice cakes and other flotsam. It would take quite a while to clear the mess and allow the boat to be launched. His only course of immediate action would be to launch the station's fishing boat and use his children as a crew. Morgan, his eldest son James, and Edith would muster at the oars, and little Frank would man the rudder. The station fishing boat was little more than a small sailboat that could be rowed as well, and placing it onto the storm-raked lake would surely place the entire Morgan family in serious danger. Those breaking seas near the station could easily swamp or capsize the fishing boat and that would certainly spell the end for some or all of the Morgans. Today such an act would likely see Morgan prosecuted for child endangerment, but in 1878, on the Lake Michigan coast, this desperate measure was one that this lifesaving family simply felt duty-bound to take. The Morgans did not see this as endangerment, they simply saw it as a demonstration of Morgan family values.

Using all of the strength, and most of the will power that the Morgan family had, the fishing boat was headed out against Lake Michigan. There were three lines of breakers to breech, the first was the surf breaking on the beach itself, and the second and third involved the two sand bars located off shore. The initial launching was a cold drenching affair as the lake shoved ice water surf at the tiny boat and showered the Morgans with freezing spray. Soaked and shivering, Edith pulled at her oar as each wave struck her from behind in a bitter cold slap. Soon the boat was among the sand bars and their marching surf. This time, the strength of the Morgan clan would not be enough to overcome the waves. In a frigid swirl the little fishing boat went out of control, broached and was nearly swamped. Keeper Morgan saw then that Lake Michigan was not in the mood to be tempted, and he elected to turn his family around and head back to the station. Once the fishing sloop was landed, Morgan sent his eldest son, James, on a run to town to obtain enough men to launch the surf boat. While James was gone to muster the volunteer crew, Edith and her father set about the task of clearing the launch ways of the winter rubble. This was a task that could have kept an oxen busy, but the two Morgans had it finished by the time that James returned with the makeshift crew. Together the volunteers were able to properly launch the station's surf boat which was designed to breech the breaking waves, and shortly thereafter Edith stood and watched as they pulled off toward the capsized sloop. Soaked by the excursion in the fishing boat, and stung by the cold bluster of the wind, Edith shivered as she watched the surf boat shrink toward the stricken sloop. She would not be a firsthand participant in this rescue, but she had come close.

Only one of the two men who were clinging to the capsized sloop managed to live long enough to be rescued that day. The U.S.L.S.S. narrative of the action simply states that two men were holding onto the overturned boat, and then later says nothing more than the surf boat "...put out to the rescue." The official record of that action presents the number of lives lost as "1." Apparently, the bitter cold of the lake's water sapped the life from one of the luckless sailors while the Morgan family tried desperately to accomplish the rescue.

For nearly the next two years Edith continued on as "the station keeper's daughter," taking on all of the mundane tasks that go with such status. With the closing of navigation in November of 1879, the lifesaving station again reverted from its role of government outpost to its winter role of Morgan family household. Out on the lakes, the official close of navigation was the date upon which the insurance underwriters, by policy, discontinued coverage. For many vessel operators the un-official close of navigation, however, was the day when the ice became so thick that the boats could no longer make it to open water or break away from the dock. In quest of additional earnings these operators were willing to risk their boats, cargoes, crews and passengers while running without insurance coverage. In a few cases, out of season insurance could be purchased, but it often was at a premium so high that it essentially negated any additional profits. So it was that vessels kept sailing long into December.

On the evening of Sunday, December 21, 1879, the snow that was blowing in off of Lake Michigan pelted at the windows of District 11's Life Saving Station Number 6. The station, however, was now acting as the Morgan household and so the family stove was kept stoked and the house remained warm. This weather was typical for late December, and through the short hours of daylight, Edith tended to her Sunday chores as the afternoon grew dark. Soon it was time to begin lighting the lamps. A wintry snugness had enveloped the Morgan family and it seemed as if that would be the way of things for the next few months. Hidden behind the curtain of snow out on the lake, however, a very different story was taking shape. Lake Michigan was also pelting the pilothouse windows of the 413-ton steamer *City of Toledo* with an unending onslaught of thick snow. Through an open window, Captain Beron did his best to see and hear beyond the gale as the boat thrashed ahead. He had taken his boat out of the port of Milwaukee on the western side of Lake Michigan and was now bound for the harbor of Ludington. His normal course would have been to sail on a 046 and one-half degree course for the 93-mile trip northeast to Ludington. In the normal navigation season this is an easy matter, you simply assume the proper course and watch for the Little Point au Sable Light to appear on the starboard horizon. The appearance of that white light which was varied by white flashes at 30 second intervals indicated that your boat was angling in toward Ludington with about 36 miles left to run. Next the Grand Point au Sable Light would come into view out of the pilothouse window on the horizon on the port quarter. This steady white light would indicate less than a dozen miles to go and shortly there after the Ludington Pierhead light would appear and could be used to guide the vessel the rest of the way into the safety of the harbor. Tonight, however, Beron had no such comfort to aid in guiding his boat. One of the other disadvantages to sailing after the close of navigation was that the lighthouses were closed much the same as the life-saving stations. Granted that on occasion if a bad storm were to blow up, some lighthouse keepers would make a point to get their light running. Again, such an effort would have done the *City of Toledo* little good because the December blizzard that was currently blowing had cut the visibility to near zero. Beron's only choices were to stop his engine and drift with the storm, drop his anchor and hope that it may take hold, turn back and hope that the weather was better toward Milwaukee, or keep steaming ahead into the blizzard and hope that there was a break in the weather. Anchoring was out of the question as the *City of Toledo* was currently steaming in one of the deepest areas of Lake Michigan, and drifting with the storm was not really what the captain had in mind for dealing with the gale. Humanly speaking, one of the most difficult things for a navigator to do is to "turn back." Indeed, Beron decided to press ahead blindly and hope for the blizzard to let up.

At about nine o'clock on that snowy Sunday night, the *City of Toledo* had a jolting collision—with the Lower Peninsula of Michigan! Captain Beron had overshot the port of Ludington by more than six miles and was a full eight miles west of his proper course. *City of Toledo* ran onto a sandbar 300 yards off shore and within a mile of the Grand Point au Sable Lighthouse. Oddly, if he had been just a few hundred feet farther off course to the west he would have overshot the whole eastern shore. The

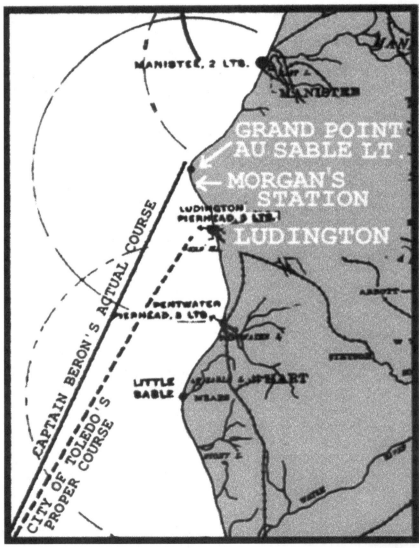

A map of the City Of Toledo's *course.*

position where the vessel ran aground could hardly have been more remote. She was several miles north of the Morgan family's station and 16 miles south of Manistee. She was, however, right on the doorstep of the Grand Point au Sable Lighthouse. It is likely that the captain never saw the 100-foot-tall, yellow brick tower. In fact, it was snowing so hard that he probably did not have a clue to his position, even after the boat grounded.

A series of standard backing maneuvers could not free the *City of Toledo*, and forward thrust would not budge her either. Soon Captain Beron came to the conclusion that there would be no chance of backing his boat off of the sand bar, and he decided that the only way to find any relief for his boat would be to go ashore and seek help. He and some of his crew took to the steamer's yawl and struck out for the beach. Unfortunately, a short distance from dry land, their boat was shoved into the ice cakes and had its hull stove in. As they dragged it onto the beach it was certain that there was no way that they were returning to the *City of Toledo* in that boat. On foot they began the trek to civilization.

It was not until late the following morning that Keeper Morgan received news of the *City of Toledo's* wreck. By that time the blizzard that had blinded Captain Beron on the previous evening had been blown well to the east and the sky had turned a brilliant blue. The winds, however, were now blowing a howling deep winter gale and the temperatures had plummeted to far below the freezing mark. Lake Michigan's water was in the mood to turn to ice and freeze on contact with anything that may be touched by their frigid presence. At three o'clock that afternoon, Keeper Morgan reached the scene of the *City of Toledo's* grounding. Located 1,000 feet from the shore, the steamer looked like a giant iceberg as thundering surf exploded over it caking on more ice with each wave. Apparently, the crew that had gone ashore had managed to secure the use of a tug out of one of the local harbors, but it had not been able to pull the *City of Toledo* from the sand bar that Beron had run her onto at full speed. Keeper Morgan saw immediately that the poor souls marooned out on the ship had one and only one chance of survival, and that was by way of his lifesaving skills. Unfortunately, Morgan's station was closed for the season and most of its staff were scattered to their off-season lives. He decided to head back to the station and muster a volunteer crew, then find a way to launch the surf boat. If he could not find a way to rescue the people of the *City of Toledo* right now, the only way they would be coming ashore would be when the lake froze solid, and then they could be chipped out of the ice as frozen cadavers!

On his way back to his station, Keeper Morgan met one of the local men who was headed in the opposite direction, hauling the lifesaving station's wagon and surf boat. Daughter Edith was not going to be left at the station this time, and had come along to help work the rescue. By the time that the surf boat was hauled to Hamlin Harbor, through the 18-inch-deep snow, enough male bodies had been mustered to work the oars, and it appeared as if Edith was again to be robbed of her chance at being a real lifesaver. Lake Michigan, however, had different plans for Edith. With swamping seas, the lake reached out and easily overwhelmed the surf boat and its crew of volunteer lifesavers. In an icy swirl, the water invaded every corner of the boat and then the bitter cold breath of the winds turned the incoming water to solid ice. Soon the tholepins that made up the pivots by which the oars were swiveled became so caked with ice that the boat could not be rowed. Before the lifeboat had gotten beyond the end of the piers, it was a useless drifting mass of ice which was then simply blown back into the harbor. If the survivors of the *City of Toledo* wreck were to be reached, it was not going to be done by way of rowing a surf boat. Keeper Morgan procured a team of horses and headed back to his station in order to obtain his beach equipment. No doubt Edith was at his side as the beach apparatus was gathered and hauled back to the wreck.

Armed with his Lyle gun and lines, Keeper Morgan proceeded back to the stricken ship. Judging the wind, it was found that the most opportune placement of the gun would be on an ice bank due east of the wreck. Still, the boat was nearly 300 yards away and the shot would have to be fired into the wind. Morgan took aim and fired the gun. The projectile flew gracefully on the gale winds and the line that was attached dropped directly across the *City of Toledo*. Remarkably, he hit the wreck with the very first shot. Now the whipline was hauled in by the crew on the wreck and the attached hawser was brought aboard. The ice that was caked aboard the vessel, however, kept the breeches buoy from being rigged any higher up than the hurricane deck. This meant that whoever occupied the breeches buoy was going to find themselves sagging down into the glacial surf for the greatest length of the ride. Also, the hawser and rigging had been pulled through the water on the way out to the wreck, and so like the tholepins on the surf boat, ice had formed and the lines were now solidly frozen.

As the first of the *City of Toledo's* crew attempted to begin the trip toward land, it became clear that there was not enough elbow grease on the other end of the ice-encrusted hawser to pull him in. It was then that Edith Morgan kicked her way through the 15 inches of snow and took her proper place with the other lifesavers. Hours passed as the crew ashore struggled to get just two people off of the wreck. Both of the survivors had to be pulled through the ice water surf for most of their trip and were near to death once they were landed. Keeper Morgan determined that if they continued with the breeches buoy, they were likely to lose some of their people in this process. There had to be a better way he reasoned. It was decided to toss the surf boat's painterline over the hawser leading to the wreck, and then, by use of the oars, pull the surf boat out to the *City of*

Ice encrusted, the City of Toledo takes the breeches buoy as the waves pound her. (Author's concept)

Toledo, while remaining attached to the hawser. In order for this plan to work, someone would have to remain ashore and keep the hawser secure. A five-mile-per-hour current was running off shore, and if the hawser slipped, the surf boat and everyone in it could be easily lost. Again, Edith took on the difficult and numbing cold job of holding that line secure. For over five hours, Edith Morgan tended the line to the *City of Toledo* which meant the difference between life and death for all involved in the event. By nightfall, she returned to the Morgan family lifesaving station, and set about the chore of thawing her frostbitten body parts. That cold was the price paid in the rescue of 18 souls from the wreck of the ill-fated ship.

On the ninth day of November, 1880, Edith Morgan was awarded a silver medal for lifesaving by the United States Life Saving Service for her acts of courage and determination while at her father's station. Officially the record read that the medal was presented for "Rescuing and assisting to rescue two fishermen whose boat had capsized (Mar. 23, 1878), and the crew of the wrecked steamer City of Toledo (Dec. 21, 1879), near Grande Pointe au Sable, Mich."

What the official report does not mention is what can be found by a careful study of the records of the issue of lifesaving medals. You see, there is a little fact that has been lost in the passage of time. In much the same way that the wreck of the *City of Toledo* has disappeared, and Station Number 6 has vanished into what is today the Ludington State Park, and even the yellow lighthouse has been painted over into black and white. The fact that Edith Morgan was the first female to ever receive a medal for lifesaving has been overlooked.

Eight months after Edith Morgan became the first woman to receive a medal for lifesaving, Ida Lewis-Wilson received a gold medal for a series of rescues that she accomplished while acting as keeper of the Lime Rock Lighthouse in Rhode Island. So famed did Ida's exploits become that she was featured in *Harper's Weekly Magazine,* and later the lighthouse was renamed in her honor. In later years, a nearby yacht club was named for her, and most recently, a new Coast Guard vessel was given her name. Delivered on November 1, 1996, the tender WLM551 was named for Ida Lewis. Today, scores of females serve in the Coast Guard in every job imaginable. Certainly, most think that it was Ida Lewis who broke the gender barrier and when they see her namesake vessels doing its duty they will recall her exploits paved the way for females serving in the modern Coast Guard. It is, however, this author's pleasure to point to the facts and say, "...but Edith Morgan was the first." Some may say that Edith's role in the rescues consisted of little more than getting her feet wet and it was her father who did all of the actual rescuing. A valid point when viewing history and the recorded accounts through the eyes of modern times. But, when considering a "woman's proper place" from the perspective of Edith's era, her award was indeed special. In light of Ida Lewis' accomplishments, we may tend to want to make little of Edith's medal, and certainly other services awarded medals for valor and lifesaving to females before Edith's, but hers was the first presented to a woman by the newly-established United States Life Saving Service, and no modern scoffer can change that fact. Sadly, however, she is all but forgotten as there is no lighthouse or yacht club or Coast Guard vessel named after her. In fact, as far as my research shows, there is not even a photo to be found of her. To honor Edith Morgan, there exists only this story and those of you who have read it.

ARE WE THERE YET?

There is a "route" in Upper Michigan that does not lead to the middle of nowhere, it actually leads to the definition of "nowhere." This modern trail of blacktop two-lane highway can be found to officially change names on occasion from "Six Mile Road" to "USFS 3150" to "State Highway 123" to "Wire Road," and long and winding enough to make even the most patient of tourist begin to groan "are we there yet?"

From Interstate 75, it is a simple matter to pick up the road to nowhere by trekking along State Highway 28 to the town of Brimley. From that point the road leads through the Bay Mills Indian Reservation and the past the gem that is their new casino and hotel. Still, lighthouse and shipwreck people do not venture this way simply to gamble, and the one thing that most who make this trip know for sure is that the "road to nowhere" is studded with two lighthouse and shipwreck jewels. The first of these treasures is just beyond the casino, and is a lighthouse buff's dream come true.

Located just a half-dozen miles up the road from the casinos is a spot where the roadside trees that separate Whitefish Bay from the pavement suddenly open up. There, gleaming white like a fresh-fallen coat of Upper Peninsula snow, is the Point Iroquois Lighthouse. Now owned by the U.S. Forest Service and considered to be a part of the Hiawatha National Forest, the sight of this beautiful lighthouse is enough to make any passing tourist slam on the brakes. Manicured to perfection, the grounds invite you in and compel a stroll around the property. Within the east side of the living quarters a terrific lighthouse museum has been created, and there are photo albums waiting for the visitor to browse. On display is a fourth order Fresnel lens in mint condition which can be examined at close range. The lighthouse tower is one of few that the visitor can actually climb. While standing in the lamproom, the view of the bay can be worth the entire

43

The Point Iroquois Lighthouse Circa 1950. (Superior View Photo)

journey along the route to nowhere. There is a zigzagging boardwalk that leads down to the sand beach where Whitefish Bay meets the lighthouse grounds. The best part of all is that the entire visit is absolutely free. Your tax dollars have already paid for your visit, although a dollar or two in the donation can is welcomed.

Skirting the lighthouse grounds is a short fence made of stones which are stacked and mortared together. This decorative fence, itself, has an interesting history, and the visitor can get the overall picture better by venturing down the boardwalk to the beach. There, the first thing noticed is the abundance of wave-smoothed stones that seem to lay everywhere. Visitors have always had the urge to grab a few stones and haul them up from the beach, so in the mid-1930s, Lighthouse Keeper John Soldenski decided to start construction on the small rock fence. As time went on, visitors who went down to the beach were asked, sort of as the price of admission, simply to bring a few rocks back up with them to aid in the fence's construction. In 1937, Soldenski finished the fence that stands today, and it was done largely with the help of rock-toting tourists. Often, even now, tourists will come sneaking up from the beach with armloads of rocks trying to avoid the sight of the caretakers. When apparently caught, the rock-runners will ask, "Do 'ya mind?" to which the caretakers reply, "Nope, there will be more rocks down there next spring."

Caretaking of this lighthouse is an addictive venture. Currently, each family of caretakers is given a one-year contract with the option of a second year. In mid-July, such a toil may seem like a vacation, but one must consider the unseen side of this coin. Although the Point Iroquois Lighthouse is opened to the public from the 15th of May through the 15th of October, the caretakers must remain there every day the year around. By the time that the first snows begin to fall, this lighthouse can become quite isolated. The nearest substantial city, Sault Saint Marie, is nearly an hour's drive away, and that is when the weather is good. By the first week of January, even the lakeboats stop passing by. There is no cable television, few radio stations and even fewer neighbors. Still, the concern over the caretakers is not one of isolation, but rather one of passiveness. At other

The Point Iroquois Light today, remains one of few that visitors can climb. (Author's Photo)

lighthouses, some caretakers who were placed there on long-term contracts have come to think of the lighthouse as their own property. There is even one case where a caretaker used a shotgun to fend off authorities who tried to remove him at the end of his contract. Although this has never happened at the Point Iroquois Lighthouse, the Forest Service is not taking any chances. After all, who would not want to eventually possess a jewel such as this? It is only human nature to grow attached to such surroundings.

One such attachment at the Point Iroquois Lighthouse has managed to keep someone there long after their mortal time on earth had expired. The folks who volunteer at the facility only talk reluctantly about their ghost for fear that too much "hype" will overshadow all of the other wonderful features of the facility. In fact, by lighthouse standards, this isn't much of a ghost at all. It is openly referred to simply as a "presence." Some feel that it is a child, because of the activity around one of the museum displays. Located in the west wing of the living quarters, where most of the activity seems to take place, is a section of the building that has been preserved to appear much as it did in the early part of the 20th century. The living room is set up with all sorts of "everyday" items that were once used by those who lived at the station. One such item is a child's puzzle with large cutout pieces. The entire room is sealed with sheets of Plexiglas, so that the

These stairs lead to the lamproom of the Point Iroquois Light. (Author's Photo)

Although inactive, the Point Iroquois Light has become a major tourist attraction. (Author's Photo)

visitors can look at, but never touch, the items contained within. Access is done only through a locked door, yet pieces of the puzzle are sometimes moved and have even been found as far outside of the glass as the kitchen. This, along with the usual slamming and opening of locked doors associated with most lighthouses, does not make for a grand ghost story. That's exactly the way that the folks who work the Point Iroquois Lighthouse want to keep it.

Originally, this site was established in 1855 to help in the navigation needs of the traffic passing through the newly opened Soo Locks. This first light displayed a fixed white light through a sixth order lens. The original tower stood only 45 feet tall and had a focal plane of just 65 feet. Thus it was visible for a scant eight miles in clear weather. By 1870, however, the Whitefish Bay winters had taken their toll on the original structure and the brick lighthouse that stands today was constructed as a replacement. The new tower was listed as having a white light that flashed at 30 second intervals and was visible for 15 miles in clear weather. A fourth order lens was placed atop the 55-foot-high tower giving the new station a focal

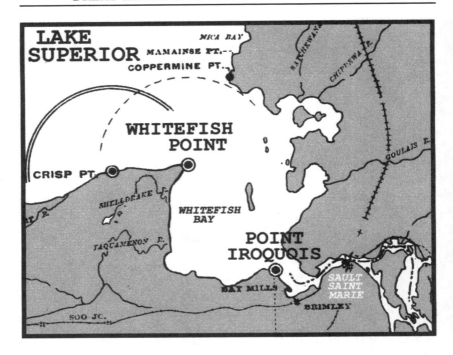

plane of 72 feet above the level of the lake. This light operated until 1962 when it was deactivated after being replaced by a new offshore light. Fortunately, local historical societies and the U.S. Forest Service saw fit to save the light for future generations of tourists to visit. This lighthouse, however, is only one of the two jewels that wait along the route to nowhere. In order to find the next treasure, the tourist must go to nowhere itself—Whitefish Point.

If you were to draw a straight line from the Point Iroquois Lighthouse to the Whitefish Point Lighthouse the distance between the two would measure more than two dozen miles, and all of that would still be across Whitefish Bay. This is a part of the Great Lakes where distances are large, the water is deep, the winters are long and the best way to get to any point on the shore is still by boat. The route that takes you to the tip of Whitefish Point and the lighthouse located there can not be traveled in a straight line, rather it curves along the shore with the bay. At highway speeds it can take well over an hour to get from Point Iroquois to the tip of Whitefish Point, and after an isolated drive such as that, the visitor is not prepared for what they are likely to find.

The first thing that greets the fair-weather visitor to the Whitefish Point Station is a large parking lot that is usually filled to capacity with the cars and R/Vs of other visitors! In fact, this lighthouse can likely lay claim to being the most highly-visited light on the Great Lakes. By count, more than half a million visitors annually make the trek along the route to nowhere to visit this lightstation. Included on the grounds is the iron skeletal light tower, an attached keeper's quarters, a shipwreck and lighthouse theater, a fog signal building, and one of the most outstanding shipwreck and lighthouse museums in the nation. The museum alone contains displays of Great Lakes shipping that are far better than those found at the Smithsonian. One item on display within the museum that no other museum will ever hold is the actual ship's bell from the wreck of the *Edmund Fitzgerald* which rests in Lake Superior just 17 miles north of the museum.

This station was first established in 1847. It is listed as having a fixed white light with 13 lamps that shown through 14-inch reflectors. Later, the 1863 refit of the lighthouse shows the site as having a third order lens. It was this Civil War-era rebuild that established the present-day 80-foot-tall iron skeletal tower.

This light has always been an important symbol to mariners. In fact, while there this author overheard one former lake mariner saying, "Whenever we saw this light downbound, we always knew that we'd made it, we were safe. When we saw it on the way up, we knew that there was a long long way ta go."

Those words, coming from one who sailed the lakes to one who has found himself charged with the duty of documenting their history, are

Thousands of tourists visit the light at Whitefish Point each summer. (Author's Photo)

highly profound. Considering all of the mariners who have sailed past this station at Whitefish Point and then sailed on into oblivion, it is true that this place marks the boundary between existence and nowhere. On a fine summer day it is a gleaming white Oz for the lighthouse and maritime buff. In foul weather it is the symbol that represents either safety or the passage into what could well become nowhere—depending on which way you are going.

GUESTS FROM THE STORM

When Mrs. Bisonette peeked from the window of her lakeside home toward the first hints of Wednesday, October 5, 1932, the morning looked nearly as melancholy as the economic times. From her window, the distance across Lake Erie was the color of cement. As usual—the lake was brewing up an ugly climate and casting it upon New York's Chautaqua County shore. So cold and depressing was the scene that Mrs. Bisonette allowed herself only a brief glimpse toward the lake before pulling her hand from the curtain and allowing it to silently slam shut on the foulness beyond the window. Turning to her household chores, she set about brewing coffee and getting a start on the drab day that lay ahead. If, however, Mrs. Joseph Bisonette had taken the time to look just a bit closer and just a bit longer out that window toward the lake, she may have spotted a tiny speck tossing in the distance upon Lake Erie's ragged surface. It would be that tiny speck that in just a few hours would put Mrs. Bisonette on the front page of the *Buffalo Times*, put her village of Portland on the map, and put her largest coffee kettles to work overtime. That forsaken speck was where the lake's act of life and death was being played out and 16 souls were gripping on the thin line between Lake Erie's vengeance and Mrs. Bisonette's hospitality. Puttering in her kitchen, Mrs. Bisonette had no idea of the drama being acted out just beyond her window or of the predicament that would soon knock at her door.

By October of 1932 the dark cold cloak of the Great Depression had planted its shadow firmly over the entire civilized world. Today the myopic news media enjoys comparing any economic slowdown to the Depression of the 1930s—but in truth there is no comparison. Hinged on the stock market crash in the autumn of 1929, the economy of the nation entered a death spiral. There was no social safety net for the millions of people who were about to lose any means of earning a living. Soon nearly

51

every family in the United States would be touched by the cold hand of the Depression. On the Great Lakes the wildfire of financial disaster had cataclysmic results on the maritime industry. New and modern lakeboats were left at their lay-up berths, as there was simply no market for the cargoes that would be put in their holds. Prior to the stock market crash the lakes shipping industry had been a hodgepodge of hundreds of small and independent fleets scurrying around the ankles of the giant operators. Many wooden lakers still remained in service feeding on the fringes of the industry. When the hard times came, the corporate giants were able to put their excess vessels in lay-up and take their losses. For the smaller operators, however, the onset of the economic downturn was a death stroke. Many shipping companies simply disintegrated in the Depression, abandoning their boats where they had last been laid up. This was particularly true for the wooden fleets. In fact, the Great Depression spelled the end of the wooden-hulled laker.

In 1929 the total bulk tonnage of cargo shipped on the lakes was just over 138.5 million tons; in 1932 that total would drop to just over 41.6 million tons! The single bright spot seemed to be in the shipment of coal. During 1929 more than 39.2 million tons of coal had been transported around the lakes. That figure would be at a low of 24.8 million tons by the end of the depressed 1932 season. Although it was a dramatic reduction, it was not in proportion to the overall tonnage depression. This was, in part, due to the fact that coal was a primary fuel and used practically as a utility. Its shipment, however, was accomplished in the smaller, handy vessels due to the fact that contracts for the fossil fuel were usually in small quantities. Such was the niche that Captain Scott Misener, the president of the Sarnia Steamship Company, had found for his canaller *John J. Boland Jr.*

Attending to the *Boland's* every need was a crew of 19 who were thankful simply to be employed. Serving in the pilothouse along with the captain were First Mate M. Smith and Second Mate A. Burtenshaw who, on their respective watches, gave orders to either Wheelsmen Pender or Vernard. A sharp eye was kept on the safety of the *Boland* by Watchmen McLeod and Scott as they traded duty. Aft, the steamer's engine room was commanded by Chief Engineer Mille Roche who was backed up by William Byers and G. Irwin who, oddly, were both rostered as second engineers. The lubrication schedule of each of the engine's moving parts was attended by 32-year-old Sidney Brooks and 41-year-old Harry Jobes. So hard was the work of shoveling the coal that fed the steamer's boilers that a crew of three men was required to rotate that toil. They were F. Shager, S. Campbell and George Keary. deckhands G. Bennett, A. Verard and C. Goodier played the part of ship's roustabouts, along with the handling required to transition the locks and manipulate the hatches. Most important of all the crew, however, were the Chief Cook, Mrs. J. Smith, who was no relation to the first mate, and Second Cook, Miss Jean

McIntyre, a 24-year-old native of Welland, Ontario. These two ladies of the lakes were charged with providing the crew with an unending supply of that which so many of the Depression victims ashore were missing— hot meals. In all, this group of escapees from the troubled economy were the living element that made the *Boland* function. The boat's crew were all Canadians and most hailed from shipping towns such as St. Catharines, Sarnia and Hamilton. The *Boland* was truly a Canadian boat designed to perform her chores in Canadian waters.

Somehow, in the gloom of the Depression, Misener had managed to secure a few meager contracts to shuttle coal around to assorted lake ports. In the last hours of Tuesday, October 4, 1932, the *Boland* eased her beam up beneath the coal trestle at the port city of Erie, Pennsylvania, on the southeastern shore of Lake Erie. Like so many other ports of call around the lakes, the harbor of Erie, just two years earlier, had been a bustling din of lakeboat activity. Now, in the hollow economic times it was deathly quiet. As the *Boland* tied up, the general darkness of the night covered the hulks of the big steel lakers laid up nearby, as well as the wooden boats left abandoned. With their crews laid off, the big oreboats simply hibernated without so much as a lamp to mark their existence. Daylight, however,

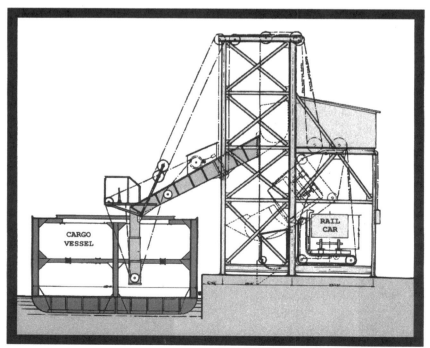

Dump loader similar to that used to load the John J. Boland *before her last trip.*
(Author's Collection)

53

would reveal the sad sight of steel hulled boats tied in convenient slips as if winter lay-up had been indefinitely extended. The oak-hulled vessels would be harder to find as most of them had been shoved into the overgrown backwaters and were already beginning to sink into the landscape. The sight of the depressed armada always brought one fact to mind—tomorrow it might be the *Boland* that sits idle in the slip, and her crew would then be on the street among the millions of people looking for work of any kind. It was all just as well because Captain Hawman planned on having the *Boland* loaded and underway long before dawn. His departure would be prior to the daylight's revelation of those beleaguered lakers, but then again, every port on the lakes had a depressed fleet in lay-up. There would be plenty of gloom to go around wherever the *Boland* may tie up.

Loading of coal was an interesting process. At some docks, railroad cars filled with the combustible rocks would be pushed into a loading gantry, locked down and then rolled completely over so that their contents were dumped into a hopper. That hopper was then hoisted over the open hatchway of a lakeboat and dumped using a trap door. In other cases, such as the side-dump method, a rail car was chained down to an elevating platform and hoisted to the top of a large gantry. There the rail car was tipped over and its coal cargo was dumped into a hopper-like funnel and directly loaded into the lakeboat. One of these "McMyler Side Dump" units is known to have existed at the port of Erie. Although no record exists of exactly which dock put the *Boland's* cargo aboard, it is highly likely that she used this unit at the Erie and Pittsburgh Railway Dock. The process, regardless of which type was used, was quick and efficient, resulting in the *Boland* being fully loaded before three o'clock Wednesday morning. It was likely nothing more than pure economics that caused Captain Hammond to make one of the traditionally dumbest decisions that a captain of a lakeboat can make in the autumn season. In order to carry as much cargo as possible, he not only ordered his hold filled with coal, but also had a deckload piled upon his tiny command. To keep the loading time to an absolute minimum, he also did not have his hatchcovers placed or secured. This was a process that would have required placing dozens of large planks across each hatch opening and then wedging them in place with long steel rods. After that a tarpaulin had to be stretched across each hatch and made secure in order to make the whole rig watertight. All of this had to be done by hand and the work would take hours. So, the time between filling the hold and adding the deckload would be considerable if the hatches were to be secured. Instead, Captain Hammond elected to save time and simply add the deckload immediately after the cargo hold was full.

Hamilton, Ontario, had been assigned as the vessel's destination. The trip would require steaming to the easternmost end of Lake Erie, through the Welland Canal, and onto Lake Ontario. It was a short haul that would

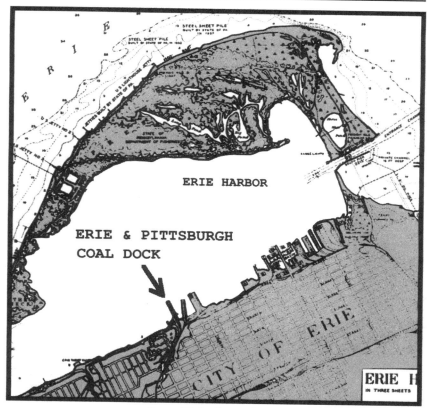

Port of Erie, Pennsylvania

take the little canaller the better part of two days to complete, but it was honest work. The problem was that there could very well be a representative of the Sarnia Steamship Company waiting at end of the line with lay-up instructions in mind and severance pay in hand. Just that quickly the crew of the *Boland* could go from sailing the lakes to selling pencils on the street. Such were the times of the Great Depression. Today the media is fond of saying that every family is just a paycheck away from homelessness, a faddish fib that ignores the true state of the world. They would do well to take a hard look back to 1932, to a time when living on the street *actually* was just a paycheck away. Seeing the world from that perspective, we can understand Captain Hammond's motivation in sailing the *Boland* in an overloaded condition.

No one really took notice as the *Boland* slipped through the pierheads and onto Lake Erie. The early October weather was rude and dark with an insulting wind that came whipping at the little steamer. A continuous heavy rain fell across the whole of the eastern lakes region, and in many areas flood conditions were prevalent. It was a nasty autumn night that was nearly as discouraging as the financial atmosphere. By Great Lakes standards the *John J. Boland Jr.* was considered a new boat. Her assembly had taken place less than four years earlier in 1928 at Wallsend-on-Tyne, England. Christened *Tyneville* at the time of her birth, hull number 1282 was given the name *John J. Boland Jr.* shortly after her launching. Typical of most canallers, the *Boland* was engineered to fit the confines of the Welland Canal at that time. Her length overall was a bantam 258 feet—the maximum for the locks of both the Welland Canal and St. Lawrence River in 1928. Interestingly, at that time the Welland Canal was nearing the completion of a project to expand the locks from 270 feet to 820 feet. This "off-again and on-again" project was started in 1913 and completed in 1932, reducing the number of locks needed to lower or lift the boats the 326-foot difference in elevation between Lakes Erie and Ontario. The 22 locks along the St. Lawrence River, however, would not be expanded until the end of the 1950s, so although she was soon to be outmoded on the Welland, there would be plenty of use for the *Boland* on the St. Lawrence.

Bearing in mind that canallers were designed to spend most of their working time within the protected waters of the rivers that made up the seaways, and that their primary challenge was in repeatedly passing through the 48 locks in that system, their utilitarian construction makes sense. Most canallers were basically a cargo hold built around a boiler with a pilothouse stuck on for good measure. Their job was simply to haul products through the restrictions of the canals and locks, so little effort was made in most canaller designs to aid in fighting off an enraged open sea. When loaded, the vessels had meager freeboard. In other words, the distance between the deck and the water was just a few feet. Additionally, their fo'c'sle decks were often "half raised." This meant that the forward cabin's roof was only about one-half of the normal cabin height, with only a hint of gunwale at the forepeak. On an angered lake the seas would easily take advantage of a canaller's low profile and climb aboard. These elements were all constructed into the *Boland*; when fully loaded she could have less than six feet of freeboard. Yet, when it came to effectively toting cargo through the locks and in and out of restricted waterways—she was a model of efficiency. Although a canaller such as the *Boland* had a normally low posture when fully loaded, add a deckload to such a lakeboat and the thing is nearly a submarine.

Driven by a 40-mile-per-hour wind Lake Erie lashed at the steel bow plating and sent spray completely over her pilothouse. In gray billows the foaming lake came on deck and swirled playfully around the hatch combings before departing through the scuppers. The night was ink-black and the winds were making that familiar and musical hum in the wires of the steamer's rigging. It was just after four o'clock on Wednesday morning

Steamer John J. Boland. *(Author's Concept)*

the fifth day of October, 1932. Although he had no inkling of events to come, Captain Hawman was standing the last few minutes of his command aboard the *Boland*. At six o'clock that morning the Interlake steamer *Cygnus* passed the *Boland* about an hour out of Erie, and the little canaller appeared to be making good weather of it. Still, the hand of doom waited over the little lakeboat, but seemed to want her when she was alone. As if the wind and waves and rain had not made for a rude enough setting—the frigid air that was passing across the relatively warmer lake now formed a fog. The *Cygnus* sailed on into Erie.

Huffing her way toward the east-northeast, the little laker was just settling into her routine posture for the stormy passage across Lake Erie when the vengeful lake decided to take her. There is no record as to who was standing what watch, or at the wheel, or even exactly what time the event occurred, but the *Boland* was about 10 miles off of Barcelona, New York, just after 6 a.m. when the end came. From the written accounts that exist it is clear that there was a great deal of confusion aboard as the boat's steering apparatus reportedly jammed. Moments later, the wind and waves took control of the steamer and swung her completely around into the sea trough. So overpowered was the boat that now her bow was pointed back toward Erie. At that point, the minimal freeboard that had been designed into the these canallers became very important. What had been a modest sea in weather that was only slightly more than ugly, now swept the *Boland* like the worst of Lake Erie's gales.

Waves came solidly over the *Boland's* beam and attacked her open hatches through her deckload. A sharp list to the starboard side was the first telltale sign of the boat's impending demise. In just a matter of minutes all of the crew knew that their boat was doomed. Chaos reigned atop the *Boland's* aft deckhouse as the crew mustered in the effort to abandon her. The lake's tossing of the steamer and the extreme listing of the deck signaled the crew in a manner that no general alarm bell could have accomplished. Each person that gathered near the lifeboats knew that they had to get off of the boat, and they had to do it immediately. The port side lifeboat was useless because the listing hull of the *Boland* now came between the lifeboat and the lake effectively blocking its being lowered. The crew now concentrated on the lowering of the starboard boat as the *Boland* began to founder beneath their feet. All around the winds sent the waves to beat down the steamer as the decks tilted toward the depths. Panicked hands pulled at the lines and swung the lifeboat out over the encroaching water. In a matter of seconds the yawl was being lowered as the crew clamored aboard. Apparently, however, the sense that the steamer was on the brink of turning turtle was overwhelming for some of the crew. Not wanting to wait for the yawl to be launched, several of the crew simply went "over the side." In a blind panic, oilers Sidney Brooks and Harry Jobes, as well as Fireman George Keary and Second Cook Jean McIntyre,

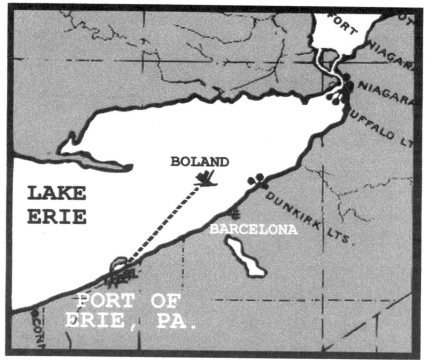

Map of the Boland *wreck site.*

were among the group who jumped into the lake and attempted to make a swim for it. Just where these four thought that they would swim to was known only to them—the nearest land was eight miles away!

No sooner had the lifeboat been set free of the *Boland* than the steamer began to roll over. For a single empty moment the wind, the cold, the waves and the ice water that sloshed among the numb feet of those in the lifeboat meant nothing as each person watched their workplace capsize. No one, not even the most experienced of the crewmembers, could have imagined that a vessel the size of the *Boland* could roll over so quickly, but roll she did, like a floating log. A rumble that resembled an earthquake filled the night as everything that had once been attached to the steamer suddenly found itself up side down. Boilers, cargo, equipment of all kinds ripped lose as gravity pulled at them and the lake exploded into every compartment. To the witnesses in the lifeboat it appeared as if the *Boland* went completely over with her keel pointing straight up. A heartbeat later and the vessel plunged toward the depths shooting a plume of steam into the air and turning the lake's surface into a hill of frothing water. Then, there was only the sound of the whipping wind and whitecapped waves. As suddenly as the demise of the *John J. Boland Jr.* had started, the event was over.

Surrounded by nothing other than a heaving lake in every direction, the *Boland's* survivors now had nothing between them and certain doom other than a small wooden lifeboat. Of the entire crew, all but Harry Jobes, George Keary, Sidney Brooks and Jean McIntyre had managed to get aboard the lifeboat. Their panicked leap into the lake had been a deadly mistake, and now all four were gone. Waves of frigid Lake Erie now cascaded aboard the tossing yawl bringing with them an indescribable cold that seemed to pierce through every person the water touched. Each member of the crew had just enough time to escape with the clothing that they had been wearing when the *Boland's* steering gear jammed. Mrs. Smith had been able to grab a light jacket from the hook and throw it on over her cooking dress. As she sat on the cold bench of the tossing yawl, the lake had already soaked her thoroughly. Now it seemed as if the stinging water was out to sap the very life from her body. Her teeth began to chatter in spite of her best efforts to keep still and her very fiber trembled, partly from the cold and partly from the shock. Others in the lifeboat took turns bailing, rowing and shivering. The night was as black as death and there was not a light to be seen. There is no written account of how the group navigated the yawl, but it is likely that a compass was aboard in the lifeboat's emergency equipment, and using it they would have made a heading for the southern shore—a distance of eight miles in waves that had just made short work of a 250-foot steel steamer. A stormy night that seemed to swallow them as a group would be the obstacle they had to overcome.

Dawn came grudgingly and turned the black storm to gray, but there was no warmth with the daylight. Instead the pain of the stinging cold seas that came aboard at every opportunity simply persisted. Aboard the yawl, there was not much to do or say in this sorrowful position, there was only shivering and numbing as Lake Erie toyed with its victims. After the first few hours had melted together, the distant tossing horizon ahead appeared to grow much darker. Indeed it was the south shore of Lake Erie, but it was still a long distance away. Yawls have been known to upset within wading distance of dry land and send all of their occupants to their doom. For that reason, the sight of the shore was really not insurance of survival. The beach was ahead all right, but it could very well be a lifetime away.

Rowing and bailing for the better part of six hours, the castaways eventually ran into the southern shore. It was about 11 o'clock in the morning when the yawl skidded onto dry land and left behind a vengeful Lake Erie. Although benumbed by the cold and exhausted from their calamity, the castaways managed to safely cross the breaking surf. The ordeal in the little boat had lasted nearly six hours and left every member of the lifeboat nearly spent from exhaustion and cold. From the narrow stretch of beach, a ladder led up the bluff toward the Bisonette home which was about 100 yards inland. It took the last ounce of strength for some of the crew to make that climb, but soon the whole group had gathered at the top of the small bluff. Happy just to be on dry land the refugees at once sighted the Bisonette house and headed off to seek its shelter. Involved in her daily routine, Mrs. Bisonette was suddenly distracted by an unexpected and loud knock at her door. When she opened the entry she was startled to come face-to-face with a large group of weather-beaten, soaking wet castaways. Certainly she must have thought that her home was about to be invaded by a gang of hobos. A second look, however, told her a different story. Several of the survivors were hardly able to stand up and all were shivering uncontrollably. Mrs. Smith, the chief cook, was nearly in a state of collapse from the ordeal in the lifeboat and had to be held up by two of the crew. After only a brief explanation from the survivors, Mrs Bisonette realized their dilemma. With a loud shout she summoned her husband, and a moment later the Bisonette home was opened to shelter the shipwrecked crew.

Putting to work her two biggest pots and her two largest kettles, the homemaker-turned-lifesaver quickly brewed an amount of coffee that seemed large enough to warm a small army. The survivors emptied all four containers in less than five minutes. A large loaf of fresh baked bread and a dish of butter was quickly brought out and Mrs. Bisonette cut a large slice and started to butter it. But, before a stroke of butter could be applied, the hand of a starving mariner snatched away the slice and it was gobbled up. More coffee was definitely in order and the stove went back to work. As the second batch was brewing, Joseph Bisonette was out enlisting the help of the neighborhood. Soon the most exhausted of the crew were tucked into dry beds and everyone was provided with all of the old clothing that could be found around the neighborhood. Jackets, pants, shirts and sweaters that were once considered as useless now had a purpose. They may have been hand-me-downs, but at least they were dry and no one from the *Boland* was about to complain. No one concerned themselves with the fact that these were hard economic times, and that most folks in the area could scarcely afford to feed themselves. There was no deal struck for reimbursement, or contract for services rendered. The neighborhood and the Bisonettes simply opened their arms to the mariners in need. Once clothed and filled with hot coffee, most of the crew began to rapidly recover. Without really knowing it, Mrs. Bisonette had turned her home into a lifesaving station. By tradition, these stations not only were established to rescue mariners from the seas, but also to shelter and cloth those who were cast ashore. Without Mrs. Bisonette's hot coffee, warm stove and dry clothing the survivors of the *Boland* may have died on the open beach. In a time when those who gave were likely more destitute than those who came calling for aid, the Bisonettes and their neighbors opened their doors to mariners in distress and kept the valor in the finest traditions of the people who live around the lakes.

By nightfall every member of the crew who had reached land alive had recovered fully and the entire crew boarded a bus for Buffalo. By that time the news of the sinking had spread and the local newspaper buzzards descended on the Bisonette home. Popping flash bulbs and sharpened pencils now went to work as an eager housewife told her side of the story that would be the next day's front-page news. In the tradition of the news media, they only managed to publish most of the facts, and forgot one important detail—Mrs. Bisonette's full name. By the time that the survivors transferred to a Canadian bus, the homemaker turned life-saver was left with a mountain of dishes and a scatter of blankets as her reward. It mattered little, because in her heart Mrs. Bisonette knew that she had done the right thing for all of the right reasons. By opening her home she had come to the rescue, and that was all that mattered.

The following morning the fishing tug *Betty And Jean* putted out into the predawn darkness in an effort to net what fish harvest the lake might see fit to offer. Perhaps, if Lake Erie was willing, there may be enough fish in the nets to sell for a decent day's wages. Of course, in the depths of the Great Depression, anything that should come back with the netting would probably be a welcomed catch—or so they thought. Unfortunately, the fishermen had no idea what kind of a grim harvest Lake Erie had in store. The gulls screamed in their normal begging screech as the fishing tug's nets were hauled up, but the weight in the snare was not that of a mass of fish, it was the remains of Second Cook Jean McIntyre from the *John J. Boland Jr.* For a moment the gulls seemed to silence as the shock of the catch smothered the background clamor. The implications of having a woman's dead body hanging in their net were not lost among the fishermen. It is a good bet that there was even thought of putting the cadaver back into the lake. At length, it was decided to just return to Westfield and turn the poor lady over to the proper authorities. By the following day, Miss McIntyre, like the *Boland's* survivors, was on her way home to Canada.

With eight years more of the Depression remaining, followed by a world war, a cold war and the re-expansion and redecline of the Great Lakes maritime industry, the sinking of the *Boland* was forgotten by nearly everyone. Other vessels later carried the name *John J. Boland Jr.* across the lakes—the most recent being the third, and given that name in 1953. As of this writing, it is in active service on the lakes. Books were written of the shipwrecks of the lakes popularizing the most disastrous and mysterious of those events. Researchers, boat-buffs and divers were inspired by these texts and the efforts to find the glamour wrecks seemed always drawn from the written accounts. With all of this, it is easy to see how the 1932 shipwreck of the *Boland* could have been obscured. And so it was, with the *Boland* being an afterthought, that research diver Jack O'Keefe went looking for the long-lost wooden steamer *Dean Richmond* off of Barcelona, New York. Using a magnetometer, it was his hope to discover the giant metal boilers and engine works of that long lost steamer. During the search, a large mass of metal was discovered by the O'Keefe team. In 140 feet of water and eight and one-half miles northwest of Barcelona, the object was a bit too deep for the team and the decision was made to engage a professional wreck diver. Enter research diver Paul Ehorn into the tale of the *Boland*. What Paul discovered at the location was not the *Richmond*, but the *Boland*. Laying three-quarters inverted on her starboard side, the boat rested with her bow pointed to the west-southwest. Even with her bow slammed 10 feet into the clay bottom, it was clearly the *Boland*.

After half a century of laying forgotten on the bottom of Lake Erie, the *Boland* had been rediscovered. There was not much to see, she was simply a big steel hulk that would forever rest on the bottom of the lake. Once Paul Ehorn had made the identification, there was little more to do other than continuing the search for the *Richmond*. Compared to the long-lost *Richmond*, the *Boland* had little historical significance. The *Richmond* had vanished with hardly a trace, but everyone knew what had happened aboard the *Boland*. Perhaps for that reason alone, her wreck had been relegated to the pages of Great Lakes obscurity. The highlight of the *Boland's* story seems to be the actions of the Bisonette family and their neighbors. Unfortunately, the Bisonettes seem as swallowed by obscurity as was their story. Efforts toward finding them or their kinfolk were fruitless. Should anyone who happens to reside along the southeast Lake Erie shore read this account and recognize the persons named here please contact the author. Of persons, such as the Bisonettes, we all would like to know more.

Today, the port city of Erie boasts a waterfront that no one could have possibly imagined in 1932. Hardly a trace of the Depression's industrial rot remains. In the place of coal docks and railheads are now upscale marinas and a bayside library of the most modern sort. Additionally, there is a convention center and maritime museum which sparkle like the fresh water of the bay beyond their windows. Certainly, the lakeboats still tie up at Erie, but the prospect are, as of this writing, far brighter for the mariners than they were on that October night in 1932 when the *Boland* made Erie her final port of call.

A SCIENTIFIC PERSON
RESIDING AT
MILWAUKEE SAYS...

O n Tuesday, September 11, 1883 the steamer *Don M. Dickinson* pulled the schooner-barge *N.P. Goodell* into the Saginaw River and dropped her off at the Bay City, Michigan dock of the Beard Company to load 230,000 board feet of lumber. Three days later, at the end of the *Dickinson's* towline once more, the *Goodell* followed faithfully out of that same port. Included in the tow was the schooner-barge *G.W. Bissell*, her deck also being stacked high with 400,000 board feet of freshly-cut lumber. All three boats were bound for Toledo where their cargoes would be unloaded and distributed across the growing nation. A nasty bit of autumn weather was blowing on Saginaw Bay as the steamer and her tow plowed up toward the tip of the thumb and all of the boats in the *Dickinson's* tow began to roll drunkenly in the waves. The widely-published weather prediction of a "scientific person residing in Milwaukee" seemed to be coming true. Yet for those who made their living on the lakes this was just another fall blow. That was certainly the way that Captain Emery, master of the *Goodell* saw things.

The modern science of meteorology is largely taken for granted as being routinely correct in predicting the weather to come. Satellites hover in geo-synchronous orbits over the earth and gather data of all kinds beaming it back to super-computers where it is converted into weather models. Every form of news media carries the concise weather picture and manages to make it available to nearly every person concerned. In the 1880s the distribution of weather information was quite different, often depending on the farmer's almanac and local barometer movements, or any other tidbits that may indicate the conditions ahead. On the first Friday of September, 1883, a prediction of weather to come was submitted to the *Chicago Tribune* and published in marine columns around the lakes. When turning to the marine section of port city papers Captain Emery and his fellow mariners would have come upon the following prediction:

Vesselmen are warned against impending storms of unusual violence during the remainder of the season. A scientific person residing at Milwaukee says: 'Present appearances indicate unusually violent equinoctial storms, universal in extent and disastrous in effect, and it will be well if vessel owners take extra precautions for the safety of their vessels and crews during the next three months. In particular they ought to use extra caution during the last 16 or 18 days of this and the next two ensuing months. The moon's influence upon terrestrial matter will be exceedingly strong between the 15th and 22nd...', and no doubt we shall hear of further calamities from earthquakes or volcanic action that week."

Adding a bit of editorial comment the newspaper article continued, "It may be possible that the alleged weather prophet doesn't know what he is talking about, but ten-to-one every sailor who reads this will cut it out and use it as an argument in favor of higher wages." Certainly, if Captain Emery or mariner Abbot Way would have had any idea as to what level of truth that stormy prediction had in store for them, they would have demanded a higher wage for this current trip from Cleveland and Toledo, Ohio to Bay City, Michigan and back—much higher!

Lake Huron's bright blue turned into her stormy autumn gray as the foul clouds appeared to race along the lake's surface driven by a bitter wind that foretold the coming of the worst of the navigation season. The rain mixed with spray and hissed across the vessels, not cold enough to freeze, but frigid enough to send a shiver through the most seasoned lake mariner. Somewhere in the middle of the turmoil, Captain Emery noticed that his boat had jammed her fly. The boat's "fly" is a small windsock-like flag or pennant that is used to gage the winds as they are applied to the boat. Knowing that this small cloth tool was often needed, Emery could not tolerate the thought of it being tangled and he climbed over to free it. Before doing this he probably should have taken greater heed in that "scientific person's" warning to use extra caution during the last 16 days of the month. There were exactly 16 days remaining in the month, when a sudden wave caused the *Goodell* to lurch beneath Emery as he tried to clear the fly. A moment later the startled master found himself submersed in the shocking cold of Lake Huron. Instinctively he righted himself and clawed for the surface. Breaking his head above the water, his eyes cleared just in time to get a closeup view of the *Goodell's* hull timbers as they slid past him. As if attempting to catch a giant greased pig he pawed at the slimy, slick, oak hull but could find nothing on which to get a grip. The skipper knew only too well that if he could not grab onto the boat she would leave him behind for the lake to keep, and the prospect of treading water in the middle of a Lake Huron gale was surely one of which nightmares are made. Seeking any crack or spike that may be protruding from the hull, the frantic master tried desperately to grapple his boat, but it was quickly becoming too late, the stern of the *Goodell* was coming up fast and when it passed, so would Emery's fate be sealed. Indeed, he truly should have paid attention to that "scientific person residing in Milwaukee."

Unfortunately, at the moment that the scientific person was penning his prediction and preparing to send it off to the local media, Captain Emery had been busy supervising the matters of the unloading of the *Goodell* at Toledo. He did not have a clue as to the icy cold bath that was in his near future and little time for such highbrowed foreshadowing on the events to come. Likewise, seaman Abbot Way was busy singling up the lines onboard the vessel of his employ, the schooner-barge *Colorado*. When she was constructed at Fairport, Ohio in 1866, the sailing vessel *Colorado* joined a massive fleet of wind-powered vessels making a good living on the Great Lakes. But, the age of sail was about to rapidly give way to the age of steam power, and within two decades the 118-foot-long *Colorado*, like the *Goodell*, could no longer earn her way alone. She soon discovered a new era of profitability at the end of a steamer's towline and thus joined another massive class of lakeboats, that of former schooners being used as barges. Much the same as the *Goodell*, the *Colorado's* new life represented a mixed blessing to her crew and owners. When the winds were scarce or from an undesirable direction, it mattered little because her consort steamer simply towed her across the lakes in spite of the winds. On the other hand, when the winds were favorable and the vessels that were still rigged as sailing craft raced gracefully to their destinations, the old schooner-barge was obligated to depend on her steamer. It was a toil of far less elegance than that of wind-grabbing, but it extended the careers of small vessels, such as the *Colorado* far past their normal useful life. Thus, the *Colorado* was pulled from Cleveland harbor at the end of the steamer *Dickinson's* towing hawser.

Running with an empty cargo hold, the *Colorado* was bound for the port of Bay City, but due to her dependence on the *Dickinson's* steam plant for propulsion, she would be forced to follow the steamer on a little side trip. Waiting at the port of Toledo, the schooner-barge *Goodell* would soon join the *Colorado* in the trip upbound with the *Dickinson*. In the resigned labor of a tow-barge, the *Colorado* and her crew had no choice other than to tag along into Toledo. To Abbot Way this side trip was of little consequence. He earned the same wage regardless of being in port or out on the lake. His duties of handling lines, opening and closing hatches, chipping and painting and shoving lumber with the dock crews never really changed much, it was only the seasons that made his job change. So, as the port of Cleveland faded astern it may as well have been Alpena, or Muskegon or Kenosha, it really made no difference to Abbot Way. Early in the afternoon of Thursday, September 6th, 1883, the *Dickinson* and her consort slithered into the Maumee River and through the heart of Toledo.

By dinner time the *Goodell* was attached to the tow line directly behind the steamer with the *Colorado* bringing up the rear and all was ready for the upbound passage to Bay City.

Command of the *Colorado* was the responsibility of Captain Patterson, and aboard were his wife and three children. In this era of Great Lakes navigation, captains and seamen often found themselves away from home from the opening of the season of navigation in April until its close in December. For this reason, officers on vessels often took their wives sailing with them. Although in modern times, union contracts allow extended periods away from the boat during the navigation season, the tradition of taking a spouse along for some sailing still continues. So, the fact that Captain Patterson had his wife and children along on the *Colorado* was nothing new, nor was it anything unusual, it was just the way of things on the lakes.

Once the whole tow had been properly assembled, the *Dickinson* headed outbound. No sooner had the trip started than the *Colorado* began to give the entire group a headache. As the string of lakers began to pass through the Pennsylvania Bridge over the Maumee River, the *Colorado* decided to take a sheer to the starboard side and before Captain Patterson could get her under control, she struck the draw. The sudden stress parted the towing hawser like a pipestem and the schooner swung across the channel. Leaving the stranded barge behind, the master of the *Dickinson* proceeded to Ironwood where he dropped the rest of his tow and then headed back for the *Colorado*. Once the wayward schooner-barge had been recovered, and the whole tow had been reassembled, the captain of the *Dickinson* set his course for Turtle Island and the upbound track through the Detroit and St. Clair Rivers. Eventually, the tow would pass Port Huron and the open expanse of Lake Huron would lay ahead.

It is unclear who exactly was in charge of the *Dickinson* on this trip. Local newspaper accounts do not specifically say who the captain was, but some give indirect reference to a man called "Captain Blanchard," stating that "his barge" was the *Colorado*. Considering that the official accounts of the events surrounding this particular trip clearly list Captain Patterson as the schooner-barge's master, we may consider that Blanchard was in charge of the tow via the steamer, and thus considered the *Colorado* as "his." This bit of confusion is in step with the whole background of the *Dickinson* itself. Born of saltwater at Wilmington, Delaware, in 1858, the iron-hulled steamer had originally been christened *Ellen S. Terry*. While on the ocean waters the 148-foot vessel went through a number of owners. In fact, at least one document shows as many as 16 changes prior to her coming to the lakes in 1881. Her home port was eventually listed as Detroit on April 15, 1881, and she appeared to have found a home on freshwater, even if no clear record of her captain was kept.

All night on Thursday, the sixth of September, 1883, and most of the following morning were taken up by the trek of the boats toward Lake

Huron. When the tow passed Port Huron on Friday afternoon, the sky above was growing gray and threatening. A nasty autumn storm was in the making and of that there could be no doubt. Pushing the *Dickinson* for all that the boat's dwarf steam engine could muster her captain was in hope of nearing the port of Sand Beach, Michigan, before the weather set in. Sand Beach, now known as Harbor Beach, was being groomed as one of the best storm shelters on the lakes. Construction on a massive three-legged breakwater was just being finished, and if the *Dickinson* was anywhere near that port when the storm came up, it would be an easy matter to duck in and wait out the blow. As the sun set, the gale exploded across the thumb of Michigan and set upon the boats on the open lake. The *Dickinson* was just south of Sand Beach at the time, and started her run for the south entrance to the port's breakwater. It was a good plan, but the *Colorado* had other ideas.

When the gale hit it brought winds out of the northeast that rapidly blew away the last traces of summer and sent an ugly sea against the *Dickinson* and her consorts. With the lamps of the harbor entrance in sight, all looked perfect for the run for shelter and in short order the *Dickinson* entered the calmed waters of Sand Beach harbor. Minutes later the *Goodell* came rolling through the breakwater at the end of the steamer's hawser. For the *Colorado* and Abbot Way, however, the story took an abrupt turn. Just as the schooner-barge was approaching the entrance to the breakwater, that same towing hawser that had parted in Toledo the previous day let go once again. His mariner's savvy told Captain Patterson that his boat had just enough inertia to make the breakwater before the storm winds grabbed her. Having that in mind he ordered Abbot Way to snatch a line and jump to the breakwater when it came near. Once there he was to attempt to secure the *Colorado* to the pier. Without a moment's hesitation Way dashed forward and clutched the first mooring line at hand, and telling one of the other crewmen to get the other end, Abbot poised on the schooner-barge's rail ready to jump. As if slowed by an invisible tug, the *Colorado* traded her forward speed against the power of the gale as she slid up nearly parallel to the pier for nearly a thousand feet. Gradually the rocks of the breakwater neared as Abbot Way waited for exactly the right moment, and then he leaped.

Being out on a breakwater in the calm of a pleasant summer day can be a bit unnerving with the land seeming to be an unreachable distance away. But during the insanity of an autumn gale it must have been a terrifying spot for Abbot Way. Lake Huron blasted waves of exploding ice water over the pier as Way struggled to find a spot to secure the line. The top of the incomplete breakwater was a riprap of timbers and boulders that was slickened by the lake washing atop it. To make matters worse, there was not a single lamp to split the darkness—and there was also not a moment to lose in securing the line! Slipping and stumbling in the dark, the bruised crewman somehow found a place to tie off the line and, as fast

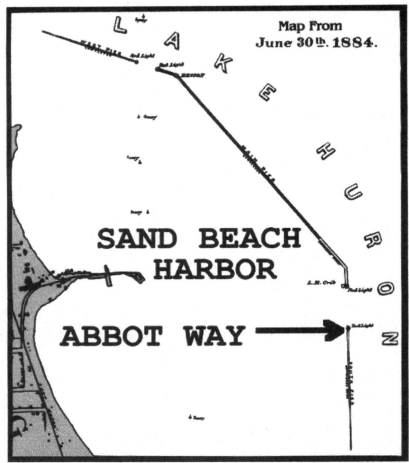

Map showing Abbot Way's *position after being stranded by the* Colorado.

as his benumbed hands could maneuver, he tied a quick sailor's knot. Instantly the slack was taken up on the line as the wind took the *Colorado*. Apparently, the vessel's mooring lines were in worse condition than her towing hawser, because no sooner had the line tightened than it parted at the knot. Scrambling, Way managed to grab the line and resecure it, but it promptly parted again. Once more he managed to grab the line and attempted to retie it. This time, however, the *Colorado's* movement had not left enough line to make a good knot and it simply slipped away and snaked into the lake. Now the schooner-barge rapidly vanished into the night—carried by the storm. Abbot Way was left behind, marooned on the breakwater. Every few seconds a wave smashed against the pier and drenched the castaway with a cascade of Lake Huron, as the wind howled in a spooky storm-song. Suddenly, Way felt very much alone and the realization of where he had planted himself came upon him. The gap of the south entrance to the harbor stood between him and dry land, and now the lake was washing completely over the breakwater. There was only one hope, a thousand feet across the frothing water at the gap of the east entrance, the spar to which the red entrance light was mounted was elevated well above the water. Attached to mast was the ladder that was normally used to reach and light the entrance lamp. If Abbot could get to the spar he could climb above the waves. The sweeping seas attempted to continually wash him from the wall as he tripped and stumbled toward the refuge. Once he had managed to transcend the incomplete portion of the breakwater, Abbot came upon the planked walkway that lead to the mast. By this time, however, the waves were rolling six feet deep over the pier, and he could only make progress by sticking his fingers between the planks and dragging himself along through the deluge. Each ice water avalanche sapped his strength and slowed his progress. Way had started as volunteer with a line in hand, selflessly seeking only to save his boat. Now he found himself firmly in Lake Huron's deadly grasp.

At this same time, the lookout at the Sand Beach Lifesaving Station observed a signal from the keeper of the lighthouse located at the eastern gap of the breakwater. Thinking that the keeper may be in some kind of distress, the lifesavers launched their surf boat and pulled across the inner harbor to the lighthouse. Once there they were informed by the lightkeeper that he had witnessed a schooner-barge break loose from her tow and strike the south breakwall. Unknown to both the lightkeeper and the lifesavers, that schooner-barge had been the *Colorado*, and she had deposited Abbot Way into the grip of Lake Huron. Concerned that the loose vessel had been damaged in the process of meeting the wall, and may have drifted away to its doom, the lighthouse keeper had summoned the station crew to go to the rescue. From the lighthouse the lifesavers rowed back across the harbor to the south of the breakwater and commenced a search for the wayward schooner-barge. They found nothing—no sign of a vessel and, more importantly, no sign of Abbot Way. After more than a hour's search, the lifesavers returned to the station at nine o'clock. They logged in and dispatched the beach patrols to the north and south. From the sternrail of the *Goodell*, Captain Emery observed the activity of the lifesavers along the breakwall. As the station crew returned, he assumed that all was well—despite the severed towing hawser that now rested in a jumble on the *Goodell's* deck. He was wrong.

Blasting from the northeast, the gale continued to intensify with sheets of rain and a wind that seemed intent on making the prediction of that scientific person living in Milwaukee ring true. Two hours after the lifesavers had stowed their surf boat, the surfman who had been on the south patrol came dashing back to the station excitedly reporting that a vessel was stranded a mile and a half south of the station at Crane Point.

The famed Marquette lifesavers are seen here posing in their lifeboat on the launching ways. Note several items in this photo, such as the careful stowage of the rescue gear in the surfboat in the foreground and the massive stacks of lumber in the background. These make up the setting in which the lifesaver's adventures were played out. (Superior View photo)

Instantly, the station crew mustered in preparation to row to the rescue. Just as they were ready to launch, the north patrol came running into the station. He reported that the captain of the passenger steamer *City Of Concord*, which had just come into the Sand Beach harbor through the east gap, had hailed him as the boat anchored to report an odd observation. As the *City Of Concord* passed through the gap her crew had observed a most unusual sight. The lamp at the entrance appeared to be blinking, and as they drew closer they could see clinging high up on the spar that supported the light was a drenched man who was shouting for help at the top of his lungs. It was Abbot Way! By momentarily covering the lamp, probably using his hat, Abbot had signaled the steamer, but the crew of the vessel could do nothing other than sail past helplessly. Once again, Way was left behind on the south breakwater.

Pulling with all of their strength, the surfmen headed for the east gap. This time they knew exactly what to look for, and where to look. Nearing the gap they saw Way attached to the lamp mast and continuing to shout for help. The waves were running so high that their crests were nearly reaching his legs, and the only thing that had allowed him to survive this long was the fact that the air temperature was around 48 degrees. If the gale had taken place just a few weeks later in the autumn season, the temperature would have dropped below freezing and Abbot would have surely perished on the mast. Now, as the surf boat drew near, the towering waves actually worked in the stranded crewman's favor. The seas lifted the surf boat and the lifesavers closer to the shivering castaway, and he was able to jump into the waiting arms of the surfmen who shuttled him to the lifesaving station. So sapped was Abbot's strength that he seemed to melt into the surf boat and was unable to move. Once safely in the protection and warmth of the station, however, the stranded mariner rapidly recovered and was able to tell his tale. Wasting no time, the surfmen procured a team of horses and headed up the beach to where the *Colorado* had stranded. Arriving at the boat at one o'clock in the morning, the lifesavers found her "lying easily with her head to the wind." In fact, so secure was the boat's position that the crew and the captain's wife and children felt no need to be rescued. For the Sand Beach lifesavers, that was enough. Without additional concern they returned to the station and waited for their next call to action.

By the following evening, the gale had blown itself out and navigation on Lake Huron was returning to normal. The lifesaving crew of Sand Beach returned to the *Colorado* and, at the request of Captain Patterson, procured a scow. Once at the stranded schooner-barge, the surfmen helped her crew strip the vessel of her storm-sail, spars and other items that the lake may attempt to remove in some new fit of wind and wave. The appliances were then transferred to the steamer *Dickinson* for transport to Bay City. The plan now was to refloat the *Colorado* and tow her to the Bay City drydock where she could be repaired and returned to service. Once the *Colorado's* gear had been secured aboard the *Dickinson*, the steamer took her remaining consort, the *Goodell*, and steamed out onto Lake Huron. From the *Goodell's* rail, Captain Emery could see the beaten *Colorado* fetched up on Crain Point as his vessel was pulled onto Lake Huron. The grounded schooner-barge looked like a real mess, and Emery felt a bit lucky that the lake had seen fit to spare him.

Only a week later, Emery found that the lake had her sights set on him, personally, as he thrashed about in the storm-churned sea after being tossed overboard. With the *Goodell's* hull rapidly passing by it appeared as if the captain was about to meet his doom in the big lake. Fortunately, the ire of Lake Huron can not undo the course of Providence, and with a desperate reach Emery snagged the *Goodell's* rudder guyline and managed to hold on. At the top of his lungs he shouted to his crew above, who had been frantically running along the rail in search of any sign of their captain gone overboard. Hearing the shouts, the crew gathered at the sternrail and saw Emery dragging near the rudder—and being submerged with every roll of the boat. As fast as they could move, the crew snatched a ladder and lowered it within reach of the floundering captain. In a few shivering moments Lake Huron was robbed of its vengeance and Captain Emery was pulled safely to the deck of his boat. The lake had missed its opportunity at Emery and the *N.P. Goodell* by the width of a guywire.

By the time that Emery was dried out and fully recovered from his unplanned swim, the *Dickinson* was hauling her tow past the port of Sand Beach. In the distance the brooding hulk of the *Colorado* could be seen along the shoreline. Surely she was a sorry sight with her hull badly holed and her rigging down. The thought that he had gotten off lucky on this trip with a simple soaking must have run through Emery's thoughts. Certainly the *Colorado* looked as if she would be a total loss as the *Goodell* left her behind. That perception, however, turned out to be wrong. Shortly after the *Dickinson* and *Goodell* passed Sand Beach, the tug *William Park* arrived from Bay City with the intent of salvaging the *Colorado*. Ten days after the work had been started on the *Colorado,* she was tugged into Wheeler's dry dock in Bay City. There she was put back into shape and resumed he career as the 1884 season opened.

No one really knows what happened to Abbot Way after his misadventure on the Sand Beach breakwater. As of this writing, all that is known is that he faded into the throngs of able-bodied mariners working the lakes. Perhaps his name will pop up in a story yet to be uncovered. The *Colorado* was subsequently repaired and put back to work on the lakes. Serving a protracted career, she was left idle and abandoned in 1902. Perhaps this was an unfitting fate for so faithful a vessel, but it was the way that those of the wooden-hulled sailing fleet were commonly retired. The *Don M. Dickinson* and *N.P. Goodell* were not so lucky as to fade quietly into backwater obscurity. Just over five years after the *Colorado* had gotten away from her, the *Dickinson* caught fire and burned to a total loss. The date was November 12, 1888 and the iron-hulled steamer found her end at the foot of the Belle Isle Lighthouse at Detroit. Three seasons later, nearly to the day, the *Goodell* vanished in a wild Lake Huron gale. The complete story of that loss can be found in this author's book *Stormy Disasters*.

Overall, the autumn sailing season of 1883 was one of the most damaging to lakes shipping in history. Wooden vessels of nearly every description were tossed ashore, wrecked, damaged or otherwise assaulted in some manner by the bad weather. From Chicago to Duluth to Buffalo the shores of all of the Great Lakes were strewn with tangled wreckage from oak-hulled vessels—and the occasional body of a luckless mariner— by the time that winter's ice put an end to the mayhem. Countless stories, such as those of Abbot Way and Captain Emery, can be found when examining that season. We do not know if that "scientific person living in Milwaukee" possessed the correct formula for predicting the disastrous season to come, or simply happened to publish his theory just in time for one of the worst autumns in lakes history. What we do know is that if Way, Emery and a throng of other mariners had known how accurate that prediction was going to be, they would have surely used it to demand extra money—a lot of extra money!

WHAT BERT HUBBARD
FOUND ON THE WAY
TO SCHOOL

T hrough Wednesday, October 20, 1886, a heavy gale was blowing across all of Lake Huron. In the middle of it all the 149-foot schooner *E.W. Rathbun* was beating her way toward her home port of Goderich, Ontario. Aboard the boat was a crew of five men and a single female cook. Among the drenched crewmen was a hardworking mariner by the name of Thomas Cox. The people who worked the vessels of this era were a transient lot, moving from one vessel to another almost as commonly as they would change winter jackets, and Cox was no exception. One of the roust-about class of mariners, Cox often worked different boats in different seasons on different lakes. At present, he just happened to be working the *Rathbun*. In the schooner's belly was a cargo of coal that had been taken aboard at Toledo and was bound to Goderich, consigned to Ogilvles and Hutchison. As the *Rathbun* heeled toward the port's entrance, however, it was about to become clear that Lake Huron had other ideas for the boat's cargo. Just how it happened is unexplained. Perhaps the autumn storms had caused the sands to form a shoal across the entrance channel, or the boat's captain misjudged the approach course, or the winds picked that moment to gust extra hard. For whatever the reason, the *Rathbun* found the lake bottom just outside of the harbor and went from ship to shipwreck.

Minutes after the boat grounded, Lake Huron pounced upon her. Giant waves burst over her rail and swept the hull taking down her masts and rigging. Thomas Cox found himself clinging to the wreck as wave after wave of numbing ice water rolled over him. Fortunately, the *Rathbun* had found the bottom just outside Goderich harbor, and well within reach of the local lifesavers. Manning their surf boat, the Canadian lifesavers launched and pulled out to the wreck. Soon, all of the crew, including Cox were removed from the shipwreck and safely taken to dry land. Landing on the safety of Canadian soil, Cox's soaked shoes made an icy sloshing sound as he wobbled toward the warmth of the lifeboat station. He was now unemployed, and had lost all of his belongings on the *Rathbun*. He needed to find a new job—and fast. In the days that followed, the *Rathbun* was broken to pieces by the surf. Her coal cargo was spread across the lake bottom and mixed with the sand. The whole event was buried just as efficiently within the sands of time and the waves of Great Lakes maritime events. Thomas Cox moved on, looking for another lakeboat and another paycheck. Even though the season was growing late, it was certain that he could find a new job, and the idea far-fetched that he would again find himself shipwrecked. After all, considering the odds, Cox was probably the last mariner on the lakes fated to be wrecked in the single month that remained in the 1886 season.

Nearly every day that was not in the planting or harvest season Alberto "Bert" Hubbard walked to school along a twisting dirt road. Without regard to the weather, the lad trudged toward the one-room Woodville, New York, schoolhouse where the basics of his education were presented. Rain or shine he made that walk "uphill both ways" that so many of us have heard our parents reminisce about. The stretch of dirt road that led from the Hubbard farm to Bert's school ran close to the east shore of Lake Ontario along northern Mexico Bay. With nothing more to look forward to other than another day in the classroom, the view of the lake was normally the best part of Bert's walk to school. Rising substantially above the lake, the bluff on which the road ran provided a bird's-eye view of the water beyond, with clusters of trees being the only obstruction. Sometimes a faraway lakeboat could be seen in the distance and—if Albert was really lucky—the smudges of smoke from a far-off steamer may be on the horizon. Such images caused the imagination of a schoolboy to run wild with the thoughts of adventure at sea. Such thoughts also included the excitement of shipwreck and the adventures of the courageous lifesavers at the nearby Big Sandy Station. On this particular morning, the second day of December, 1886, Bert's walk to school was being hampered by a gale-force wind and thick snow shooting in due west from off the lake. As the plucky schoolboy tipped the brim of his hat against the wind and snow, his wildest imagination could not place him in the middle of the adventure that a vengeful Lake Ontario had arranged for him just a few steps ahead. Very soon Hubbard and his neighbors would all play parts in an adventure that normally could only be found in a school boy's day dreams.

Normally, in the era of 1880s lake commerce, the coming of the month of December brought the end of the navigation season. Most of the lakeboats had been laid up beginning as early as the end of October, while those with a thirst for profits or attempting to meet tonnage commitments continued to run through the evils of November. By December the weather was almost always foul, and the cold temperatures locked the rivers with sheets of ice. The closing of the season was something that 23-year-old Captain Hugh McKay and his 68-year-old father, Sutherland McKay, the boat's first mate, were determined to fend off for that "one last trip." Heading out of Oswego on the 18th of November, 1886, Captain McKay was bound for Bath, Ontario, on the Canadian coast. Although the two men held joint ownership in the 138-ton schooner *Ariadne*, they were not men of wealth. In fact, the family income was gained by the scarcest of margins, earned by the ship. At least one official record describes the McKays as "comparatively poor men," yet they not only owned the $3,000 *Ariadne*, but they worked it as a family. And that was an asset that no ledger could reflect. Before laying up the *Ariadne*, the McKays desperately needed to make one last haul of a profitable cargo across Lake Ontario. This would allow the crew to be properly paid off for the season, and may just provide enough cash to perform the winter maintenance on the boat. Lake Ontario, however, had a different season's end in store for the McKay family business.

Adjacent to Prince Edward Bay on the ragged northeastern coast of Lake Ontario, the port of Bath was neatly tucked behind Amherst Island and well-protected from the temper of the open lake. By Friday, November 26, the *Ariadne* had taken aboard 10,000 bushels of Canadian barley and Captain McKay gave the orders to cast off. This load held the promise of a tidy profit if the cargo could be promptly gotten to the Oswego, New York, elevator for the Gaylord & Downey Company where it had been assigned. In calculating his profit margin, McKay had carefully factored in the expense of retaining his crew for the time required to cross the lake, load the cargo, and sail back across to deliver the barley. The round trip of 112 miles should have taken less than 24 hours sailing time. Unloading would be another matter if there happened to be a vessel at the elevator ahead of the *Ariadne*. Once the schooner was tied below the Oswego elevator, the crew would no longer be required and, in order to minimize expenses, the crew would be immediately paid off and the McKays would tend to the unloading and laying up of the schooner. Lake Ontario did not see it that way and seemed determined to rob the McKays of any hint of profit. Through the last days of November, McKay had tried a number of times to cross the lake, but each time adverse winds had blown the *Ariadne* right back to the Canadian coast.

Upon his attempt at crossing the lake as the *Ariadne* cleared Prince Edward Point, Captain McKay found a nasty sea rolling. It was far more than the little schooner could handle. Turning the boat around, he ducked behind South Bay Point. For the next two days the *Ariadne* squatted behind the point with the schooner *Wave Crest*. Also with a cargo of Canadian barley aboard, the *Wave Crest* was, like the *Ariadne*, bound for Oswego. Unlike the *Wave Crest*, a much greater sense of urgency was beginning to develop aboard the *Ariadne*. Each storm-bound hour that passed ate into the McKay's family income. McKay had calculated his costs on this run very closely and they did not include hiding behind the point for several days. Not being able to pay the crew their expected wage would surely lead to someone "libeling" the boat for owed wages. In that situation the boat would be tied to the wall and arrested by the local marshal until the McKays could come up with the money—which they could not earn unless the boat was sailing. By Sunday night it is a sure bet that the captain and his first mate were itching to go. On Monday the *Ariadne* made another try at Lake Ontario. The wind was bitter cold and every drop of spray that contacted the boat froze instantly as the little schooner tasted the gale. The seas were still rolling high, as the lake continued in a rage. The *Ariadne* was forced back once again and had to drop anchor behind the point. By the time November expired into December, the McKays had said goodbye to any thought of profit, and would be lucky if they did not have to pay some dock owner to lay the boat up in Canada.

The morning of the first day of December, 1886, presented the long-awaited favorable winds and the *Ariadne* departed South Bay headed for Oswego. The atmosphere of a happy departure hung all around the schooner as the crew congratulated one another on having been granted such a fine break in the weather. A fair wind was blowing out of the west-northwest and the sky was clear and blue as the schooner set out. By this time every member of the crew were relieved to see South Bay Point fading steadily behind them. Food and accommodations aboard the boat were not the best when she was earning good money, so when the owners were attempting to squeeze the last penny of the season out of her, even the wood needed to heat the galley stove was getting scarce. Now that the *Ariadne* was finally underway, the problem was how the McKays would squeeze enough cash out of the load to pay off crewmen Charles Dean, Thomas Cox, Edward Mulligan, and Maurice Young. This trip had rapidly become a losing venture for the McKay family and the proportion of the loss would be directly linked to the time required to make the port of Oswego. By two o'clock in the afternoon the McKay clan's losing venture had reached the midpoint of the crossing. It was here that Lake Ontario decided that Captain McKay's worries over simply paying his crew would now come to an end. This trip, the lake determined, was going to cost more—much more—than McKay had ever calculated.

Catching the *Ariadne* smack in the middle of its clutches, Lake Ontario turned out a thick blanket of snow as that friendly wind turned into a roaring gale from due west. Having more than 100 miles to build, an endless series of combing waves came to attack the *Ariadne* and board her decks. Rocking insanely and heeled to the point where her rail was dipping into the lake, the luckless schooner had no alternative other than to continue on toward Oswego. At six o'clock that evening, the first glimpse of the Oswego Lighthouse was seen from the *Ariadne*. From the sighting of those initial flashes, it appeared as if the boat was running on course. Two hours later, however, when the Oswego Light became clearly visible, the ship found herself downwind of the harbor entrance. Now the boat would be required to tack into the wind to make the harbor.

Lake Ontario had played a cruel trick on the McKays and their schooner. There were two choices—they could turn the boat and tack her against the gale toward Oswego, or they could put the wind on her heels and run for shelter somewhere toward the east. Either option was going to impose a beating on the boat, but McKay's decision was influenced more by economics than by the thrashing gale. If he could make the harbor he could deliver his cargo and collect his fee. If, however, he ran east the boat would likely end up frozen into an east-end port for the winter. He decided to turn the boat and tack for Oswego. The snows came in smothering squalls that appeared out of the blackness to swirl around the *Ariadne,* then lift only to soon return. The surface of the lakes belongs to winter after the gales of November have expired, and any mariner who would challenge December's ownership would certainly pay a penalty.

By the time that the lights of Oswego glowed on the horizon ahead of the *Ariadne*, she was not alone in her plight. The *Wave Crest* had beaten her to the harbor and, heeling in with the wind on her stern quarter, she slickly made the entrance. Waiting on the schooner's arrival, the tug *Redford* had managed to bring the *Wave Crest* the rest of the way in. Unfortunately, as the *Ariadne* neared the breakwater, the seas were running higher and at a 90-degree angle to the harbor entrance, effectively blocking the schooner from entering the harbor on her own. Additionally, when she came out of the snowsqualls at the end of her tack, she had actually lost ground against the wind. The boat got within two miles of the breakwater and signaled for a tug by raising a torch to the masthead. Unfortunately, the same seas that prevented the *Ariadne* from running in, also kept the harbor tugs from running out to pick her up. An agonizing period of time lapsed as the schooner just sat there rolling madly within a few thousand feet of shelter.

For what it was worth, her plight did not go unnoticed by those ashore. The lookout at the Oswego Lifesaving Station saw the *Ariadne's* situation, and expecting trouble he rang the alarm. In an effort to signal incoming vessels of the shallows near the breakwater and to also signal that the lifesavers were on the alert, the keeper ordered some signal rockets fired. It was their hope that the fact the storm-warriors were standing ready would influence Captain McKay to attempt a run into the harbor.

Time passed and McKay appeared to make no move toward the entrance. Increasing in strength, the gale seemed determined to keep the *Ariadne* from passing through the harbor entrance as it now sent waves exploding over the breakwater. The channel that lead to safety was nothing more than a mass of heaving water that no vessel could pass. Still McKay had hope of making Oswego, and he turned the boat into another tacking maneuver. That was just the opportunity that the vengeful lake had been awaiting. With a single gust the wind blasted the schooner's jibsail to shreds. Jibbing the boat into and out of the wind and sea trough would now be impossible and the option of tacking was also gone. To make matters worse, rolling in the heavy seas by this time had caused the *Ariadne's* timbers to grind against her caulk. Now the boat began to leak and it was discovered that she had three feet of water in her hold. Captain McKay's only option now was to turn and run with the storm at his stern. Interestingly, the three feet of water in the hold had probably ruined the boat's cargo of barley long before the boat reached the vicinity of Oswego. For some reason, the lake appeared determined to take everything from the McKays. From the schooner's deck, her crew could hear the whistles of the harbor tugs and clearly see the beckoning rockets of the lifesavers. It was not easy to sail away and leave the comfort of Oswego behind, but Lake Ontario offered no other choice. The odds were that even if the boat could have been jibbed around and stood into the harbor, she would have been smashed on the breakwater, and her people dumped into the raging seas. While the lifesavers watched helplessly, the lamps of the *Ariadne* headed back out onto the open lake and vanished into the snow squalls.

Lake Ontario had set Captain McKay up so that now he could only run toward the east until he ran out of lake or the *Ariadne* sank beneath him. Such a dilemma was not acceptable to her captain. The master of the schooner may not have been a man of wealth, but he was rich in navigational savvy. By turning from due east to the northeast he would take a bit more pounding by the waves. But in about 35 miles, he could run into Henderson Bay or behind the Galloo or Stony Islands. It was a big gamble, but the *Ariadne* was both his home and business and he seemed determined to fight Lake Ontario for her to the end.

No record exists of how long it took before the flashes of the Stoney Point Lighthouse came into view from the wallowing *Ariadne*. The time consumed in the run from Oswego was apparently enough to allow Lake Ontario to apply mortal punishment to the schooner's hull. The wooden hand pumps used to keep the hull free of water were becoming clogged with ice and were nearly useless. Water now came pouring in through every seam and the *Ariadne* was making sounds deep within her hull that gave a dismal warning that the vessel was sinking. Maneuvering into the shelter of Henderson Bay would now cost time that McKay did not think was his to spend. He decided, instead, that he would turn due east and attempt to beach his boat in Mexico Bay. This was an act of pure survival that would allow the *Ariadne* to sink in shallow rather than deep water. Perhaps then she may be salvaged when the weather moderated.

The lake, however, was not yet done with the McKay family business. While the crew manipulated the sails in the effort to come around, the main boom came loose and swept to the portside. When the boom reached the end of its swing the stop was so sudden that the boom itself snapped in half, and with that ripped the mainsail to a rag. Now the schooner was completely uncontrollable, but the breaking of the boom had another implication that was even more deadly. A broken portion of the boom fell to the deck an slammed directly onto the hand pumps. The hand-worked bilgepumps, although almost completely clogged with ice, had been the only thing keeping the schooner afloat. The result of the smashing boom was that now the *Ariadne* was not only out of control, but her pumps were totally useless. McKay and his crew had only one chance for survival — that the winds would shove the schooner on the beach, and soon.

Everyone aboard knew too well what the boat's situation was as she drifted eastward into the night. This was particularly true for Thomas Cox. For the second time in just seven weeks, he was going to be shipwrecked. It was only a matter of time before Lake Ontario reached out to take the schooner and her crew. Just over a mile from the beach at Mexico Bay the hull suddenly jolted. A moment passed before the boat slammed hard and jolted a second time as it suddenly crushed to a stop. The waves now burst over the rail and the rocking of the schooner ceased. Drowned Island Shoal was the spot where the *Ariadne's* career and the McKay family business came to an end. At the time the schooner met the shoal, eight feet of water covered Drowned Island, but the foundering ship was wallowing in waves nearly that high. It was almost as if she had been run onto dry land. Realizing that their duties as sailors were now over, the crew sought shelter in the deckhouse. The hull was flooded and shattered, but the deckhouse was still intact. Once inside the confines of the cabin the cookstove was fired up and a pot of coffee was started brewing. Now that the rolling of the boat had stopped it was finally possible to actually set a pot on the stove and not have it flung across the galley. So long as the boat held together, her people were relatively safe. The crew of the *Ariadne*, unfortunately, were far from being in a position of comfort, and their time around a warm stove would be short lived.

It was two o'clock in the morning on the second day of December, and the scene in the *Ariadne's* galley was pretty grim. The boat was squatting with her hull broken on a submerged shoal more than a mile from land. Outside the storm was growing in its power and waves marching the full length of Lake Ontario were crashing into the wounded vessel. A blizzard lashed at her and temperature dropped below 18 degrees. Certainly, the crew may be sheltered long enough for a cup of coffee, but not much longer than that. To add to the dilemma, the boat had fetched-up in what still is one of the most remote areas of Lake Ontario. The site of the wreck was more than five miles north of the Big Sandy Lifesaving Station, and

Map showing Ariadine's *wreck site.*

out of the range of the station's beach patrol by more than a mile. If the weather were clear and had it been daylight, the patrol may have spotted the schooner in the distance. In the blizzard and dark of night, the chance that the boat would be spotted by the lifesavers was nil.

As with the rest of the *Ariadne's* saga, Lake Ontario was now going to make the situation worse. Two hours after the crew took refuge in the deckhouse, the broken boat's stern began to sink and the water soon forced the mariners from the shelter of the cabin. While they evacuated, a giant wave plowed over the stern and ripped the roof from the deckhouse. The crew climbed into the standing rigging of the mainmast and held on for their lives. Exposed to the wind and snow, they would at least be out of the water—for the time being. Their soaked clothing was frozen stiff nearly as soon as the men gained the rigging, and the bitter wind stung their skin to the point where the pain was only stopped by the numbing cold. Each line in the rigging was coated with ice three inches thick, and holding on was like gripping icicles. Just as it appeared that refuge in the main rigging would be possible, the decking below the mainmast came apart and the mast unshipped. Fortunately, the mast only toppled into the foremast and wedged there. Thinking that the mainspar was about to go over the side, the crew, with the exception of Captain McKay, abandoned its rigging and fought their way into the foremast's lines. McKay was left struggling like a bug in a web among the wreckage left behind by the departing deckhouse roof and the mainspar. Shouting over the howl of the wind, the crew pleaded with their captain to join them high up in the rigging, but McKay was helpless. Then, as if to target its vengeance on him alone, Lake Ontario sent another huge sea exploding aboard the *Ariadne* and swept the entire deckhouse away along with McKay. A heart-beat later the cabin was tumbling in the ice water surf, and for just a moment Captain McKay was seen attempting to hold on to a piece of planking. The results of that struggle were the same as his struggle to bring his cargo into Oswego—he lost! His effort had no sooner started than he vanished into the darkness of the blizzard.

Sorrow over the loss of their captain turned into the thoughts that his image had been a foretelling of all their ends, as the shattered hull of the *Ariadne* began to shift beneath the crew once more. So gutted had the schooner's hull become that her cargo had spilled out, and much of the lower workings had broken lose. Now the ship regained some buoyancy and lost enough of her lower hull to allow her to be washed from the shoal. For more than an hour the shifting and grinding of the seas worked at the wreck until the hulk was floated free. It seemed as if there was no limit to the lake's treachery as the *Ariadne*, which was now more of a raft than a vessel, was blown toward the surf a mile away.

Miraculously, the wreck did not crumble when it hit the shallows just over 100 yards from dry land. With each wave the deck rippled and flexed and soon the foremast appeared about to fall. The only part of the boat that remained above water was the bow. It ended up being the last refuge for the crew as the foremast swayed drunkenly, held in place by only its spring-stay. Waves burst over the remains of the bow as the ice-encrusted survivors waited to join Captain McKay in an ice water doom.

Somehow the scene seems always to repeat: benumbed shipwreck survivors drenched in a vengeful lake and forced to watch as the cold saps the life from their shipmates, one at a time. The ice coating on the wreck grew steadily thicker as each wave that broke over the hulk left behind its frosting. Soon the pain and frostbite grew so great that the castaways could do little more than huddle stiffly on the iceberg that had once been their boat. Charles Dean spent the last two hours of his life crouched in that bitter cold torment as his body slowly froze. Sometime around eight o'clock that morning he murmured the name of his wife, asked for mercy upon his soul from God, and slumped into death. Sliding down the canted deck, the expired mariner froze into a solid lump at the feet of his shipmates. Sutherland McKay had been weakened by the cold to the point where he was raving, apparently blind, and unable to hear the encouragement's of his shipmates. Lake Ontario was sure to claim him before long.

Morning did not bring any relief from the storm, but the daylight did bring Bert Hubbard. While taking one of his gazes across the lake, Bert happened to spot the top of the *Ariadne's* swaying foremast in the distance. For a moment the schoolboy pondered the image in disbelief, but then correctly rationalized that if a vessel's mast was that close to the bluff, she must be run ashore. Making his way up to through the thicket of trees that stood between him and a clear view of the lake below, Bert cast his eyes on what he had daydreamed about so often. There in front of him, distorted by the blowing snow and the tearing of his eyes caused by the wind were the remains of the *Ariadne* pounding in the surf. Holding the branches apart with his arms, Bert could hardly believe his eyes as he whispered into the driving wind, "Shipwreck!"

Two farmhouses were a short distance off and Bert dashed to them and began to beat on the doors. "Shipwreck!" he shouted, "Shipwreck!" The wheels of community action his alarm started into motion were really quite remarkable. First in the action of joining in the alarm was Marshall Forbes, a boy who, like Bert, was about to go out the door to school. From the Forbes farm the two boys made a dash down to the lake. Once on the beach they proceeded to shout and beckon in the direction of the wreck. Only a portion of the *Ariadne's* bow and foremast were above the water, and the boys could clearly see the five crewmen huddled on the structure. Then, one of the castaways waved back. Seeing that, the boys turned and made a run back up to the road. Bert headed off to alert his father while the Forbes boy struck out to alert the rest of the neighbors. When Forbes reached the Southwick farm, Mr. Southwick listened to his story and then immediately headed out for the Lake View Hotel, a summer resort and also the location of the only telephone in the area. There he called the only other telephone in the region which was at the Woodville Post Office. His call was to request that a runner be sent to the Big Sandy Lifesaving Station and alert the crew. The runner was dispatched, but found the passage to the station blocked by the infamous "Wind Gap"—the outlet from a small lake a few miles inland called Wood's Pond. In the fair-weather months the Gap was little more than a wide creek, but in a gale-force wind blowing on shore from due west, the Gap was a raging river that was nearly a mile wide. Figuring this, the post office runner elected to go instead to the home of Captain William A. Jenkins, the well-known master of the local schooner *Fiat*. Captain Jenkins knew just what to do. First he went out to his boat which was laid up for the season right outside his back door, and raised the *Fiat's* flag to the top of her mast with the union down as a sign of distress. The mast was high enough that the lookout in the Big Sandy Station's watch tower would probably be able to see it. Next he grabbed the schooner's foghorn and headed out around Wood's Pond, sounding the horn along the way in an effort to alert the lifesavers.

While the effort to alert the lifesavers was going on, Bert Hubbard and Marshall Forbes continued to alert the locals. Among those who were given the word was farmer James Wood, who would play a most important role in the rescue effort. Keeper William Fish of the Big Sandy Station had made an advance arrangement with Wood that if ever a wreck should occur north of the gap, the farmer should rig a team of horses and wait above the Gap. This way the lifesavers could use their beach cart to move the lifeboat and equipment as far as the Gap, then leave their team and float their gear across in the surf boat, and pick up Wood's team on the other side. This advanced planning was made with the images in mind of the botched rescue of the crew of the schooner *Cortez* six years earlier. In that case the lifesavers got snarled in the Wind Gap and before they could get to the scene, local fishermen using a condemned fishing dory had rescued the crew. The repercussions over the botched rescue resulted in the dismissal of Keeper W.E. Van Alstine. Certainly Keeper Fish was not going to fall into the same trap. This time, the crew of the Big Sandy Station would use every asset in their efforts.

As soon as he was alerted to the wreck, James Wood hitched up his team of horses and headed for the beach north of the Gap. Actually, the arrangement was that if the station hoisted one flag to the top of the flagpole it meant they were proceeding via the beach. While two flags meant that they were taking the longer inland route. The weather, however, was so bad that Wood could not see as far as the station from his house, so he just guessed that the lifesavers would use the beach route. With a crowd of locals in tow he proceeded to the Gap and waited.

Captain Jenkins' foghorn could not be heard by the station lookout, but his odd behavior was seen. Through his glass the lookout focused on the man jumping about near Pond Brook, and recognized him as Captain Jenkins. Sounding the station alarm, the lookout alerted his fellow storm-warriors. Keeper Fish had Surfman Wheeler dispatched to Pond Brook, hauling a skiff rigged with ice runners. The ice on the brook was not thick enough to support a man's weight so the skiff would make crossing possible. As soon as Wheeler reached Jenkins, the two men hastened back to the station and the rescue effort went into high gear. Lifesaving stations of this era were normally equipped with two boats to be used in rescues. The lightweight "surf boat" was used when speed and maneuverability were required. In other cases the "lifeboat," which was heavier and had a larger capacity than the surf boat, was used in very heavy seas. In the mid-1880s the famed "Dobbins Lifeboat" was thought of as the ultimate rescue craft, and many stations kept it in reserve for the worst of weather. Dobbins boats were self-bailing, self-righting, and self-ballasting, and the lifesavers thought that the boats were nearly invincible. To respond to the *Ariadne's* rescue, Fish ordered the station's Dobbins Boat launched. For that reason alone, everyone of the station's crew knew that the situation was very serious.

Launching the boat, Fish and two surfmen manned the vessel while the others, including Captain Jenkins, walked the beach with a line attached to the lifeboat and pulled it up the coast. The surf rolled the boat wildly and water poured over the rail, but the boat's self-righting and self-bailing characteristics kept it afloat, while the crew pulling on the beach hurried the trip toward the wreck site. Any standard lifeboat would have swamped and rolled over, but the Dobbins kept itself upright even if the two men inside did take a bitter cold soaking. When the boat reached the Gap, it was angled into shore and everyone jumped aboard and rowed to the other side. Waiting on the north side was farmer Wood and a large crowd of local residents. Reaching the north side, they beached the boat and dropped off everyone but the keeper and two oarsmen. Again the boat was angled out into the surf, but this time she was towed by hitching a line to the back axle of Wood's wagon. Now the boat was rushed northward using the power of the team of horses and the hands of the entire community. Doubtless that among those pulling in the tug of war against Lake Ontario were the hands of Bert Hubbard. The trip from the lifesaving station to the wreck site, a distance of just over five miles, took two hours. Often the folks pulling along the beach were waist deep in the thrashing surf that ran up as high as the foot of the bluffs. Wood's team of horses were bathed in the stinging cold surf, and both the team as well as the wagon took on a thick load of ice. For a time it was feared that the horses may not survive the pull to the wreck. The temperature was less than 20 degrees and the winds blew off of the lake at gale force. At times the team of horses showed signs of being near death. The thought that kept everyone pulling up the beach was that if it was this bad on the shore what must it be like out on that wreck?

Once the lifesavers reached the wreck site they again beached the Dobbins boat, knocked the ice from the oars and rowlocks, as well as from their clothing, and prepared to launch. From the crowd of locals, dry mittens were donated in exchange for the soaking ones the surfmen were wearing. James Wood hastened his horses to the barn. The poor animals appeared about to collapse and not a moment could be lost in getting them to shelter. It was just after three o'clock in the afternoon and the men on the wreck had been drenched in the freezing lake for nearly 12 hours. Now they appeared as nothing more than frozen lumps on a tiny iceberg. As Bert watched, the fearless storm-warriors, with the help of a dozen local residents, launched the lifeboat. The crest of the first wave had it standing nearly on end. A moment later the Dobbins boat slammed down the back side of the wave and challenged the next. Spray seemed to erupt in every direction as the lifeboat crashed one wave after another and the surfmen pulled at the oars like supermen. Every time that the boat defeated another wave, Bert, like the rest of the crowd, did not even breathe until the boat reappeared. The temperature was now 16 degrees, but those on the beach were too entranced by the dramatic scene to shiver. Freezing spray burst, ice splintered, oars creaked, surfmen groaned, and Lake Ontario howled in objection as the battle went on. Betting their own lives on only the possibility that someone may still be alive out on that frozen wreck the lifesavers pulled on. Driven by duty alone they kept the valor. At times it appeared as if the lifeboat was standing still as the waves came at it, but slowly the surfmen made progress.

What the lifesavers could not know was that just two hours after Lake Ontario had overcome Charles Dean, it had decided to take the life from Sutherland McKay. At about ten o'clock that morning, the elder McKay quieted from his hypothermic-induced rantings and became very still. He looked up blindly between the unrelenting waves and said softly to his shipmates, "Tell my poor wife how I died and that my last thoughts were of her." A moment later he spoke his wife's name and expired at the feet of his shipmates. As the lifesavers approached the wreck they would be six hours too late for two of the crew, but three others remained alive.

Nearing the wreck, Keeper Fish could see a nothing more than a large white iceberg. The foremast had unshipped, but was being held up by the spring-stays and teetering as if about to fall at any moment. Wreckage and mainmast was strewn down-wind of the remains, and five figures were cowering as high up on the sloping deck as they could crawl. Maneuvering up to the submerged port rail, the lifesavers called to the crewmen to slide down to the lifeboat. Maurice Young and Thomas Cox readily slid down and were helped aboard the lifeboat. Edward Mulligan was too weakened by the cold to do much other than slide down. The surfmen teamed up to take hold of the dazed crewman and muscled him into the safety of the Dobbins. Sutherland McKay remained crouched on the deck—frozen into a solid heap with Charles Dean. The lifesavers pulled away toward the beach leaving the two expired crewmen encased in the ice with the *Ariadne*. Along the way Mulligan regained enough of his senses to inquire about the fate of Captain McKay. It was the first time that the lifesavers had any clue that anyone, other than the five persons that were huddled on the bow, had been aboard the boat. McKay's remains were nowhere in sight as the surfmen pulled back toward the beach. Oddly, at least one account of the wreck published in more recent years details the use of the Lyle gun by the lifesavers in the rescue operation at the *Ariadne's* wreck. In the official record of the Life Saving Service, and the local news reports concerning the wreck, no mention is made of the firing of the gun. In fact, the reports indicate that the lifesavers did not bring the gun with them when they left the station. This rescue was done by frost-bitten hands pulling at ice-coated oars.

Immediately upon making dry land, the shipwrecked crew were taken into the care of the local residents. A bonfire had been burning on the beach and dry horse blankets were at the ready in an attempt to revive the survivors, but it was clear that this was not enough. Dr. Chapman, a local physician had found his way to the scene and without hesitation went to the treatment of the three castaways. An 1880s-version of a rescue squad, a horse-drawn sleigh was used to transport the three mariners, with Dr. Chapman in attendance, to the Whitney family home in Woodville. In the meantime, the lifesavers packed up their equipment and with the help of some local volunteers, began pulling the Dobbins boat back to the Big Sandy Station. The crowd that had gathered on the beach was now beginning to splinter and head for their homes as well. Among the locals, Bert Hubbard and Marshall Forbes watched as the shipwreck adventure came to a close. Bert had caused quite a commotion with his discovery on the way to school. Although he probably did not realize it, he had saved the lives of the three mariners who were now on their way to the Whitney house. Bert, Marshall and the whole community had done their share in pulling off the rescue of the *Adriane's* survivors. Certainly, Bert felt it was better than a day at school!

For three days after the wreck occurred, the lake continued its tantrum and the seas raged to the point where no attempt to recover the bodies could be made. It was not until Sunday that the storm quieted and the lifesavers were able to go out to the wreck and chip the ice-shrouded remains of Sutherland McKay and Charles Dean from the wreck of the *Ariadne*. Captain McKay, according to the *Annual Report of the United States Life Saving Service* was never found. Newspapers at the time reported that he was recovered six days after the wreck. As to which report is correct, only the reader of this story can guess.

Headed for Oswego after having spent four days recovering at the home of the Whitney family, the three surviving members of the *Ariadne's* crew thanked the local residents for all of their efforts. Upon their departure, a letter of thanks was left for the crew of the lifesaving station, allegedly composed by the mariners. Such letters often turned up after an action by a station crew, and were dutifully forwarded to the district superintendent. They were later published in the service's *Annual Report,* which was submitted to Congress, and aided in funding justification. Some of these letters of gratitude could be considered of dubious origin because their content seems just a bit too self-serving, and the wording is sometimes not quite what you would expect from common mariners. The letter that was supposedly submitted by the survivors of the *Ariadne* was a good example of this, it read:

> To the captain of the life-boat and the gallant crew
> at Big Sandy:
>
> We can not help paying a little tribute to the great bravery
> and courage which you showed in your gallant behavior
> when saving us from the terrible wreck of the *Ariadne* of
> New Castle. We can not express our feelings of gratitude
> to you and your gallant crew. To you alone, next to
> Almighty God, we three owe our lives. If ever courage

and bravery were exercised, it were on the 2nd of December, 1886, when you and your gallant crew saved us from a dreadful state on the schooner *Ariadne*, running the greatest risk of your own lives and forever setting all brave men an example which can never be surpassed. The life-saving crews of the United States of America have often showed great bravery and depend on it, if a life-long gratitude could repay a part of the debt we owe to you and your crew we will think ourselves vary fortunate. May God never fail to shower blessings on your heads is the sincere wish of —

> Maurice Young
> Edward Mulligan
> Thomas Cox

Considering that the letter reads like it slipped from the desk of a local politician, and that the word "gallant" was used three times and the reference to bravery was given four times in a single paragraph, the conclusion that the letter's origin was not from the common seamen from the *Ariadne* may be valid. The most clear evidence that the letter was not written by someone who was involved in that day's events comes from the fact that one critical part is missing. For all of the praise that is heaped upon the lifesavers, the persons most responsible for the rescue of the crew are not mentioned. Missing is credit to the community of Woodville and Bert Hubbard.

Thomas Cox ended his star-crossed season with the wreck of the *Ariadne*. On his way through Oswego he had commented that he would gladly give up sailing if he could manage to make a living ashore. It is doubtful that he accomplished either. The odds are that Cox returned to the schooners and barges and leaky lakeboats as soon as the ice cleared in the spring of 1887. As of this writing there has been no discovery of where he went. Mariners of his ilk were a transient bunch, rousting about from one boat to another, being paid in cash and often never having their presence recorded. But, who knows, perhaps with a close look at another obscure adventure such as the *Ariadne*, maybe the name of Thomas Cox will again show up. In part we would like to know of his further exploits, but then again the research into these events often turns up the names of those lost to the lakes. In that case, maybe we do not want to find the name Thomas Cox in the jumble of Great Lakes history.

A BEACH HE'D
RATHER FORGET

For those who keep the valor of the unending struggle with the Great Lakes, the elevation through the ranks from subordinate to command can be a lifelong affair. Many a vesselman, lightman, and lifesaver has managed to work up through the ranks only to find the test of command to be rigged in favor of a cheating lake. For some this means returning to their previous rank in the hope of one day being able to again test the lake with a bit more savvy. For many, the failure to pass the test of the lakes means leaving their career pursuit and never returning. Their names appear in relation to a single event and then fade away forever. It is easy to envision these individuals spending the rest of their days feeling much more than just a bit cheated by their decisive encounter with the Great Lakes, but unlike so much in our civilization, the lakes have absolutely no sense of fairness. Such was the lesson that Captain Barney Alonzo Cross would learn on a beach that which he would rather forget. In looking back at Captain Cross' test with the lake, some narrow-minded, and short-sighted reviewers of history have had occasion to use words such as "bumbling." Those short-sighted narrators need to look beyond that lone, dark event in this man's life, and find that he met Lake Michigan many times—and on all of those occasions always was more than a match for the sweetwater sea. In fact, Cross had a long and highly-distinguished career as a lake man that extended far beyond the date of his test. But, as is commonplace in the media of his day and our day, his whole existence is judged within a myopic kaleidoscope of one single event and the rushing time of just a few days. This judgment and distortion of the facts is nearly as unfair to this good captain as was the circumstance that Lake Michigan chose to deliver upon him. In this chapter, we will look at the whole story of Captain Barney Alonzo Cross, who was not a clod or bumbler or misfit by any stretch of the imagination.

On Thursday, February 17, 1887, the choice of the station keeper of the South Haven, Michigan, Lifesaving Station was officially made, and two days later the *South Haven Sentinel* made the announcement that the locals already knew. Barney Cross, a local resident, would be in command. This was really not news as he had been occupying the newly-constructed building since late November. On the first day of April, the lifesaving station at South Haven was officially opened. In command of the crew was Station Keeper Cross and acting as his second in command was number one surfman, Fletcher Stillson. There is no doubt that both men were looking forward to the tests of the inaugural season ahead. At age 33, Cross himself had served for several seasons as the number one surfman at the Muskegon, Michigan station. Additionally, at least one source says that he served at Ludington and was also known as "Lon" by those close to him. When the crew selection for the new South Haven Station was made, Cross had been picked from the ranks of number one Surfmen to command the new facility by District 11 Superintendent Rogers for his "... unflinching courage, many times put to the test while a surfman... honesty of purpose, and his apparent general fitness for the duties of the office." The Muskegon Station had always been one of great activity and Cross had served well while there. From dragging for the bodies of drowning victims, to fighting lumber fires on the pier, to pulling with the rest of the crew to the aid of storm-tossed lakeboats—Cross had proven himself worthy of a chance to keep the valor at a station of his own. If the events at South Haven were to play out well enough, Stillson would soon follow with a command of his own. Together the two lifesavers greeted the spring breezes of the first days of April with an anticipation of the tests that the lake would one day present. Both knew that there would be no warning and that their lives as well as those of persons unknown would depend on how the crew of the station performed in the test by Lake Michigan. As it would turn out, the names of those in the lake's ultimate test would be Captain P.W. Costello, Mate Frank Wood, and Crewmen A.T. Slater, Henry Brakett, John Williams, Thomas Hoitman and Patrick O'Leary—all of whom were residents of Chicago. The test would soon be coming and the results would be most harsh.

Through the months of spring the surfmen of the South Haven Station practiced with their equipment, tended the station grounds and apparatus, patrolled the beaches and kept a 24-hour, seven-day-a-week watch on Lake Michigan. Every Thursday, Keeper Cross thrilled the locals with the firing of the Lyle gun and the weekly beach drill. The Lyle gun being a small cannon-like device that fired a projectile with a line attached in an effort to get the line over the rigging of a stranded vessel. Once the "shotline" was fired over the stranded vessel, the shipwrecked crew would use it to pull in a loop of thicker line by which the breeches buoy would be gotten to the wreck and the crew then would be hauled ashore. For the purposes of practice a simulated ship's mast attached to a stand was used. At a distance of about 75 yards the "wreck-pole" was easy work for the Lyle gun delivery system which could handily find a range of 600 yards. On special occasions—such as holidays and local festivals—the lifesavers would select a lucky lady from the crowd to ride in the breeches buoy. In practice, Keeper Cross had amazed the crowd and impressed his surfmen by accurately throwing a number seven line, which was 7/32 of an inch thick, more than 200 yards long, using only a two-ounce "drill charge" of powder in the gun. Constant readiness, however, was the best means of preparation for what the lake may deliver, and Cross saw to it that his men were ready. As for himself, he took advice from other keepers throughout District 11. Words of sound advice, the most common being, " Never go to a wreck without a number nine line," were often sent his way. A number nine line was a shotline of 9/32 inch thickness and was the heaviest

The Lyle gun, used to fire the lines to stranded vessels. The gun's wooden carriage was cracked by the cannon's over-charging in the City Of Green Bay's *rescue. (Author's Photo)*

Faking box, in which the lines to be fired from the Lyle gun were spooled.
(Author's Photo)

94

allowed for use in the service. In a heavy gale, the strength of a number nine line would surely carry against any storm. Truly, other keepers were providing Cross with good advice.

Wednesday was normally the day scheduled for practice with the international code of signals, and on Wednesday the eighth day of June, 1887, that was just what the surfmen of the South Haven Station went about doing. A thick summer atmosphere hung over Lake Michigan and the temperature began to slowly creep upward toward a swelter. In the lookout tower atop the station boathouse, the surfman on watch had all eight windows open in an attempt to take advantage of any breeze that may come calling. Out on the lake, the sails of dozens of small pleasure sloops dotted the distance as the amateur sailors set out with their guests to beat the heat of an early summer day. It was a mixture of careful sailing enthusiasts, peppered by an occasional careless boater—all in a state of escape on an indifferent lake. Watchful eyes from the lifesaving station kept tabs on them all as the day quietly passed.

Just after two o'clock in the afternoon, the horizon to the west began to grow darker in contrast to the rest of the bright blue sky, and within an hour the westward distance became black and threatening. As the conditions grew foul, the pleasure boaters formed a parade back into the safety of South Haven harbor, and by the time that the flashes of lightning and distant squall line were in sight, just one sloop remained out on the lake. From the lifesaving station's lookout tower, the surfman trained his binoculars on the diminutive craft and saw a clear sense of panic among the persons on the boat. For a moment he hesitated. What if he rang the alarm and the lifesaving station's first ever action turned out to be a false alarm? Then again, the oncoming squall gave every sign of being about to run down the sloop like a freight train. Doubts or not, the watchman rang the station's alarm for the first time and Keeper Cross' crew were called to action. It only took Cross a heartbeat to get to the watchtower and one glance over the situation was enough for him to order the surf boat launched. With the whole station crew pulling at the oars and Cross at the steering oar, the surf boat was alongside the sloop in minutes. There the lifesavers found a group of men and ladies all in a state of near panic. Not one person on board had any experience in the handling of a sailboat and with the fast-approaching squall they were all in line to become fodder for Lake Michigan. The arrival of the highly-skilled lifesavers was indeed a welcome event. Without hesitation several of the surfmen boarded the sloop, and together the surf boat and pleasure boat worked safely into the harbor just as the blackened green squall line smashed into the Michigan shore. Later back at the station, the surfmen congratulated themselves as the thunder boomed in the distance and the wind spit rain against the windows. They had been called to action and performed their duty for the first time, and they had successfully saved lives.

A dozen days after their rescue of the panicked pleasure sailors, the station crew was awakened to attend to a far less glamorous mission. At half past four o'clock on that Monday morning, the crew was summoned to the harbor to aid in the salvage of the bantam steamer *Myrtle L. McCluer*. During the night the winds had shifted to a stiff blow out of the east. As a result the water in the harbor had blown back into the lake, thus dropping the water level quite significantly. The *McCluer,* loaded with a cargo of bottles of soda water and ginger ale, was moored to a pier. As the water level dropped, her rail caught on a spile. Listing sharply, the boat began to fill and sink before her crew of two men could stop the event. Armed with the station force-pump, Keeper Cross' crew managed to pump the boat clear by midday. The crew of the South Haven Station returned this time with a better idea of just how wide the scope of their services could be.

Three days into the month of July the South Haven surfmen were again pulling into a late afternoon squall line to the rescue of another pleasure sloop. This time the five persons aboard had been overtaken by the squall, three miles out on the lake, and their boat was dismasted in the conflict. After a lengthily pull the lifesaving crew managed to reach the sloop, clear her wreckage, and tow her back to safety behind the surf boat. A month and a week later on August 10, they went to the aid of the schooner *Lilly Amoit* which had arrived at South Haven with a cargo of cobble-stones, and in a leaking condition. Once more the station's force-pump was used and the boat was saved. Six days later the little schooner *Norman* missed the South Haven harbor entrance and, being unable to get an anchor to hold, she was in danger of going aground. The lifesavers rowed out and towed her to safety using only their surf boat. As they returned once more to the station, the crew stowed their equipment, the surfmen slipped back into their routine with a sense of invulnerability. As discreetly as possible, Number One Surfman Stillson reminded everyone that autumn was right around the corner and that the worst that Lake Michigan could offer was surely waiting just a few weeks ahead.

Passively, the bright blue days of the summer of 1887 faded away along the shores of Lake Michigan and gave way to the gray gloom of rain-spattered autumn. In the lookout tower of the South Haven Lifesaving Station, the eight windows were more often closed than open as the weather outside tended to be more foul. Each surfman who stood watch in the tower now set his gaze across a steel gray lake with threatening whitecaps. On those days and nights when the weather looked ugly, the lookouts scanned the distance for the slightest hint of mariners in distress. Autumn was not long in delivering exactly what the lifesavers had been waiting for. On Thursday, September 8, a southerly gale began to blow and Lake Michigan roared up in front of the South Haven Station. Through the day the winds blew a full gale and by sundown began to shift to the southwest. By midday on Friday the blow shifted to the west and later toward the north. Across all of the lakes this classic cyclonic pattern caused trouble and made a hard time for the mariners. In the South Haven Station each surfman stood his watch with a sharpening eye toward the lake as the storm blew on.

When the winds began to shift from out of the north, Captain Nelson ordered the lines of his command, the 135-ton schooner *W.H. Hawkins*, cast off and took on a tug. A cargo of fresh cut lumber valued at $1,000 was neatly stacked aboard and consigned to the port of Michigan City, Indiana. Nelson had been waiting out the blow after loading at Muskegon, and now that the winds were out of near due north, it was his chance to make a speedy run down the lake with the wind at his heels. Once out on the lake, however, both the *Hawkins* and her crew of seven mariners found that the conditions were much more than they had expected. The rapidly shifting gale had left the waves rolling in contrast to the wind, and a "confused sea" resulted. Now the schooner plowed ahead in near opposition to the seas and her hull began to show the stress. Shortly after the boat had ventured onto the open lake, the twisting of her hull caused her seams to begin to open and cascades of water came aboard. Manning the hand pumps the crew of the *Hawkins* worked in a futile effort to expel the water, but the lake simply came in at a rate far greater than the hand pumps could match. The old schooner was sinking and that was certain. Hardly had 50 miles been gained toward Michigan City before the schooner had become totally waterlogged. Only the buoyancy of the lumber crammed below her deck kept the beaten laker from sliding to her doom. Just above South Haven, Nelson ordered one of the crew to hoist the ship's flag at half-mast as a signal of distress, from that time on all that there was to do was wait. Either help would find them, or the lake would rip them completely apart.

A tardy dawn came the following morning and found the waterlogged *Hawkins* wallowing in a full northerly gale a half-dozen miles above South Haven. The station lookout spotted the distress signal and for the first time Keeper Cross' crew were going to do battle with an actual gale. The surf boat was launched and the storm-warriors went pulling against Lake Michigan. Surprisingly, it took only half of an hour for the surfmen to reach the *Hawkins*, and once there they found that a local tug was close behind. As the lifesavers relieved the schooner's crew at the pumps, the tug took a haul on the weathered laker and the safety of the harbor was made in short order. After four hours of work at the schooner's pump as well as the station's force-pump, the *Hawkins* was free of lake water. The whole event seemed to somehow be anticlimactic. Although they did provide shelter at the station for two of the schooner's crew for a total of five days, there was once again little left for the lifesavers to do other than return to their routine and wait for Lake Michigan's next test. If matters of true terror and deadly consequence were what the crew of the South Haven

A schooner of the period showing standing rigging similar to the City Of Green Bay. (Author's Collection)

Station were in want of, it was a sure bet that Lake Michigan would be able to deliver.

In the first days of October, 1887, the industry of transporting iron ore across the Great Lakes was in the latter part of its infancy. Transportation of lumber was king in the realm of lake commerce, followed closely by coal, grain, and passengers. Iron ore would not take its rightful place at the top of the list until the 1888 season. Additionally, the ports to which the ore was commonly unloaded were not as established as they would be just a decade later. The port cites of Cleveland and Lorain, Ohio, and Gary, Indiana, would soon become standard unloading points for iron ore. The ports of Superior, Wisconsin, Marquette, Michigan, and Two Harbors, Minnesota, became the common shipping points. In 1887, however, the ore sometimes went to places a bit more obscure than the legendary ports it was being shipped from. A good example was moored to the loading dock at Escanaba, Michigan, and taking on a cargo of iron ore on the first day of October of that same year. It was the 346-ton schooner *City Of Green Bay*, and being loaded into her hold was a cargo of ore consigned to St. Joseph, Michigan. Located at the northernmost end of Lake Michigan, Escanaba is the only iron ore port that has direct access to the lower lakes without the need for the lakeboats to navigate the bottleneck at the Soo Locks. The first ore cargo was shipped from there in 1863, mined from the Menominee Range. A year later, a giant ore loading dock was under construction, and by the time that the *City Of Green Bay* took her load in October of 1887, the Escanaba dock was feeding every hungry blast furnace on the lower lakes.

As the *City Of Green Bay* squatted below the loading bins and the clumps of iron ore came tumbling down into her hold, a dense bitter cold fog hung all around and swallowed every sound. In fact, all of the lower lakes were shrouded in a dense autumn muddle. Condensation formed a soaking dew that found its way onto every surface of the schooner. When loading was about to finish, Captain P.W. Costello stepped from his cabin and into the clouded gloom. An odd silence seemed to draw his senses into the befuddlement. The soaked oak planking beneath his feet had become a rude mixture of red ore dust and damp condensation. There would be little point in attempting to get a tug out of the harbor, there was no wind to fill the schooner's canvas sails. Once released onto the open lake, the becalmed sailing vessel would likely be run down in the fog by some passing steamer. It would be best to simply work the *City Of Green Bay* out from under the loading dock and tie up with the other schooners waiting to depart. Captain Costello gave those instructions to the mate, Frank Wood, who was busy attending to the closing of the boat's hatches. A cargo of 675 tons of iron ore formed a pile that hardly took up half of the schooner's cargo space. This is common with cargoes of iron ore, as the substance is so dense that if the hold of a vessel was to be completely filled, the boat would sink long before the hold became full. Together, Thomas Hoitman, John Williams, A.T. Slater, and Henry Brackett all were at work laying the planks across the schooner's hatch openings and then sealing each opening with a tarp. Once that chore was complete, the task of moving the loaded schooner was started. When the day's work was finished there would be nothing left to do but loiter, and it is likely that everyone gathered in Cook Patrick O'Leary's galley for hot coffee to chase off the foggy chill. With that finished the crew of the wind-grabber would do what all mariners do best—they waited.

There are no records as to exactly when the *City Of Green Bay* finished loading, or her movements in the harbor area in those first few fog-shrouded days of October, 1887. In fact, there are no records of exactly when she did leave Escanaba, but using the existing reports of vessels in the same time period and recorded weather conditions, as well as the few records of the schooner's movement shortly after her departure, we can speculate on the boat's activity. Late on the second day of October, a hefty west wind came up on northern Lake Michigan, and the odds are good that the masters of the becalmed schooners made haste in getting out on the lake and getting up sail. Oddly, the wind did not blow away the fog, but in many areas it only grew more dense. From existing records it is gathered that the *City Of Green Bay* departed about midday on October 2. By sunset, the winds had grown to gale force and gained the fog as its partner. This combination caused no end of problems in the Great Lakes maritime industry and caught Captain Costello in some very bad circumstances. Once leaving Escanaba, his vessel was exposed in the upper pocket of Lake Michigan with a west wind sending a vile cross sea against his beam. The schooner wallowed and rolled madly as the waves grew ever higher, and she heeled over as the powerful wind filled her sails. To his south and east a number of islands studded the lake and could provide shelter—that is, if he did not slam into one of them in the fog. The other choice was to run more in the middle of the lake, exposed to the winds and seas, but clear of any obstructions. Neither of these options was desirable, but such were often the choices when it came to autumn navigation on the lakes. Costello elected to run down the open lake, and the *City Of Green Bay* pounded down through the fog, come what may.

Interestingly, the same winds that created the waves which were pounding the ships also hastened her progress down the lake. The combination of heavy seas, high winds and a dense load of ore, however, were about to become the boat's undoing. By the predawn hours of the morning, Costello could feel his boat becoming sluggish in the seas, and when the mate returned from his inspection of the hold he told the captain what everyone feared the most, the schooner had "sprung" and was taking on water. The twisting of the hull timbers had opened the seams between the boat's planks and spit her caulking. Now she had water coming in from a number of different places. At once Costello gave the order to man the pumps and the crew took to the boat's two seesaw hand pumps. Through elbow grease alone they would now have to fight off an inrushing Lake Michigan, and if they did not succeed the iron ore cargo would take the leaking schooner to the depths like a bucket filled with rocks. Before daylight, the situation obviously had become hopeless, and plans to save the boat were paramount. It was then that the flashes of the South Haven Light were spotted through the fog. Abandoning the pumps, the crew hastened to the task of dropping the anchors. The hooks went over the side four miles west-southwest of the South Haven, and the schooner's crew returned to their pumping. Five feet of red ore-stained water was now sloshing in the hold and she was rolling insanely with the anchors finally getting a bite. Costello ordered the flag hoisted upside down at half-mast as a signal of distress, in the hope that daylight would reveal the vessel's plight.

Unknown to those aboard the distressed schooner, their predicament had been seen and help was at that moment being prepared. From the lookout tower of the South Haven Station, the surfman on watch had spotted the *City Of Green Bay* in the first brightenings of dawn as it sat rolling at the ends of its anchor chains. He instantly rang the alarm and Keeper Cross joined him in the tower. There was no doubt the schooner in the distance was in real trouble and Cross brought his station to action. Ordering his crew to have the surf boat ready for immediate launching, the keeper hastened down to the harbor in an effort to engage a tug to go to the aid of the schooner. The tugmen all refused to leave the harbor, pointing out the breakers that were marching up the harbor entrance were far beyond what any of the tugs could overcome, and that the schooner's position was in water that was much too shallow. Cross had no alternative other than using his own means to effect the rescue.

Shortly after her anchors took hold, the beaten hull of the *City Of Green Bay* began to show the signs of going to pieces at the ends of her chains. The deck twisted in an odd manner, and the hull below began making loud groaning sounds that could be heard over the noise of the howling gale. Captain Costello now saw clearly that the battle with Lake Michigan was lost and that the best hope for his crew to survive was to let slip the anchors and beach the boat. Having the pins hammered out, her anchor chains rattled out and dropped into the lake, and Costello put the boat's wheel hard over. Under the power of her foresail the schooner turned her heels to the wind and began to drive toward the shoreline. As the outer sand bar off of South Haven loomed up ahead of the schooner's keel, she slammed into it with the force of 1,021 tons total burden behind her. With a brutal jolt the doomed wind-grabber struck the submerged bar and plunged right through. An agonizing moment later the boat jolted a second time and twisted around broadside to the seas. No sooner had she shuddered into the shallows than the first of the waves that would soon destroy her exploded against her beam. Like fleeing insects, the schooner's crew scrambled into the standing rigging in an effort to get some distance between them and the seas. While the crew made their climb, Lake Michigan slammed repeatedly at their vessel's beam and drove her closer and closer toward shore. Finally, 188 yards from the beach, the *City Of Green Bay* impaled herself on the lake bottom and made the transition from ship to shipwreck.

The situation was critical and the only chance for the schooner's crew was with the lifesavers. Keeper Cross had dashed back to his station and ordered the beach apparatus prepared. The schooner had fetched up opposite a high clay bank and was surrounded on all sides by a furious gauntlet of breaking waves. Keeping this in mind, and figuring that there was not enough beach space to launch the surf boat Cross judged that a rescue by breeches buoy would be best. Procuring a team of horses, the cart with the beach equipment aboard was hitched up and the crew departed. In the beach cart was everything that the crew should need to effect the rescue—that was what was required by the regulations of the Life Saving Service. But, for reasons unknown, Keeper Cross' cart was short one critical item. As the cart was hustled off toward the disaster scene it was lacking a number nine line.

Splitting into two squads, the surfmen took two routes toward the wreck. The first team went on foot via the most direct route, and the second team, hauling the beach cart, was forced to go a half-mile out of their way crossing "the river bridge" and covering a full three miles of total distance to the wreck. Once there the teams regrouped at the top of the clay bank adjacent to where the *City Of Green Bay* had fetched up. At that moment it was realized that there was plenty of beach to allow for the launching of the surf boat, and leaving it behind had been a critical error. No matter, Cross quickly put the breeches buoy plan into action. The Lyle gun was lowered 30 feet down the embankment, set up on the beach, and at an inclination of 25 degrees, the first projectile with a number seven line attached was shot from the miniature cannon. An ear-splitting bang blotted out the storm winds and a billow of white smoke filled the wind as the gun recoiled across the beach nearly to the bluff. Only 50 feet of the line came out of the box before the bullet-like projectile parted from the line and went whizzing over the wreck. As fast as their hands could work, the surfmen pulled back the line and "faked" it back into the fakebox. This task consisted of carefully coiling the line around a series of pins about a foot high in a box formation. The objective was not to entangle the line as it was pulled away by the projectile. It was lucky that the line had parted so close to the box, because refaking a fully-expended line could take from a half-hour to nearly a full hour, under extreme circumstances. Once more, Keeper Cross took aim and fired. Once again the gun recoiled a great distance amid a cloud of smoke. This time the projectile parted instantly and left the line in the faking box. Knowing that there were only three projectiles in the beach cart, Cross ordered two of the surfmen to return to the station for the surf boat, additional shots, and most importantly, a number nine line.

Lake Michigan was well into her test of Keeper Cross, and he was rapidly falling into the trap. Astonishingly, Cross took the line that had already parted twice and attached it to his only remaining projectile. As the shot was fired, the projectile predictably parted from the line and hurtled into the distance taking the fate of the *City Of Green Bay's* crew with it. Cross' frustration now turned into desperation as he commandeered a nearby horse and galloped off toward the station saying that he was going off to hurry the surf boat and supplies. For a long moment the remaining surfmen stood in silence as the waves crashed against the beach and the wind roared past their ears. Less than two football fields away the *City Of Green Bay* was being beaten by the lake with her crew holding on for their lives in the rigging, and the only men who could do anything about it were left helpless with nothing more than an empty Lyle gun and a box of number seven line. That moment of helpless tension began to drag out until three-quarters of an hour later one of the surfmen who had been sent back to the station returned to the wreck site with a number nine line. The schooner's mizzen mast had already fallen over and she was starting to break up. There was not a moment to lose. Keeper Cross was nowhere to be found, so the surfman elected to act on his own. Stuffing a four-ounce charge of powder and a new projectile into the gun, he attached the number nine line and fired. This time the gun recoiled just a few feet back. From the white cloud of smoke the projectile hurtled out toward the wreck as the number nine line whizzed out of the fakebox and arced gracefully over the wreck. The shipwrecked crew got hold of the line and proceeded to pull it in and attempted to rig it. Unfortunately, the schooner was now rapidly going to pieces, and no sooner was the line rigged to the crosstrees of the foremast, than the mainmast was unshipped and went over the side. Now the wreck's crew feared that the foremast would fall next and come down from the rigging onto the wave-swept deck. At once the lifesavers began to pull on the line to the schooner, but the vesselmen on the wreck had failed to properly rig it. As soon as the slack was taken in, the line fouled and became useless. The only hope for the people on the *City Of Green Bay* was now the station's surf boat.

More than an hour after he had departed the wreck site, Keeper Cross returned with the surf-boat. By then the schooner was quickly breaking up and the surrounding surf was filled with a churning field of wreckage. Into the tossing flotsam Cross launched his surf boat, but unknown to him and his surfmen, the lake had already started to claim the *City Of Green Bay's* crew. When the boat's mainmast toppled, cook Patrick O'Leary was struck and killed by the falling spar. Shortly after, a monster wave caught Captain

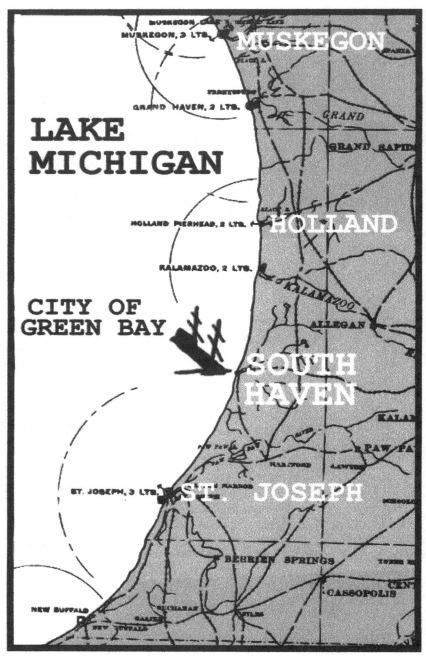

Map showing City Of Green Bay's *wreck site.*

Costello off-guard while attempting to clear the line that had been fired from the beach. In the wink of an eye he was clutched by Lake Michigan and taken over the side to his doom. Then the mighty lake set its ire toward the rest of the vessel's crew, as if to draw Keeper Cross and his storm-warriors more deeply into its snare. From the beach the locals watched in horror as every wave claimed more of the vessel, and the lifesavers floundered in the wreckage field less than 400 feet from shore.

Just a ship's length away from the luckless vessel, the wreckage field became so impassable that the surf boat could go no farther. Now the lifesavers were trapped in the heaving mass of debris, captured by Lake Michigan, and forced to watch as it took out a dreadful vengeance on the crew of the *City Of Green Bay*. One-by-one the five remaining crewmen were either washed over the side or leaped into the lake as the schooner went completely to bits beneath them. The lake, however, was not satisfied with simply putting on a horror show for the surfmen. It next elected to reap a personal vengeance on Keeper Cross. Sending a rogue wave, the lake spit debris against the stern of the surf boat smacking the steering oar on which Cross had a tight hold. The resulting shock catapulted the keeper out of the boat and landed him 15 feet away in the water. When he surfaced he was battered by wave-tossed wreckage of all kinds, as one breaking wave after another cascaded the wreck's rubbish down upon him. Using every ounce of oarsmanship the lifesavers maneuvered in the direction of the struggling keeper and benumbed hands reached out to save him. Tumbling wreckage pummeled and dented the surf boat itself as the crew attempted to recover their leader. But even as the surfmen were pulling in their distressed commander, the lake reached out once again. This time the whole surf-boat was lifted on the back of a wave and dropped squarely atop the thrashing station keeper in a final effort to smite the rescue.

Keeper Cross was successfully pulled from the grip of Lake Michigan, but the lake had released him only in the physical sense. Shortly after the keeper was pulled back aboard the surf boat, the captain of the *City Of Green Bay* was discovered floating face down among the flotsam and pulled from the lake. Clearly no trace of life remained in his body, but the surfmen recovered him anyhow. Next, a castaway was found clutching a chunk of the schooner's deck tossing in the wreckage field. It was A.T. Slater who had elected to go over the side and grab anything floatable. As he was pulled aboard the battered surf boat, he was very near death and hardly aware that he had been rescued. Now the surf boat was headed back to the beach where the occupants spilled out in an exhausted condition. Cross was suffering from several broken ribs on his right side, but still made a painful effort at reviving Captain Costello. It was no use; he was long dead and no human effort would bring him back. It was rapidly becoming evident that the only member of the *City Of Green Bay's* crew who would come ashore alive was A.T. Slater.

As soon as the lifesavers had cleared the surf boat of the water and debris, they decided to launch once again. Keeper Cross, however, was in no condition to man the steering oar. To make matters worse the station's lifeboat was badly damaged having its forward deck shattered and two of the seats, or "thwarts," smashed. Worst of all, the lock to which the steering oar was attached was sheared away.

As if unaware of all of this, Cross turned in a wounded daze to his Number One Surfman, Fletcher Stillson, and growled an order, "Take the boat and go get those men."

Puzzled, Stillson attempted to bring Cross to his senses. Clearly there was no one left alive out in that jumble of surf-tossed wreckage, and the surf boat would be completely unmanageable with its steering lock damaged.

Half in argument and half in attempting to bring the stunned keeper into reality Stillson protested, "Not 'till the steering lock is fixed."

Cross, apparently now totally consumed by the fog of the disastrous failure of the rescue effort and the intense pain of his own injuries, glanced toward the beached surf boat, "Is she hurt?" he asked, as if blinded by the befuddlement of the events.

"The steering lock is broken," Stillson replied as if explaining the obvious, "two of the thwarts are broken and the deck forward is torn loose."

For a long moment the beaten station keeper stood wavering as the lake roared in its disastrous delight on one side, and a disgruntled mob of local residents gathered on the other. At that moment, amid the greatest defeat that the lake could impose on him, Cross did not interpret Stillson's protest as a projection of common sense, but rather as an act of insubordination. In his eyes, Stillson was no longer worthy of taking command,

"George Smith has got my belt," Cross announced loudly as his glazed eyes locked on those of Stillson, "and he will take charge of the boat."

Exactly who Captain George Smith was or what his relation was to Cross is not recorded, but clearly the broken station keeper's sense of defeat had turned into a feeling of general distrust in the loyalty of his own crew. It is after all human nature that under great stress an individual may pass the blame and frustration of his own down fall to those around him. Such may have been the case between Cross and Stillson.

Using what equipment was available, the surfmen made a cobbled repair to their boat's steering lock and shoved off once again into the wreckage-peppered lake. Stillson made certain that he was the first man into the boat—in effect demonstrating his continued courage in the matters of surf and disaster. For a time the surf boat clamored among the pieces of the former *City Of Green Bay*, but the point was moot. There was nothing to be saved, not a life nor a dollar's worth of property. Lake Michigan had imposed its most difficult test on Keeper Cross and the lake's victory had been harsh and complete. By the time the surf boat returned, the sandy beach was a strewn mess of wreckage and Cross' command was as much a wreck as the ship itself.

Three days after the wreck, Lieutenant Rogers and Captain Robbins arrived at the South Haven Station to conduct the standard investigation that followed any loss of life under the jurisdiction of the Life Saving Service. Apparently, Keeper Cross' ill-will toward Surfman Stillson remained, and the investigators were hungry for scapegoats. No sooner had the two investigators arrived than Stillson was informed that he was being demoted from the number one surfman to the number seven surfman. This, Stillson wanted no part of. He felt no guilt in the event and found the demotion completely wrong. He tendered his resignation on the spot and informed the investigators that he would remain at the station only long enough to allow for a replacement to be found. Stillson's resignation, however, would not be the end of the repercussions over the loss of the crew of the *City Of Green Bay*. In fact, the investigation was just starting.

In the cold silence of the South Haven Lifesaving Station, and under the crushing gaze of Rogers and Robbins, Keeper Cross was questioned about the details of the event. It was his claim that the line had parted when shot toward the wreck for reasons that he could not explain. There was a rumor that the lines were rotted, but this was proven wrong when the investigators hung weights up to 403 pounds from a selected sample of the line. Additionally, the break points of the line were examined and found to be clean as if cut with a knife. Such a clean snap is normally caused by sudden and extreme force being applied. On the same day that the investigation was started, a convenient squall came blowing across the lake giving the investigators a chance to fire exactly the same line under similar circumstances. Several shots were made into the squall, and not one time did the line part. As Cross stood watching, it seemed as if Lake Michigan had sent that squall just to seal his personal fate. Shots were fired more than 300 yards, and no indication of flaw was found.

Next the Lyle gun was examined. The wooden carriage on which the gun was mounted consisted of a pair of 30-and-one-quarter-inch-long by two-inch-thick brackets. These hefty wooden mounts were cracked, but the two-and-one-half-inch bore gun barrel was undamaged. While at the beach, the investigating officers also reviewed the recoil distance of the gun as witnessed by those on the scene. The length of the recoil was strikingly similar to the firings at Nantucket the previous October. In those tests, larger than normal charges of powder were used in an effort to determine how they would effect the gun. The damages to the Lyle gun and the recoil distances were found to be consistent with those of an overcharged gun. Moreover, the breaking of the line was also consistent with an overcharged firing. In all, the evidence gathered seemed quite condemning toward Keeper Cross.

When the investigation was finished, so was the command of Barney Alonzo Cross. The team of officers found a number of areas where Cross seemed to have inexplicably made the most incorrect of judgments. His leaving the station without a number nine line and, even more importantly, the surf boat, started the chain of events that lead to the loss of six lives. Just why he apparently overcharged the gun, which supposedly led to the breaking of the line, as well as why he used the same line that had previously broken, was beyond explanation. In the United States Life Saving Service there was no room for error and no excuses were valid. Along with the minimum pay went a maximum responsibility, and the blame for the loss of those aboard the *City Of Green Bay* now was placed squarely onto Keeper Cross. Upon the conclusion of the investigation, Cross was immediately relieved of his command of the South Haven Station. John Brooks was appointed Keeper in his place.

From an historical perspective it would be easy to call Barney Cross a "bumbler" and place the entire blame of the *City Of Green Bay* tragedy in his lap. Unfortunately, far too many tellers of Great Lakes tales take the easy route, and the memory of good people, such as Captain Cross, suffers for that shortcut. It is a bit more difficult to look beyond that single moment in time. Out of all of the number one surfmen on the lakes, Cross was selected to open the new station at South Haven, based completely on his past performance in the service. Certainly, if Cross was a "bumbler," that trait would have shown itself long before his promotion. Keepers of lifesaving stations were hand picked and carefully screened, so this is clear evidence that, prior to the *City Of Green Bay's* wreck, Cross' record was not only clean, but exemplary. So those who would look back and call this man a bumbler are dealing in tabloid history and not true research. Some also have reported that Cross' separation from the Life Saving Service was the end of him on the Great Lakes, and that also is simply wrong—let alone being too easy of a conclusion to draw. The fact is that Barney Cross, upon ending his career with the lifesavers, did exactly what most former surfmen had done—he acquired a better job as a Great Lakes mariner. His new career was begun as an officer, and later a master, aboard the South Haven Line boats, beginning with the steamer *Glenn*. In later seasons he commanded the *City Of Kalamazoo* before switching to another transportation company. As master of the steamer *Arundell* for the Chicago-Saugatuck Line, Cross ended his sailing career in 1910 after 23 years as a respected mariner. He spent the next four years in South Haven where he died of a heart ailment on October 8, 1914—37 years, nearly to the day, after his separation from the Life Saving Service. This was obviously not the career of a "bumbler" by any stretch of the imagination. Cross was, in fact, a well-respected and highly successful Great Lakes mariner.

So, if Captain Cross was indeed a competent individual, why then did he come to such a disastrous end in the Life Saving Service? Perhaps he simply found himself amid circumstances beyond his control, and as a result was swept up into turmoil. Then again, maybe Lake Michigan found the one moment when he happened to leave himself vulnerable, and it picked that instance to surprise him with its most difficult test. For just a few horrible hours, Cross was overwhelmed by the scope of Lake Michigan's vengeance, and it is that moment that everyone seemed to focus on when looking back on him. As so many thousands of capable mariners have done, Cross had the lake get the better of him at just the wrong time. This was a mistake that he never made again for the rest of his career. Without a doubt, the stretch of beach just south of the harbor entrance to South Haven, where the pieces of the *City Of Green Bay* came ashore, was a place that Cross would rather avoid, and probably tried hard to forget.

South Haven on a fine summer's day is much the same as it was in 1887. The sails of dozens of small pleasure sloops dot the distance as the amateur sailors set out with their guests to beat the heat—all in the hope of escape on an indifferent lake. Now, however, the piers are often the places of art fairs and craft exhibits, while dozens of downtown shops market wares of every sort. Tours of the lighthouse allow the visitor to step back in time. At the foot of the bridge and adjacent to the maritime museum stands the original boathouse of the South Haven Lifesaving Station. From its rafters once hung the 403 pounds of dead weight that demonstrated the soundness of Keeper Cross' number seven line, and helped end his career in the Life Saving Service. As a matter of fact, the *City Of Green Bay,* itself, is not far away. As of this writing, it is just a few dozen yards off shore in 18 feet of water. Unlike the other features in this story, however, the wreck is not a fixture. Like most of the wrecks on the Lake Michigan shore, the skeleton of the *City Of Green Bay* moves. In 1950 the schooner's bones made a ghostly appearance within wading distance of the beach, then vanished once again below the waves. The tourists who visit the beach near the wreck may want to look carefully, because no one knows when the ship will make another visit to the beach that Captain Cross would rather forget.

OUTSIDE OF THE
LEXINGTON WINDOW

A long the shore that stretches from Pointe aux Barques to Port Huron, the state of Michigan is currently enjoying a rebirth. Gone is the lumber industry, and going is the auto industry. Yet some entrepreneurs see a new livelihood in Michigan's greatest natural resource—the lakeshore itself. All along the shore the seeds of investment are beginning to sprout returns, and in the process inventors are breathing new life into the Great Lakes region. These are steadfast individualists for whom terms such as "no" are simply the fuel that is used to motivate their projects. Myopic politicians and status quo locals are no match for such true "doers." A good example of this is the "Smackwater Development" block that is now open in Lexington, Michigan. The brain child of Adam Buschbacher, the development is constructed from the ground up to resemble an old brick building that has been hollowed out and restored as a series of new shops. Upscale yet friendly with a first-class coffee shop and restaurant, the block is a departure from the moccasin-and-mug gift shop mentality that has been the way of things for so long in the Michigan tourist trade. It is just the kind of draw that will pull tourists and their dollars into the thumb as well as providing local folks with a first-class place to eat. While dining or sipping cappuccino, the visiting tourist or relaxing local person may look out upon the lake and ponder wild storms and shipwreck adventures. Their pondering would rightly include the keeping of valor—which actually occurred right outside the windows through which they gaze.

It would be safe to say that January 10, 1891, was one of the high-points in the Great Lakes maritime career of Captain Alfred Mitchell. This apogee of his many years of service on the inland seas had its roots in an Act of Congress passed on June 20, 1874. The act was renewed on June 18, 1878, and again on May 4, 1882. It provided the Secretary of the

111

Treasury with the power to award medals of valor through the United States Life Saving Service for acts of lifesaving both civilian and service-related. The medals were in two forms—silver for acts of courage or assisting in acts of bravery, and gold for acts of extreme valor. By the first month of 1891, the Secretary of the Treasury had dispensed 159 silver awards and 151 gold awards to individuals for acts of courage. Captain Mitchell was presented with the 152nd gold medal and was only the second vessel master on the Great Lakes to be given such an honor. Pondering the gold medallion, it was easy for the captain to remember the events that inspired the award. That dreadful morning of October 20, 1890, was not far in the past, and Captain Alfred Mitchell had indeed become a hero on that date. Now, of course, he had the medal to prove it.

A loathsome north-to-northeast wind was blowing on lower Lake Huron in the predawn hours of Monday, October 20, 1890. At Port Huron, Michigan, Sergeant of the Signal Service, H.L. Boyce, observed and dutifully recorded a wind blowing at 12 to 20 miles per hour, with gusts of 32 miles per hour. With that nasty autumn wind, Lake Huron sent an ugly sea rolling toward Port Huron and the mouth of the St. Clair River. Tramping nearly the full length of the lake, the seas did not appear big enough to be a threat to navigation, but were indeed an annoyance. Boyce also recorded a barometric pressure of 29.89 inches of mercury, and a temperature of 48 degrees at 7:30 that morning. Although these measurements showed an increase over the previous 12 hours, it was still a nasty morning at Port Huron. Had Sergeant Boyce turned his gaze toward the lake he would have observed the normal clutter of upbound and downbound vessel lights out upon the stormy water. No doubt he could picture in his mind's eye the rude time mariners on the lakeboats were having this morning. He would not, however, have been able to imagine the terror and valor that would soon surround two of those lakeboats.

Plodding toward the open lake at six o'clock that blustery morning, the wooden lumber-hooker *Edward Smith* was pulling a string of inconspicuous schooner-barges. As his steamer cleared Port Huron and started on her course up the lake, Captain Mitchell descended from the "open-air" bridge and down into the pilothouse below. He had been standing watch over his command through the entire night as the steamer churned her way up from Lake Erie, and now that the boat was clearing the confines of the St. Clair River, he could step out of the wind and cold rain and seek shelter inside. The steam heat that came from the boat's radiators filled the pilothouse with comfort as Mitchell shed the first layers of his outdoor garb. It is certain that the all night passage had taken its normal toll on the exhausted captain. Countless vessels had been passed in the darkness and each was an ordeal of judgment, decision-making and whistle-blowing. Mitchell's upcoming nap would be well-deserved. Glancing up through stress-clouded eyes, he saw that there was one more oncoming vessel to signal. Taking the whistle-pull in hand, he took just enough time to blow the standard passing signal to the downbound oak-hulled steamer *John B. Lyon* and then he retired to the snug comfort of his cabin.

Departing a Port Huron dock and heading upbound only a quarter of an hour behind the *Smith* came the package freighter *Annie Young*. Aboard the *Young*, Captain Miller had his sights set on the *Smith* and her consorts. Running without the burden of a tail of barges, the *Young* was able to make a good deal more speed than the *Smith*, but Miller was reluctant to pass her in the confines of the upper St. Clair River. Now, as the expanse of open Lake Huron was reached, Miller's chance was at hand. He gave the order to "Let'er go," and the *Annie Young* came up to full steam. The upbound progress for the *Smith* was slow, and the shoreline seemed to hardly move at all. Although the boat was in its first season of operation, the string of barges moored to her stern greatly restricted her over-the-bottom speed. The result of the *Smith's* burden was that shortly after she had cleared the river, the *Annie Young* was upon her and pulling out to pass. In good time the package freighter had made short work of the passing operation and was swinging back on course. In just a few miles on the open lake, the *Young* had overtaken Captain Mitchell's boat and was rapidly opening up a distance between the two. To those aboard the *Smith* the whole scene was somewhat of a non-event. When you make your living towing long strings of barges, those unattached steamers are always plowing past you. Concerns aboard the *Smith* were more likely to be directed toward the weather as Lake Huron grew in her foul mood.

Daylight across the lake revealed only sullen gray clouds that reached down toward the waters of the lake. Every person on every boat knew, however, that the current conditions could rapidly change and a weather eye was kept by every watchman. Aboard the *Annie Young*, the crew was preparing for a rough passage. Hauling a combined cargo of coal, barreled oil, barreled nails and packaged freight from Buffalo to Gladstone, Michigan, the *Young* had a number of scheduled stops along the way, and in this ugly autumn weather anything not firmly tied down would be thrown about and perhaps damaged. Boats such as this were sometimes referred to as "coasters," due to their frequent callings at coastal towns and ports. This was a time when many towns along the lake shores were devoid of railroad access and local roads were little more than muddy trails. Vital supplies and goods were provided by these handy lakeboats and their arrival was always a welcomed event. Trips by the coastal package freighters were of the greatest importance in the late fall and early spring. Between the months of December and April, the winter's ice blocked access to the coastal towns, and what supplies had been stockpiled had to suffice for the local consumers. As she beat her way through the autumn bluster, every piece of merchandise carried aboard the *Young* was of great importance. Damaged goods were not likely to be sent back for repair and then returned in the same year. Thus, if any of the items in her hold were broken, the buyers were simply stuck with them. Such damage would surely cause the shippers to look to boats other than the *Young* to carry their goods next time, and there were plenty of them to choose from in 1890. With future loads in mind, Captain Miller had probably given strict orders to secure the cargo, and great care was taken to insure that no loose items were tossed about with the roll of the boat.

The oak-hulled steam propeller and package freighter *Annie Young* had started her career as a bulk freighter. Constructed at the Detroit boatyard of Campbell & Owen in 1869, the *Young* was that company's first bulk freighter. For her day she was a real giant, having dimensions of 157 feet in overall length, 32 feet in beam, 13 feet in depth, and 1006 gross tons of capacity. She was listed as "hull number nine" and assigned an official number of 1760. Just nine years after her launching, she was converted to a combination package and bulk freight carrier. Although this conversion was done for reasons unknown, it was a good move. Advances in the maritime industry were moving at an unimagined pace by the end of the 1870s, and vessels were rapidly outsizing and out-powering the *Young*. So, although the vessel's dimensions were less impressive a decade after her launch, she was very well suited for the coastal trade. By the nasty autumn morning in 1890 when she pushed passed the *Smith*, the 22-year-old *Annie Young* also pushed her way toward earning a tidy profit among a lakeboat fleet that would always be rapidly outgrowing her.

Once past the *Smith*, the *Annie Young* had made steady progress up the lake, and the distance between the two boats continued to rapidly grow. The only boat that was now on the upbound track ahead of the *Young* was the big 294-foot wooden lakeboat *Tom Adams*. For the *Young's* master, Captain Miller, the *Adams* was no factor in his navigation plans. The big steamer was 50 minutes ahead of him and now consisted of little more than a silhouette and a smudge of coal smoke on the horizon. So far as traffic was concerned, the *Young* now had clear sailing. However, the weather was another matter. Miller faced an ugly day at sea and a rude chop that was now the surface of the lake. Certainly, he was a long way from the next pleasant summer day on Lake Huron. As often happens on the Great Lakes, the danger came from more than one direction. While all aboard the *Annie Young* were focused on the weather and the cargo, no one seemed to notice the traces of smoke that were growing within her cargo hold.

Back onboard the *Edward Smith*, Captain Mitchell had just settled into his bunk when there came a banging at his cabin door. Shocked from the earliest stage of his deep nap, Captain Miller bounded to the door. The word from the pilothouse was that the *Annie Young* was burning ahead. It had been just over two hours since the *Young* had passed Captain Mitchell's boat, and now he had the *Smith* and her barges halfway between Lakeport and Lexington. The *Young*, on the other hand, was nearly a half-dozen miles ahead and directly abeam of Lexington. It was just after nine o'clock in the morning and the boats were nearly three miles off shore. As Mitchell focused his binoculars on the burning vessel ahead, it was clear that she was the *Annie Young*, and it was also clear that her crew were in a fight to save their lives. Dense smoke billowed from the stern of the boat and bright orange flames could clearly be seen. With his schooner-barges in tow, it would take Mitchell more than an hour to reach the *Young*. If the *Young* was still under power, it would take even longer for the *Smith* to catch her, and by then it may then be too late. With this in mind, Mitchell ordered his barges to be cast off. Once free of the burden of her consorts, the *Smith* would be able to muster a good deal more speed, and her time to reach the *Young* would be measured in minutes rather than hours. After dropping his towing hawser, and without regard for the safety of his own boat, Mitchell plowed to the rescue at full speed against the gale.

Captain Mitchell's guess as to the level of urgency aboard the *Annie Young* was correct. In 1890, the ways in which a fire was fought aboard a steamer was by use of a bucket brigade, or a steam hose, or both. Vessels such as the *Young* were constructed of wood and nearly everything that made up the boat could burn—including her crew. The fire had its beginnings somewhere in the aft cargo hold among the cargo itself. By the time that the boat's chief engineer discovered the smoke coming from the aft hatchway, it was already too late to save the boat. The hold was a furnace and no human efforts would change the fate of the wooden steamer. To mariners caught aboard a combusting vessel, however, the reality of such a situation is never apparent. All that can be thought of at the moment of such a fire's discovery is that they must fight the blaze and save their boat. With that in mind, the chief quickly deployed two steam hoses and the crew set to the task of "fighting" a fire that they could never possibly extinguish. What no one on deck knew was that some of those several hundred barrels of oil that were among the boat's cargo were being super-heated and were now ready to combust. As soon as the hatchway was opened, the flames were given the draft they needed, and the super-heated gasses burst through the opening. Although there is no record of it, it was probably at this point that First Mate Bogan was severely burned about his hands and face. He would have likely been at the front of the assault, and may have been caught by surprise by the intensity of the inferno as the afterhatch was opened. Now, as the crew began its fight, the *Annie Young* began to be rapidly consumed at a frightening pace.

Since the fire had started in the lower regions of the boat, the first occupied compartment to be overrun was the engine room. Shortly after the hold was opened, the engine room crew was forced to flee their stations. Unfortunately, no one bothered to stop the engine before

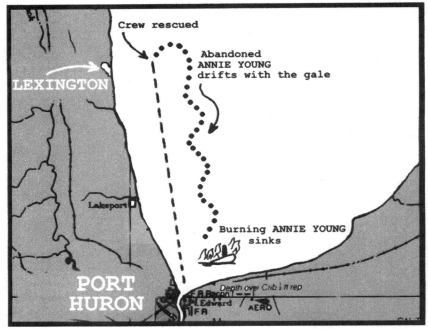

A map of the Annie Young's *last trip.*

evacuating. So, the boat went charging up the lake under a full head of steam, burning all the way with no one, other than the flames, standing watch at her engine controls. Topside, the crew were rapidly losing the battle against the flames. Captain Miller reasoned that he had to save the lifeboat which was located aft near the fire. He ordered the boat launched and moored to the side of the *Young* in the hopes that when the crew needed it the yawl would be intact. The seas were running high and the yawl was not meant to be launched while the boat was under full headway. Yet, this was to be a last resort. Although Miller told the crew to launch the yawl, but to stay aboard the steamer, they did not listen.

When faced with a fate such as being burned alive aboard a rapidly incinerating ship, any person is likely to take the matter into their own hands. Such was the case aboard the *Annie Young* that morning, as the flames grew and the crew began to panic. A dozen of the 22 crewmembers scrambled into the lifeboat as soon as it was launched. Captain Miller now had a small mutiny to deal with as well as a burning vessel. Through shouts and curse words, three of the wayward crew were convinced to return aboard the *Young*. The other nine men refused to leave the yawl, preferring to tempt the lake rather than face the flames. With that, the lake reached out and inflicted a punishment that the burning vessel could not. Between the rolling seas and the swiftly moving hull of the *Young*, the

116

waters simply swamped the yawl and the nine renegades were swallowed by Lake Huron and never seen again.

From the beach at Lexington the sight must have been awesome. Brilliant orange flames shot skyward from the stern of the distant *Annie Young* as a cloud of thick smoke reached toward the low-hanging gray sky. Residents gathered on the shore saw the flaming ship as she continued to march up the lake, and just aft of her the rescue steamer *Smith* was straining to catch up.

By the time that the *Smith* reached the *Annie Young*, the burning boat's stern was nearly consumed to the water line. Maneuvering the *Smith*, Captain Mitchell brought her along side the *Young*. Although the records are unclear, it is likely that he brought the *Smith* up on the windward side so that the gale would carry the sparks and smoke clear of the wooden rescue boat. It was obviously too late to save any part of the *Young*, so Captain Mitchell's best course of action was simply to come alongside and allow the remaining crew of the *Young* to leap to safety. As the timbers of the two lakeboats smashed together, the *Young's* people jumped to the decks of the *Smith*. Then Mitchell maneuvered clear of the flaming *Young* and left her to incinerate herself.

By the time that the *Smith* recovered her barges and headed back toward Port Huron, the *Annie Young's* engine had run out of steam pressure and she drifted like a floating bonfire. Drifting with the winds and currents of Lake Huron, the *Young* was pushed from Lexington back toward Port Huron. Eventually, she burned down to the point where the lake, itself, came aboard and extinguished the mass of flames. She finally dipped below the waves seven miles, north by east, from the Fort Gratiot Light. At four o'clock on that afternoon, the *Smith* re-entered the St. Clair River and then later deposited the survivors of the *Annie Young* safely onto dry land.

Nearly a full month after Captain Mitchell had rescued the *Young's* crew, he guided the *Edward Smith* into the port of Buffalo. It was Thursday, November 13, and no sooner had the lines of the *Smith* been made fast to the pier than a messenger was aboard delivering a note to Mitchell. The note was from a Mr. Evans who was manager of the Anchor Line, which had been the owner of the *Annie Young*. Mitchell was asked to come to the Buffalo offices of the Anchor Line in order to meet with Mr. Evans. Once there, the good captain was awarded a gold watch and chain, as well as a set of embossed resolutions stating his valor in the saving of the crew of the *Young*. Next he was escorted to Mr. Evans' residence where a lavish dinner party was held in his honor. Two months later, Mitchell was again honored. This time it was the official awarding of a gold medal for lifesaving presented to him from the United States Life Saving Service. Now there was no doubt that he was a hero.

It is highly recommended that the reader make the trip to Lexington. Once there it is easy to locate red brick buildings of the Smackwater Block. Take some time to visit the shipwreck museum and ask about the *Annie Young*. They know the story, and will share other adventures with you. Next, take a seat in Aroma's Coffee House and, while enjoying your cupped drink gaze out onto the lake and remember well that day of gale and fire when Captain Alfred Mitchell became a hero just a short distance from where you are seated.

MARTHA HART'S
FIRST COMMAND

In Martha Hart's time, the role of a lady of the lakes was completely defined in one job—cook. The time in history was July of 1878 and the employment opportunities for females were scarce in general, but in the Great Lakes maritime business there seemed to be only one place where a lady could find work and that was in the galley. Looking back from a modern perspective, where females can be found doing every job in the maritime industry, some people may be astonished at the thought of there being only one opportunity aboard the lakeboats. In Martha Hart's day, however, the job as a cook on a laker was practically a liberating experience. Indeed, many ladies of the lakes took such positions to free themselves of the greater restrictions of life ashore. Those who sailed often gained travel, income and independence. For Martha, the job had been an "off again, on again" pursuit that she had worked at for nearly a full decade. Even at that, she had managed to become quite familiar with the waterways of the lakes, particularly Lake Ontario.

Residing in the port city of Oswego, New York, it was always easy for an experienced "one-pot" cook such as Martha to find a berth on a lakeboat that was short-handed in the galley. Although we have no records of her career aspirations, there is little doubt that Martha used sailing as a handy job to fall back on, or even to get her out of town when she had the urge. Through her 10 years on the lakes, she had gained a thorough knowledge of navigation that rivaled some of her male counterparts. As a cook, however, she never had the opportunity to exercise her knowledge other than the normal galley debates with the boat's crew. Still, Martha was no wallflower and when it came to taking charge, she was the type of person who was never shy. Without regard to her gender and "proper place" in the society of the 1870s, no one was going to wipe their boots on Martha Hart. Perhaps that was the reason that she participated in sailing as an off-again, on-again job. Many vessel masters were tyrannical in nature and, although not eager to discharge a reliable cook, they could make her world aboard their boat bad enough to cause her to resign. Unfortunately, the passage of time has obliterated most things that would allow us to find out about Martha, but there is one documented event that tells us a great deal about this stone-willed lady of the Great Lakes. That event took place during the early morning hours of July 5, 1878, and is another amazing tale of an individual who took command.

Noon on July 4th found Martha waiting to board the Canadian passenger steamer *Hastings* at Kingston, Ontario. Martha had to wait her turn to cross the gangway because she was not going aboard as an employee, but as a paying passenger bound for Oswego. Apparently she was unemployed at the moment and was free to travel. Perhaps she was just doing a bit of excursioning, or perhaps she had left her berth on a vessel that was in at Kingston. Unfortunately, that little detail in the story has been lost to us. What is on record, however, is that 300 to 400 passengers were waiting with Martha to make the seven-and-one-half-hour boat ride across the easternmost end of Lake Ontario. By half-past five o'clock that same evening, all of the passengers were aboard the *Hastings*, and the boat departed for Oswego. Being a professional cook aboard ship, the first thing that Martha noticed that was odd about the passage was that the *Hastings* was apparently not going to set out any food for its passengers. There was no serving crew to be seen anywhere aboard the boat. This was somewhat strange, but not completely unexpected. Passenger vessels of this era "fed" depending on the order and whim of the captain. A different boat in the same fleet may have put out a grand feast just because the captain wanted to attract greater business. Not putting out food for the passengers was more a kin to poor service, rather than anything that might be considered worrisome. No doubt Martha evaluated the lack of food in terms of her own abilities to serve meals on a lakeboat. She probably concluded that if she again decided to buy a ticket to cross Lake Ontario, she would be sure not to book her trip aboard the *Hastings*. In the hours to come, Martha would find many more reasons to avoid the boat in the future.

The *Hastings* had been delivered to her original owner, G.C. Daintry of Cobourg, Ontario, on July 1, 1863. At that time the brand-new sidewheel steamer was wearing the name *Rochester* in honor of one of the primary New York cities that Daintry intended for her to service. Cross-lake service was highly competitive on Lake Ontario in 1863, and a shrewd owner would use every method at his disposal to gain an advantage. Considering that his new boat would run a line between Cobourg and Port Hope, Ontario, and Rochester, New York, Daintry elected to name his boat after Rochester because he probably calculated that its residents would be more likely to book passage aboard their

Side-wheel steamer Hastings. *(Author's Concept)*

namesake vessel than aboard her competitor vessel, the *Empress*. Daintry's calculations would have been well-founded, because this was a generation when hometown prides ran deep. People of this time were far less mobile than they are now, and often local newspapers hyped the town's pride. Thus, when the *Empress* tied up near the *Rochester* in the port of Rochester, the walk-up passengers were more likely to buy their tickets aboard "their" boat. So, although the *Empress* had the reputation as being one of the fastest boats on Lake Ontario, the *Rochester* would have the hometown advantage. Construction of the *Rochester* took place at Montreal, Quebec, at the shipyard of August Cantin. Her hull was 138 feet long and 26 feet wide, not including her big paddle wheels. Equipped with a vertical-beam steam engine with 36-inch-diameter cylinders that ran an eight-foot stroke, the *Rochester* should have been able to make somewhere between seven and nine miles per hour across the lake.

After a decade of managing the *Rochester*, Daintry elected to sell the boat to C.E. Gildersleeve of Kingston, Ontario. Her new owner intended her for use in seasonal relief sailing. Gildersleeve currently operated the steamer *Bay Of Quinte*, and found that this vessel was showing her age. To remove some of the burden from the *Bay Of Quinte*, he placed the *Rochester* in reserve duty along the old steamer's routes. Over the winter lay up of 1876-77 the *Rochester* was given new boilers, overhauled and renamed *Hastings*. Her role after the overhaul remained that of a relief vessel. By the midsummer of 1878, the tourist and excursion season on Lake Ontario was at its peak and the *Hastings* was pressed into her duty hauling the excess of passengers across the lake. It was aboard this relief vessel that Martha Hart had bought her passage.

Sometime between 11 o'clock that evening and midnight, Martha noticed that the *Hastings* was turning off of her course to Oswego. Looking toward the south, she could see the steady lamp of the Oswego Lighthouse a dozen miles away, right on the horizon where it should be. But the *Hastings* was winding about—away from the lighthouse. It was clear to her that the boat had turned from the southbound track and was now steaming nearly due north. Certainly, something was amiss because they were apparently headed back to Canada. Making her way to the bow, Martha could see the lights of another steamer, and it appeared as if the *Hastings* had fallen in to follow that boat. In fact, the steamer ahead was the passenger vessel *City Of Toledo* which had left Oswego at eight o'clock that evening, headed upbound for Kingston, the port from which the *Hastings* had departed. Instinctively, Martha knew that the *Hastings* was going the wrong way. She had sailed this area many times herself and she was certain that this was not the way to Oswego. By now the Oswego Lighthouse was astern and about to disappear over the horizon. This was about enough for any mariner to determine that something must be very wrong. Martha decided to take matters into her own hands and find out just what was going on aboard the ship.

Climbing the companionway stairs to the boatdeck roof, she made her way to the steamer's bird cage pilothouse. Martha peeked in and saw only the flustered wheelsman within. Entering the wheelhouse, she found an elderly individual at the wheel who was completely overwhelmed by the events of the night. He was alone, disoriented and half-frozen with panic. Martha pointed out that the Oswego Light was aft of the *Hastings*, but the wheelsman refused to believe her. Instead, he insisted that the lights of the steamer ahead was the Oswego Lighthouse. Martha was dumfounded when she pointed out that the lights ahead were those of another vessel, but the man at the wheel refused to listen to her. Searching for the boat's charts, so she could prove her point, she was shocked to find that there was not a single chart in the entire pilothouse. It was about then that Martha realized that there apparently was not a single officer aboard the *Hastings* either! Grabbing the boat's binoculars, she discovered that they were so old and beaten that they were completely useless. The entire scene was like one of those nightmares where you run around trying to correct a situation gone terribly wrong, but nothing works and no one will hear your pleas. Martha urged the wheelsman to listen to her, but he simply stood there clutching the helm and following the lights of the *City Of Toledo*. Martha

Map of the Hastings *course.*

insisted that she had sailed these waters for 10 years and knew her way very well. Still the "pilot" at the wheel ignored her. Leaving the pilothouse she made her way through the crowd of grumbling passengers. Apparently, Martha was not the only one who had sensed that there was a problem aboard the *Hastings*. The passengers had not been assigned staterooms or berths of any kind and were apparently locked out on deck and awake to witness the waywardness of the boat. Some of the folks saw her exiting the pilothouse and asked what was going on. Martha told them that the boat was without any officers, that the wheelsman was steering it the wrong way, and he refused to change course. Someone asked about food.

"If they set a table," Martha told them, "go for it."

After some searching, Martha managed to find a passenger who had a telescoping marine glass. She borrowed it and returned to the wheelhouse. At half-past two o'clock that morning, Martha managed to determine that the *Hastings* was just below Galloo Island. Using the marine glass she sighted on Sackets Harbor and urged the wheelsman to turn around and head south. Again he refused, convinced that he was right by following the lights off of his bow. This part of Lake Ontario is no place for uncertainty or misguided conclusions, and Martha knew it. The waters in the area are studded with islands and shoals, and in 1878 many of those were unmarked by navigation lights. By her best estimation, she figured that the boat was within four miles of running aground. Now Martha had two choices, she could retreat into the crowd and wait for the boat to be run aground, or she could take command.

Storming from the pilothouse, Martha headed for the one place remaining aboard the *Hastings* where competent crew may still be found—the engine room. Making her way through the maze of companion ways and decks, she entered the engine room. Heat from the boilers hung heavy and as she walked through the doorway into the heart of the boat her face felt as if it had been held too long over a boiling pot. The light was provided by a few scattered oil lamps, and there was only the dim amber glow of those lamps to illuminate the way. The engine room was a hot, steamy, dimly-lit hell, and for a time it appeared as if there was no one down there either. As she searched about, seeking anyone who may be a member of the crew, she must have started to become more certain that this may actually be a nightmare. Over the hiss and thunder of the machinery, a perspiring Martha managed to find the boat's engineer who was probably a bit startled to have one of the passengers invading his engine room. Quickly she explained the situation and her fear that if something was not done soon, the boat would surely be run aground.

Perhaps it was the look in the eyes of the lady who stood in front of him; perhaps it was Martha's commanding presence; maybe it was something that the engineer knew about the boat's staff that Martha did not—but this time her words struck home and the engineer took action to save his boat. Unlike captains and deck officers who are often moving from one boat to another, engineers are normally "wedded" to their boats, and never willing to risk their vessel. Without hesitation, the engineer of the *Hastings* walked over and stopped the boat's engine. Within minutes, the steamer wallowed to a halt and was adrift, dead in the water. There was no wind that night and the lake was as flat as a sheet of glass, so the *Hastings* simply squatted there, in the dark and way off course. Now Martha had a more difficult task at hand, because she was going to have to convince the wheelsman to put the *Hastings* back on course for Oswego.

We can only imagine the scene in the pilothouse when Martha returned. The pilot was now completely powerless to chase his reckless course. It is without doubt that there were hot words between the wheelsman and the female cook turned self-appointed captain. Through most of the rest of the night Martha refused to let the boat proceed until the wheelsman agreed to take a more reasonable course. The main sticking point was probably the fact that, without any charts aboard and the compass either missing or broken, the wheelsman had no idea which way to steer because he had no idea of his position. What was amiss with the boat's compass is not on record, but this was an era when many vessels on the lakes either had compass equipment that was in disrepair or missing. Such was often the case with boats that did the short-haul coastal trade or that were "relief" vessels. Today the Coast Guard inspects and closely regulates every aspect of equipment used on lakeboats, but in 1878 such an idea was more than 30 years into the future. The United States Steamboat Inspection Service did boiler inspections in the 1800s and their Canadian counterparts did so in the Dominion. But the inspectors were few and their checks were scattered at best. So, it is quite possible that the *Hastings'* compass was in as good a condition as were her binoculars—in short it was useless! This was also an era when there was no real inspection of navigation equipment on most of the lakeboats, nor was there any enforced minimum of navigation equipment or crew. The only thing that had a true regulating affect on the cross-lake and excursion business was public opinion and confidence in the vessels. Many owners relied on the boat's officers to provide navigational tools of their own. Other than that they saw no need to provide their boats with any such "frills." So long as the public perceived a boat as fast, or on time, there was no reason to indulge in additional expense.

At the first hints of dawn, the planet Venus began to show as the "morning star." It was in the south-southeast sky and Martha and her wheelsman reached a compromise. He would navigate on that star until they could see the south shore, and then the boat could be successfully headed into Oswego by following the coast. With the deal set, "Captain" Martha went below and informed the engineer of the plan, and he agreed to restart the engine. At half-past five o'clock in the morning, Nine Mile Point was spotted from the *Hastings'* wheelhouse. Martha and her befuddled pilot could now agree that Oswego was to the west and the boat was headed in that direction.

Ashore at Oswego, the friends and relatives of those who were known to be aboard the *Hastings* spent a troubled night at dockside. This was also an era when many passengers sailed off onto the Great Lakes and never came back, so every overdue vessel caused great anxiety, no matter what the weather conditions happened to be. When the lights of the *Hastings* had not appeared by midnight, many began to worry, and as the night grew late the worry turned to near-panic. Likewise, the Canadian passengers, who were waiting for the *Hastings* to take them home, did not know what to do under these circumstances. Nearly 300 people spent the night wandering the Oswego streets among the closed shops and sleeping businesses, not knowing if their steamer would ever arrive. Finally, just before seven o'clock in the morning, the lights of the *Hastings* were sighted. Unexpectedly, the boat was coming in from the east rather than from the north. Following the coastline, Martha Hart had successfully brought the *Hastings* into its destination port. By half-past seven that morning, the angry passengers were making their way safely ashore at Oswego—thanks to Martha Hart.

It did not take long after the *Hastings* made the dock for the story to get out of how she was nearly eight hours overdue on a clear and calm summer night. Later that same day the local papers carried the story and repercussions soon followed. If some kind of explanation was not tendered soon, the *Hastings* may find herself with an extreme lack of passengers in the very near future. In the hope of quelling the tide of bad words, a statement was released a few days later in Kingston and published in the *Oswego Palladium* on July 12. It read:

THE STRAY STEAMER

Kingston News: The pilot [of the *Hastings*,] claims that there was a dense fog on the lake during the night, and this was the cause of his following up so closely to the lights of the propeller. It is not true they were within fifteen miles of Oswego. If they had been, they could have seen the lights and had been all right.

This initial portion of the statement is not only contradictory, but uses the oldest mariners excuse in the book. First of all, a number of witnesses stated that the night was clear and that no fog existed. The excuse contradicts itself by stating that if the "pilot" had been within 15 miles of Oswego, he would have surely seen the lighthouse, so he must have been farther out on the lake. If the Oswego Light could have been sighted at 15 miles, then where was this "dense fog" of which he spoke in the very first line of his statement? To blame any embarrassing circumstance on a "dense fog" is a dodge that has long been used by mariners, and always looks about as lame as it does in the *Hastings* incident. The statement went on to say that there were officers, compasses, and charts aboard and that they could have easily navigated the boat if it became necessary. In retrospect, we can say that since the boat had drifted for at least three hours, then the need for someone to "navigate" her must have been very apparent. Just where were these "officers"? The statement then goes on to accuse the Oswego papers of running such a scandalous piece "…in the interest of the opposition boat," or the vessel running the same route but based in Oswego. In that same article the *Palladium* editorialized its response by saying:

> The night of the *Hastings* adventure was perfectly clear and if there was a fog, nobody but the pilot could see it. Whether there have been any exaggerations or not, the fact remains, without exaggeration that a steamer with between 300 and 400 passengers left Kingston for Oswego about 5 p.m., could not find the way in a clear, still summer night, floated around in the lake, without her officers knowing where she was, till daylight, and didn't get to Oswego till nearly 8 o'clock the next morning....That Oswego papers have an interest in any boat, excited a smile here. Oswego papers are wealthy, but they haven't any navigation lines that anybody knows of.

Mr. Gildersleeve's people had taken a shot at explaining away the *Hastings* incident in print, but it was not going to work. Fortunately for Gildersleeve, the public has a short memory concerning such embarrassing events and the entire matter was soon forgotten.

In looking closely at this whole event, we have to ask, "Just where were most of the crew anyhow?" In her comments to the local press, Martha stated flatly that, "There was no captain, mate nor sailor to be seen all night" In looking back across this infinitesimal event in the annals of Great Lakes maritime history, we can draw some plausible conclusions concerning the cause of the *Hastings* incident. The first thought is that the officers were somehow incapacitated, either by overwork, or overindulgence. In mulling over this conclusion it becomes apparent that it is highly unlikely the entire navigational staff was overtaken by exhaustion or alcohol at the same time. The more probable cause of the problems with the crew is that perhaps they were never aboard in the first place!

Using pure speculation and keeping in mind that the *Hastings* was being operated as a "relief" vessel — and that the summer tourist and excursion market was at its peak — we can recreate the circumstances in which Martha Hart found herself. It was published that she noticed several oddities concerning the vessel's crew. There was no food service on the boat, and apparently no one from whom food could be purchased. There was no agent to assign passenger berths, and the pilothouse was occupied by only the elderly "pilot," alone without any watchmen or mate of any sort. Next, in reading her account, as well as the published account of the witnesses, we can find some additional oddities. First, during the entire time that the vessel drifted on the lake, no qualified mariner, other than

Martha, is mentioned as making an appearance on deck. Second, the engineer willingly shut down the vessel's steam-plant based on the story of a single female passenger. All of this added together leads us to a scenario that in our highly regulated transportation system of today seems impossible—but in the nearly unregulated days of Martha Hart is quite probable. Pulling his reserve steamer out of lay up, Mr. Gildersleeve kept her in readiness for sailing when the bookings got heavy. In order to keep his profits at a maximum and his expenses aboard the *Hastings* at a minimum, he hired only a skeleton crew to run the reserve boat between Kingston and Oswego. A couple of coal-passers who probably doubled as deckhands to work the lines, an engineer, and an old-timer supposed to be familiar with the route who would be the "pilot," would be just enough to make the boat operate. Because the run was only a few hours across the lake, Gildersleeve would harvest a hefty profit from hauling 300 to 400 paying passengers while not having to feed or berth them. He would be spared the expense of having to pay for a crew of porters, stewards, deckhands, watchmen, first mates, second mates and a bona fide ship's captain. This reasoning would also go a long way toward explaining the missing charts and otherwise useless navigational aids aboard the ship. If everything went without incident, Gildersleeve would make a real profit. The only problem was that the "pilot" who Gildersleeve hired was apparently well on in years, and probably had seen his days as a legitimate captain end through the bottom of a brown bottle. This combination probably came back together once out on the lake and he ended up in his own personal fog, taking nearly 400 people with him. Knowing full well that the boat was ill-staffed and under the guidance of a senile and/or drunkard "pilot," the engineer was more than willing to act on the words of the lady passenger who came storming into his engine room that night. Thus the *Hastings* incident occurred, and Martha Hart got her first and probably her only command.

More than a century after Martha Hart took command of the *Hastings*, all that remains of her story are three short items in the microfilm archives of the Oswego library. Even the best of historians are apt to look at her story and think of it as little more than trivia. For the purposes of this book, however, no story of any individual who sailed the lakes and took command is too trivial. Unfortunately, all that we know of Martha is contained within this story. Today, the ladies of the lakes can work in any of the maritime jobs from cook to captain. Although it is a world that Martha could hardly imagine, it is certainly one that she was capable of functioning within.

IF FOUND, PLEASE RETURN

D uring the pleasant autumn evening of October 17, 1887, the legs of 19-year-old Alfred Perry seemed not to be able to stride fast enough as he made his way up the 600 block of South Water Street in East Saginaw, Michigan. Excitedly dashing up from the nearby waterfront, "Fred" Perry could hardly wait to reach his parents' home. Finally arriving at number 608, the lad clamored up the stoop and burst through the door. Taking his mother quite by surprise, Fred announced that he had a new job aboard a lumberboat and was shipping out right away.

"Oh…," his mother moaned with a note of regret and worry, "…which one now?" she asked, while nervously wiping her hands on her apron.

"The *Dolphin*," he answered as he vanished into his room and began stuffing items of clothing into a handy duffel bag. "She's headin' out tomorrow, and the captain needs new hands for one last trip."

"You know that with your father already gone down to work the winter at Perrin's Lumber Camp, you'll be leaving me here all alone," the sprouting mariner's mom forebode, as she peered through the living room window toward the Lee Lumber Mill across the street. Clearly visible above the mill buildings were the tops of the tall masts of some obscure lakeboat tied up there. "And I'd prefer that you didn't go out on that *Dolphin*, its such an awful boat." In this the era of "king lumber," even an average housewife was familiar with the boats that called Saginaw home.

Fred, although short in stature had always been able to pacify his mother with a charming smile and soothing tone of voice. "Oh mother," he placated, "this will be a short trip, and the weather will be pleasant. Besides, you won't be all alone, sis will be here to stop in and visit."

Emerging from his room, Fred had on his best small-checked pants, vest and coat. "And," he reminded his worried mother, "I still will carry this."

Reaching into his vest pocket he removed a small book. On the flyleaf he had written his name and address. When he had shipped out on his last boat, the *D.H. Keys*, he had assured his mother that if anything were to happen to him, the persons finding his remains would discover the book and see to it that he was returned home to Saginaw. This thought seemed to settle his mother somewhat, so he always carried the book on his person, no matter if he was working out on deck or sleeping in his bunk. Perhaps he carried it for luck, or perhaps it was just to help keep his mother's mind at rest.

"Just be careful," the worried mother urged as she gave her departing mariner a hug.

"As I go by here when she goes downriver, I'll wave my handkerchief so you can see me," Fred promised as he headed out the door, plopping a soft felt hat atop his head.

In spite of his mother's urgings specifically not to ship out aboard the *Dolphin*, Fred was on his way, happy to have the work and to be back out on the lakes. His mother watched as her son strode happily off toward the

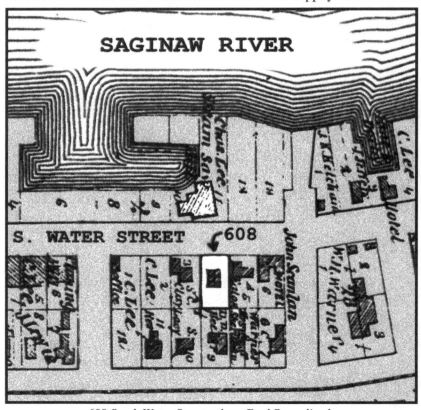

608 South Water Street, where Fred Perry lived.

130

busy waterfront, and all of the adventure that the Great Lakes had to offer. More than a century has passed since Alfred Perry left 608 South Water Street never to return. He is, however, just one of the players in the tale of the labor-worn schooner-barge *Dolphin.*

Sometimes when looking back at events across more than a century, it is difficult to understand the mind-set of the day. Events and disasters that now would draw attention for many weeks often appear to be apparently overlooked in the pre-1900s era. The news reports of the day give only casual mention of some wrecks—almost as if the lives that were ruined mattered less than the toil required to typeset the letters detailing their loss. To add to the confusion, shipwrecks occurred so frequently that as soon as the details of one disaster came to light, another and perhaps more tragic shipwreck would happen and steal the media's attention. Then, in the jumble of events, all of the facts are set aside or misplaced, perhaps to never be found. A case in point would be the saga of the schooner *Dolphin.* Today if you ask local wreck divers or boat buffs of her story, they ponder the name as if it is vaguely familiar, but have no real recollection of the boat. In short, do not look for the *Dolphin* in most accounts of well-known lakeboats or on any shipwreck chart. It turns out that her story has many characters and far-reaching circumstances all of which are nearly forgotten. With a great deal of research, and a bit of interpolation, the lost story of this threadbare lumber-barge can now be told, and we can rediscover the events that were lost so long ago.

It was a lovely autumn day when the schooner-barge *G.D. Norris* arrived at the mouth of the Saginaw River, attached to the end of a towing hawser of the 135-foot lumber carrier *Oswegatchie.* Temperatures had been in the low 50s and the sun shown brightly through the white, puffy clouds as Tuesday, October 18, 1887, stretched out. Indian Summer was in full swing and Captain J.E. Sheehan took a long breath of relief as his two-masted schooner-barge slid into the safety of the river. Unknown to Captain Currie at the time was the fact that the schooner-barge *Dolphin* would soon be tugged in his direction, and along with her would come more ill-fortune than he would care to know. For the time being, there was a break in the weather and that was reason enough to be thankful. All around the Great Lakes the storm warriors took a well-deserved break. Lighthouse keepers had little else to do other than polish their lenses and await the coming night. From the lookout towers of the assorted lifesaving stations, the surfmen on watch scanned a glassy lake as the lakeboats passed serenely. On the all-night beach patrols, others of the storm-warrior service sauntered along as if on a fair weather hike. Other than the daily drills and occasional recovery of flotsam cast ashore by the storms of the previous few weeks, there was not much for the lifesavers on beach patrol to do. Atop the pilothouses of countless steamers, barges and schooners the wheelsmen and officers stood their watches, while down on deck the crew took the opportunity to hang out some laundry and attend to other fair weather duties. September and October seemed to have gone beyond its normal storm-raked worst this year, and the current weather was indeed a welcomed change.

Built in 1856 at Cleveland, the 128-foot and 262-ton *G.D. Norris* was beginning to show her 30 years, and anytime the autumn gales came calling the boat complained as only an aged wooden boat can. This most recent passage up from the lower lakes had been particularly hard on the boat. Being a one-third owner with John E. Robinson and Captain Thomas Currie, the *Oswegatchie's* master, Captain Sheehan had a vested interest in the tired schooner-barge. It was his duty to see that the *Norris* was not only productive and profitable, but also safely brought into port. Now, in the respite of an Indian Summer day, the ship and her cargo—more than 200 tons of coal that had been hauled up from Erie, Pennsylvania—eased into the unloading berth as her master gave a silent sigh of relief. On board the *Oswegatchie*, Captain Currie also gave a small exhale of repose. In recent years, the Great Lakes had been particularly unfair to Currie, and the past two weeks were no exception. As far as could be discovered at the time of this writing, his luckless streak started when he was employed as master of the steamer *Ontonagon* on September 25, 1883, when she burned near Stag Island in the Detroit River. Also, on November 1, 1885, he was in command of the tug *Frank Moffat* when the boat's boiler exploded on the St. Clair River while towing five barges. Five of her 12-man crew were killed in this accident. None of these accidents can be directly tied to Captain Currie. In fact, it was his cool head that allowed the flaming *Ontonagon* to be run aground, and thus gave her crew the chance to escape without a single life being lost. In the case of the *Moffat*, it was determined that her boiler had likely been run dry of water causing the explosion. It is the engineer's job to keep the boiler filled, and Currie was busy "rounding" his barges at the time of the explosion. Although tradition and regulation holds the master responsible, he was clearly not at fault.

More recently, on just the previous leg, as the *Oswegatchie* was on her way up Lake Erie with the schooner-barges *Lizzie P. Betts, G.D. Norris* and *Southwest* in tow. Just west of Long Point, the 42-mile-per-hour gale-force winds through which the four boats had been beating their way, got the better of the towline and parted the *Oswegatchie* from her consorts. With his barges adrift, Captain Currie elected to turn the ship and run back to Buffalo, leaving the three barges to fend for themselves. Leaving schooner-barges on their own in a gale was a commonly-used tactic in the age of the wooden vessel on the Great Lakes that often led to the survival of the barge. So Currie did not feel that he was committing an act of abandonment by turning the *Oswegatchie* and making a run for shelter. On the three barges, however, the feeling was quite different. Captain Sheehan aboard the *Norris* was struggling with a leaking boat, and the *Southwest*,

This image of the hard-luck towing steamer Oswegatchie is a computer generated view taken from a base image of her sister vessel Garden City, since there are no known photos of her, after she was cut down to a lumber hooker. (Author's Concept)

having damaged her centerbox a week earlier, was not in much better shape. The *Betts*, which was the middle barge in the tow, had taken a real dousing, but was not in any particular danger. Casting off the *Betts* and *Norris*, the *Southwest* set out on her own. Fortunately, Captain Barnes of the *Betts* kept the towline to the *Norris* secured and raised his storm sail. In a masterful demonstration of mariner's skill, the captain grabbed the storm winds and used them to haul both of the schooner-barges to the east and under the shelter of Long Point. When the gale subsided, the steambarge *D.W. Powers* happened along and offered to take the two castaways in tow. Through megaphone shouts, Captain Sheehan stated that he would keep the *Norris* anchored in wait for the *Oswegatchie's* return. Captain Barnes, having had his fill of the *Oswegatchie's* company, was more than glad to accept the offer, and the *Betts* headed off for the Saginaw River at the end of the *Powers'* towing hawser. Later that same day, Captain Currie returned with the *Oswegatchie* and recovered the *Norris*. All that is recorded of the *Southwest* is that she proceeded up to Escanaba. How she did so we do not know. So, as Indian Summer set in, Currie had reason to feel relieved at being safely tucked in on the Saginaw River.

After dropping off the *Norris*, Currie found it convenient to swing the *Oswegatchie* parallel to the *Norris'* beam and tie up to wait his turn at the George D. Jackson Lumber Dock. His ship had arrived without cargo, but would have to wait to load, anyway, because the schooner *Golden Rule* was presently loading lumber at the Jackson dock. One board at a time, the dock-whollopers were stacking an astounding 525,000 board feet of lumber aboard the 189-foot schooner. Certainly it would take the rest of the day to load the *Golden Rule*, and Currie felt that he would be lucky if he got the *Oswegatchie* in position by the following day. There was nothing that Currie and his crew could do other than what lake mariners do best— and that is waiting. No matter the weather was fine and the coffee was hot, so Currie let the engineer know that he was finished with the powerplant, and then secured his pilothouse. The *Oswegatchie* had once been an upper cabin passenger and package cargo steamer making her living shuttling essentials to assorted ports along the lake coast. When her days as a passenger carrier drew to a close, she had her midsection cut down and was converted to the lumber trade. Upon entering that profession, the *Oswegatchie* almost immediately became a regular visitor to the Saginaw River. So, when Currie put his boat to sleep at the *Norris'* side, the steamer was right at home. Together, the *Oswegatchie*, *Norris* and *Dolphin* would later become the main players in the disaster ahead.

Within the din of the Saginaw River's marine commerce the following day, dozens of lakeboats, tugs, and ferryboats moved around the waterway. Within that Wednesday's traffic, the movement of three boats were particularly important to this story, and was almost completely overlooked. First, Captain Currie directed the *Oswegatchie* as she pulled the *Norris* clear of her unloading berth, and repositioned both boats at the dock to take on cargoes of lumber. Secondly, the 107-foot wooden schooner-barge *Dolphin* connected her line to a river tug, cleared her loading dock at East Saginaw, and headed upriver. The *Dolphin* was on her way to the Bay City anchorage in quest of a steamer that would be willing to tow her to Cleveland. Like Captain Currie, the *Dolphin's* captain, Garrett Johnson, had been having his share of hard luck in the Great Lakes maritime industry. Johnson and some fellow investors had purchased the care-worn *Dolphin* in order to start her in the 1882 season. That first season, the ship was put under the command of Captain Mart Johnson who was apparently no relation to the boat's owner, Garrett Johnson. While in the port of Sandusky, Ohio, "Captain Mart" decided to "go up the street" with the *Dolphin's* $300 freight earnings and was never seen again. Two years later, Garrett Johnson and his associates purchased the barge *Danube*, which made just a few trips before waterlogging. Now, every penny that Johnson had was invested in the *Dolphin*, and it is likely he was not about to trust any part of this investment to anyone after the problem with Captain Mart.

For most of the past two seasons, the *Dolphin* had been engaged in bringing limestone up from Lake Erie ports and then returning with lumber. Unfortunately, the tons of stone that had been dropped into the boat's hold had given her belly a good beating, and in order to make financial ends meet, Captain Johnson always hauled a hefty load. The problem was that the *Dolphin* was showing her age and fast becoming a "tender" boat, while Johnson, who was also the owner, was forced to cut every corner in an attempt to make his business pay. Apparently, the captain was losing both battles. In fact, a look at the circumstances following her October 12, 1887, arrival in East Saginaw would be a foreshadowing of events to come. It was known that Johnson usually carried his wife and 5-year-old daughter with him aboard the *Dolphin*. When the boat tied up at East Saginaw, however, he directed his family to go ashore and reportedly to stay at the "Penoyer Farm." Research shows that this was not a "farm" at all, but rather was a subdivision. Apparently the Johnson family had relatives there. At least one contemporary source stated that the action of the captain leaving his wife and child ashore was done "for fear of a storm." It also appears most, if not all, of the *Dolphin's* crew had been laid off or simply walked away after the boat's most recent trip ended in Saginaw. This supposition is drawn by the fact that the vessel remained in Saginaw for nearly seven days after her arrival. Normally, a boat would have been unloaded then repositioned, reloaded, and towed up the river within 48 hours. Instead, the *Dolphin* remained in Saginaw from October 12th to the 19th.

During the *Dolphin's* time in Saginaw, on Monday, October 17, to be precise, Captain Johnson visited Little Joe's Saloon and Restaurant at 113

Lapeer Street in Saginaw. The establishment was run by Joseph Lindlau who, along with other family members, resided in the apartment above. While there, Johnson met with Lindlau's brother-in-law, 21-year-old John Schoen. The purpose of the meeting was simple. Johnson had come to persuade Schoen to make one more trip on the *Dolphin*. Schoen had shipped out as mate on the schooner-barge at the opening of the navigation season and had remained aboard the boat until her October 12th arrival in Saginaw. Something had caused Schoen, after nearly a full season on the boat, to suddenly end up ashore. Why the boat's mate took his leave is unknown, but apparently the same reason had caused at least three members of the boat's able-bodied sailors to go "up the street" as well. Johnson, it appears, was also in the market for at least three crewmen, and no doubt made that clear to Schoen.

More than a century after the meeting at Little Joe's, we can draw some conclusions from the activity there. First, the reason why the *Dolphin* had not done a usual two-day turnaround in Saginaw could have been because her crew had walked off of the job. This is further evidenced, not only by the boat's protracted stay in Saginaw, but also by the fact that Captain Johnson had to round up an entirely new crew from the local population. Secondly, if some matter had caused the crew to leave it must have been a fairly serious situation, because her mate also went "over the rail." Johnson also had taken the precaution of sending his wife and child to stay ashore. Previous to his command of the *Dolphin*, he had been a "jobber" in the boat-loading business along the East Saginaw waterfront, and consequently knew nearly every laborer working along the river. Why then did it take him the better part of a week to contract a cargo and hire a crew in a working environment where such labor was readily available at every dock? If there was a problem aboard the *Dolphin*, was it something that would keep most people away from shipping out on her?

In this era of leaky schooner-barges and overload cargoes, only three things could have caused the lakeboat roustabouts to simultaneously vacate a berth aboard anything that floated. First was money, and if for some reason Johnson had not been able to pay his crew, they would have surely gone over the rail on him, and probably later libeled the boat for what was due. He may have been able to promise and sweet-talk to a point, and even his first mate may have set the example by staying aboard for a trip or two, but soon his crew would have left him. The second reason would be food. If a boat's cook was known to be truly awful, crews have often been known to walk off. The third reason was if the boat, itself, would have been showing some characteristic that would have foretold of certain doom to come. This would have had to be a truly ugly defect, because the locals along the Saginaw waterfront in the era of wooden lakers were known to ship out on just about any tub that would hold a cargo. In either case, the word would have quickly spread along the docks and Johnson would have been hard-pressed to continue doing business.

Another possibility for the *Dolphin's* protracted stay at Saginaw would be that when she came in on October 12th, Captain Johnson did not have another cargo arranged in advance. If this were the case, he may have paid off the entire crew and laid up his boat until another cargo could be arranged. Once paid, the crew would have scattered to other boats. There were always boats looking for crews and none of the crew would have remained "on the beach" for long. These barges were always staffed with a peppering of the most transient types of people. Desertion, theft, and drunkenness were a common problem among many of the able-bodied crewmen of the lumber barges. The fact is that just a year earlier, on September 7, 1886, while the *Dolphin* was making the dock at Marblehead, Ohio, she had lost a crewman due to these circumstances. A deckhand was so intoxicated that, while attempting to handle a fender, he fell overboard and drowned right at the dock. Considering that there was no reason to pay these crewmen while the boat was waiting for the captain to scrape up another cargo, it would make sense to pay them off and simply muster a new crew when the next cargo came along. Still, he would be taking a chance in laying off Schoen. A good first mate was hard to find, and Schoen could quickly be gone. Maybe Johnson had taken that week to scratch up an upbound and downbound cargo, then went looking for John Schoen, the only member of the crew that he really needed to have return. Then again, perhaps when the *Dolphin* came in on October 12th, Johnson may have decided to simply call it a season and be done for the winter. Thus he would have dismissed his entire crew, including Schoen. But in considering this, we have to ask what kind of a lakes mariner calls it quits in mid-October? Unlike the able-bodied crew, Schoen knew the *Dolphin* and knew how Johnson wanted things done. Further evidence that a handy cargo may have been behind all of this lays in the type of cargo that the captain managed to scrape up. A load of "mill culls" would be aboard the vessel for her trip downbound. Every lumber mill has junk lumber that consists of stumps, planks with bark, or improper cuts. These leftover remnants were called "mill culls" and were nearly worthless, so it was the equivalent of carrying scrap. This cargo was truly scraping the bottom of the barrel, and Johnson would need a big load to make any money at all. This load says much about the financial status of the *Dolphin*. This "lack of a cargo" seems to be the best explanation as to the activity of the boat and her people in that week when she sat tied to a pier in Saginaw. Perhaps the captain tied her up, dismissed his crew and sent his family ashore while he sought another cargo. When he scrounged up a load of mill culls he made haste to find a new crew for his boat, and did not bother to place his kin back aboard. His first stop in the effort to restaff the *Dolphin* would be to seek out his old mate Schoen and see if he was still available to make the trip.

There is no record as to what was in the conversation between the captain and the wayward mate that day at the restaurant, but apparently Captain Johnson said all of the right things to convince Schoen to sign back aboard the *Dolphin*. For that reason alone it is possible to conclude that if Johnson had troubles with the boat they may have been financially based. If the boat had been so unseaworthy that Schoen had walked off, no amount of talking could have gotten him back aboard her. On the other hand, if it was a matter of wages owed, or a lack of cargo, Johnson could have made a deal with him. Purely speculating, we can guess that if Johnson had sweetened the pie, some type of alternative payment may have been offered. Perhaps, a share in the ownership of the vessel, or a chance to later command the boat while Johnson managed her. Any such deal would have been more than enough for the youthful mate to go back aboard the *Dolphin*. On the other hand, if he had simply laid the boat up, why risk losing a good mate to another boat? The only reason for not keeping Schoen on the payroll and having him help to round up the needed cargo would be if Johnson could not afford to do that. Deckhands can be fired and rehired and they did not seem to care, but pay off the mate and you may well lose him. Accounts of what was arranged between the two mariners do not exist, but we know that after Johnson's visit to Little Joe's, Schoen had agreed to go back to work aboard the *Dolphin*. All that needed to be done was hire the rest of the crew. Right offhand, Schoen could think of two fellows who would be willing to ship out—his nephew, 19-year-old Joseph Lindlau Jr., and 20-year-old Fred Perry, a longtime friend.

Born at Milan, Ohio, in 1855, the *Dolphin* measured a meager 107 feet from stem to stern and just two dozen feet across her beam with a depth of nine feet. Made of oak planking, the boat's hull girthed in at 147 tons, not counting what water had seeped in over the 32 years that she had run cargoes across the lakes. In some listings and passages, she is described as a scow schooner, yet her official records remain unclear on that point. Her official number was assigned as 6152, and nearly as soon as she was put to work, the *Dolphin* blended into obscurity within the circles of Great Lakes commerce. Captain Johnson had pressed the boat into the start of the 1887 season on May 10th with a load of 100,000 board feet of lumber from Saginaw to Toledo. From that point on he had run her hard all season.

The era of the *Dolphin* was a time when the only boats that were routinely inspected were those with steam engines. Barges, for the most part sailed at their own peril, as did their crews. The marine columns of the day were peppered with quips about assorted shortcomings in the equipment and operations of barges. As if a few backhanded comments could change the way these vessels were operated. One particular marine columnist, for example, commented that some captains of steamers outbound from the Saginaw River had refused to take some barges recently. Those barges, it was said, had towing hawsers that were too rotted to withstand any amount of weather. The columnist gave a blanket praise to the masters who made such decisions. In truth, almost every lumber barge was equipped with a tattered, rotting hawser, the maintenance of which was the responsibility of the barge's master—not the towing steamer's captain. Refusing to take a barge in tow for such a matter would do little other than cost the steamer's captain the profits of the tow. It was certain that the very next steamer captain who came along would take that same hawser aboard and wink at the risk. After all, this was indeed the day of the rotting hawser and leaky barge.

Exactly which dock the *Dolphin* had delivered her inbound cargo to a week earlier is not recorded. As a matter of fact, even the boat's arrival passage is somewhat befuddled. The *Saginaw Evening News* published in the "Marine Matters" section of its October 12, 1887, edition, issue that the schooner "Dolghin" arrived with a cargo of stone from Port Clinton, Ohio. No vessel on the lakes ever carried the name "Dolghin." The true name of the arriving vessel, of course, was "Dolphin", but in this, the day when newspaper type was handset one backward letter at a time, the type-setter had inadvertently grabbed a lowercase letter "g" instead of a lowercase "p" when constructing the column. So, the *Dolphin's* arrival in Saginaw was left for us as "Dolghin." Although not recorded, the dock to which the *Dolphin* delivered her cargo was most likely the Hobson Dock. Being the only major stone dock in Saginaw during this period, the A. Hobson Stone & Lime Works was located at the foot of Carroll Street on the east side of the Saginaw River. Although it can not be positively proven, it is most probable that this is where Captain Johnson had unloaded his cargo and perhaps his crew. To add to the confusion, the boat's loading dock was also not recorded, and with dozens of lumber docks on the Saginaw river front in 1887, not even a good guess can be made as to which dock loaded her. Without regard to the best of research efforts, there are always some pieces of the Great Lakes puzzle that are simply lost.

By Tuesday October 18, 1887, Captain Johnson had nearly a full crew. It was then that Fred Perry showed up with his buddy, Adolph, who was more than willing to go aboard the old barge and begin an adventure on the Great Lakes. Adolph had never been sailing before, and the thoughts of the life as a Great Lakes mariner were so romantic that he could not resist the invitation. Those who were left ashore after the *Dolphin's* departure could scarcely recall Adolph's last name—some saying that it was "Wirtz" while others thought that perhaps it was "Mertz." To Johnson such details mattered little. He simply needed one more strong body to work aboard his boat. In the process of preparing to get the boat back to work, a cook also had been found. Now, Johnson had all the hands necessary to crew the boat and that was what mattered the most.

After the fully-manned *Dolphin* was moved to the loading slip, the dock-whollopers began throwing aboard the cargo of junk lumber. Certainly by the next day the boat would be loaded and ready to head out. Through a full workday the noise of banging mill product echoed around the dock as the lumber-shovers, aided by the *Dolphin's* new deckhands, loaded the barge by hand. Amidst Indian Summer conditions, the lumber barge finished loading and waited to catch an available tug for the trip out to Bay City. Aboard the barge Johnson had a cargo of 180,000 board feet of mill culls. This was a hefty load for the boat to be carrying in her 32nd season, but then again, these were the days of old boats and heavy loads. Happy to be working the vessel were Fred Perry, Joseph Lindlau Jr., and Adolph Wirtz—or perhaps it was Mertz. Some ashore also reported that a man named William Bannister had shipped aboard as cook, but there again the memories of those ashore were unclear exactly who was the boat's cook. All of the crew were said to be from Saginaw, with the exception of that "Bannister" fellow who was reportedly from Detroit. It was planned that once at the Bay City anchorage, the boat would await a tow to Cleveland where her lumber cargo was consigned. Sometime on Wednesday, October 19, 1887, a tug took the *Dolphin's* towline and started her toward her doom. No one took much notice as the careworn barge slipped silently up the Saginaw River on that pleasant Indian Summer day. Never again, however, would her masts pass along the river front skyline, never again would her rotting hull timbers feel the filthy waters of the Saginaw River, and never again would her crew of youthful deckhands set foot on solid ground. Every soul aboard the *Dolphin* were leaving Saginaw forever, and no one suspected it. It is much more likely, however, that Mrs. Perry was watching and waving as her son Fred slid past the Lee Mill aboard the *Dolphin*, waving his handkerchief high over his head. This was a farewell that was far more significant than anyone could imagine. Shrouded in coal smoke, and wood smoke and disguised by hooting harbor whistles, these minor movements of people and vessels were all blended into a day's work on the river. Looking back, we can see that the activity set in motion the wheels of another of the Great Lakes easily overlooked dramas. Soon, both Captain Sheehan and deckhand Perry as well as all of the other players in this story, would share the same terror—courtesy of Lake Huron. But at this moment, the *Dolphin's* novice mariners were beginning what they expected to be a great job on a fine autumn day.

For the two days following the *Dolphin's* departure, the *Oswegatchie* and *Norris* had taken aboard their own burdens of lumber, and the *Dolphin* waited in the anchorage. As this business went on, Indian Summer came to an end. By Friday a heavy northwest gale was blowing across nearly all of the lakes, and whipping snow flurries were thrown in for good measure. Saturday saw the winds shift to blowing out of the southeast accompanied by sheets of rain and sleet. The blowing precipitation was the sort that soaks through your soul and chills you to the bone, making warm weather appear to be a thing of the distant past. Rain and sleet lashed at the lumber-shovers as they stacked the last planks of cargo aboard the *Norris*. It was difficult to see much along the river, the gray of the soggy day just seemed to descend down upon the water-front and soak the life out of everything. In the middle of all this gloom, Captain Johnson had slogged through the cold muddy Bay City waterfront in search of a captain willing to engage him in a tow to Cleveland. Somewhere in his trek, the *Dolphin's* master connected with Captain Currie of the *Oswegatchie*. Having had his relationship with the schooner-barge *Betts* severed after the breakup of the tow on the previous trip, Currie was quite willing to engage the *Dolphin*.

A shivering darkness was upon the *Oswegatchie* as she pulled the *Norris* from the dock and headed off to pick up the *Dolphin*. The hiss of the rain against the pilothouse windows foretold of an ugly trip ahead, and Captain Currie strained to see each channel marker through the muddle. Somehow, even the heat from the steamer's pilothouse radiators could not warm the moment.

In speculation we can say that, like most aged vessels of this day, the *Dolphin* was probably "no fun" in the cold autumn rain and sleet. It is a sure bet that her cabins leaked, bedding was probably mildewed and molding, while the only escape from the chill was the small galley stove. As the Indian Summer weather turned to a gray, smothering rain, the novice mariners aboard the *Dolphin* were getting a good lesson in the evils of the world of the wooden schooner-barge. There was nothing to do but wait and be wet and cold. Unfortunately, very soon the terms "wet" and "cold" would take on a whole new meaning aboard the barge. On the way out of Bay City, the *Oswegatchie* took the time to stop and take the *Dolphin* in tow, an operation that delayed the departure by only a trifle, but required that the schooner-barge's mariners go on deck in the rain and sleet. It is also unlikely that they had anything close to the kind of clothing that would have protected them in this kind of weather. Odds are that when the towing hawser was made secure, the once-enthusiastic mariners returned to the relative warmth of the galley with their spirits literally dampened. Having his consorts firmly in control, Captain Currie pointed the *Oswegatchie's* steering pole northward and ventured out onto Saginaw Bay. The weather was now turning into a substantial autumn blow and rude seas met the steamer's bow as sleet froze to her rigging.

No record exists as to the exact time of the *Oswegatchie's* departure from the Saginaw River, but records indicate that the range lights of the river were left behind very late Saturday night, perhaps close to midnight. With two barges in tow, the diminutive *Oswegatchie* was ill-equipped to do battle with the angry lake. At 135 feet long, the steamer had formerly been a coastal passenger and freight hauler. When vessels of her size were deemed unprofitable for that trade, she was sold into the lumber trade and, after having her center cabins and deck cut down, started into a new career. The *Oswegatchie* had, however, been designed to dash between coastal towns, ladened only with passengers and packaged goods. In that capacity she was well able to outmaneuver all but the worst of autumn's gales. In the lumber trade, the boat was always loaded far beyond her intended burden and always assigned the hardship of a tail of barges. In good weather the boat pulled at her consorts like an enslaved snail. In a gale it would be lucky if the vessel made any forward progress at all. When she left the protection of the Saginaw River that Saturday night, the *Oswegatchie* pulled for all she was worth and clawed ahead into the ink-black night. By Sunday morning the steamer and her ducklings were rounding the tip of Michigan's thumb, a trip of just over 50 miles that she had made at an over-the-bottom speed of just about six miles per hour! Now Captain Currie felt the full power of the winds. Apparently the thumb had blocked a large portion of the southeast blow and masked the strength of the storm, because as soon as the trio hauled toward the east the seas came calling. Thrashing as far as Pointe aux Barques, the three lumber boats were nearly stopped cold by the wind and waves as the *Oswegatchie's* powerplant was readily outmatched by the lake. Nearly as soon as Currie got a taste of the gale, he decided that he wanted nothing to do with it. Turning all three boats around, the storm-weary master elected to run a half dozen miles back and anchor behind the shelter of the thumb. Approaching the Port Austin reef, Captain Currie dropped the *Oswegatchie's* anchor on the southwest side of the reef and let his tow weather vane into the deep water below the shoal.

Throughout all of the daylight hours of that stormy Sunday, the *Oswegatchie*, *Norris* and *Dolphin* huddled behind the lee of Michigan's thumb, waiting out the storm. Captain Currie had always thought himself more patient than Lake Huron, and had spent many hours tucked safely in a protected cove. The thing that troubled him now was that his position was not nearly as cozy as he wished. If the winds were to shift and start blowing out of the west, it may easily fetch his boat right up on Port Austin Reef. This entire region was a ship's graveyard, and Currie was all too familiar with the multitude of horror stories that had been played out on countless nights just like this one. That was the reason why there were no less than three lifesaving stations on the tip of the thumb. Patience, however, had always kept him from having to use the services of the lifesavers, and he would see to it that tonight would be no different. While each hour of that stormy Sunday passed, Currie kept a close eye on the winds in hope of detecting the slightest trend toward a shift. Indeed, he was more patient than Lake Huron, because the lake suddenly decided to wait no longer for the lumber trio. At five o'clock that evening the lake swept its vengeance around to out of the west-northwest and blew with winds ranging from 40 to 65 miles per hour. Currie no longer had to ponder over his next move in the storm—the lake had made that decision for him!

So swift had been the swing of the winds that the crews of the two lumber barges hardly had enough time to secure their boats before the *Oswegatchie* was pulling from the anchorage. We can only imagine what Adolf Wirtz was thinking as the waves from out on open Lake Huron came marching at the *Dolphin's* leaky hull, smashing her again and again in endless gray billows of ice water. All around Wirtz the boat groaned as if to break up right under his soaking-wet feet. His adventure in sailing had turned into a cold, shivering nightmare. Captain Currie's best chance for the *Oswegatchie* was to haul around the tip of the thumb and gain the lee of the east side before the weather became worse. At best it would be a 25-mile run for cover at Sand Beach, and the sooner that the steamer and her tow got there the better. The sudden shift of the wind, however, had not given the waves on the open lake a chance to change their direction. As a result, the three boats beat their way directly into the web of a confused sea with the waves going one way and the wind howling in another. At first, the trio appeared to make progress. But as soon as the boats were due north of the thumb off of Pointe aux Barques, Lake Huron sprung its trap. Mountainous seas that had built throughout the entire day burst around the thumb and against the bows of the three lumber carriers, while the wind suddenly exploded across their sterns. The over-the-bottom speed of the luckless lakeboats was reduced to about two miles per hour.

Looking aft from the *Oswegatchie's* pilothouse the *Norris* was scarcely visible through the storm, and the lights of the *Dolphin* were only occasionally seen. Events that were taking place onboard the *Oswegatchie* told the story of what was probably happening aboard the schooner-barges. Waves broke green over the steamer's bow as she wallowed in the lake, and the wind became so strong that it began to pick up individual planks from the boat's deck-load and fling them into the air. It was a scene unlike anything Captain Currie had ever seen in his career on the lakes. In near disbelief the *Oswegatchie's* crew watched as one after another the planks of lumber were flipped into the night's sky as if grabbed by an invisible angry giant and then went whirling up into the blackness. One individual board was ripped from the pile, swirled around a bit and was then tossed against the steamer's smokestack smashing into her steam whistle. Suddenly, the whistle began blowing on its own and would not stop. Captain Currie could only imagine what Captains Sheehan and Johnson thought of the nonstop whistle. Normally that could be considered a distress signal. If the captains of the schooner-barges thought the steamer was in trouble they may elect to cut lose, and in doing so would stand little chance of survival in the gale. For that reason, the *Oswegatchie's* skipper immediately ordered the engineer and a crewman set to work shutting off the whistle. Lashed by freezing spray mixed with sleet that impacted like bird shot, the two struggled atop the aft deckhouse roof. Reaching the whistle was no easy matter when the boat was tied up in port, the same task was almost impossible in the midst of a Lake Huron gale. Drenching ice water came from every direction and in some places ice had formed making each step a slippery risk as the chief and his assistant endeavored to find a way to shut the steam off to that blasted whistle. The sound was deafening, the rolling, pitching boat disorienting and, to make matters worse, the gale continued to pick up lumber and fling it out of the darkness. Luckily, the wind was coming from behind and was roaring so powerfully that no one aboard either of the schooner-barges was able to hear the whistle and mistake it for a distress signal. This was truly fortunate because it took a full hour to get the whistle shut off.

Just before 11 o'clock on that dreadful evening, the beleaguered lumber trio were eight miles above the shelter of Sand Beach harbor. To Captain Currie it appeared as if he may beat the lake again. Soon the lee of the land would be found and the wind would be blocked. What the good captain could not know was that by this time the luckless *Dolphin* had been so beaten by Lake Huron that she had completely waterlogged, and the only thing keeping her afloat was the buoyancy of the wood cargo she carried below her decks. Leaking badly and showing signs of structural failure, the *Norris* was in not much better condition. Those eight miles to shelter were not going to be long miles, they were now going to become impossible miles. The added burden of the floundering schooner-barges, plus the stress of the storm, was more than the towing hawser could stand. Shortly after 11 o'clock it parted. Nearly as fast as the crew of the *Oswegatchie* noticed the line parting, the two barges were swallowed behind the wall of rain and sleet that the gale had cast across the lake. Currie could do little more than watch helplessly as his consorts were pulled away by Lake Huron. Whitecapped waves of glee were all that the lake offered Currie as it continued to extract its vengeance on the mariners who would dare to venture upon it.

Limping into Sand Beach, the *Oswegatchie* was battered and in a leaking condition. Most of the steamer's deckload had been pillaged by Lake Huron and her whistle was out of order. All of the sheltered boats in the harbor of refuge took notice as the stricken lakeboat staggered through the gap in the breakwater. Clearly the boat had come out on the short end of her contest with mighty Lake Huron, but less obvious was the fact that she had left her consorts out in the storm. Captain Currie knew full well that the big lake could easily devour both of the schooner-barges and leave not a human trace, but the OSWEGATCHIE was absolutely in no condition to venture back out onto the lake tonight. Again, he could do nothing more than wait, and see how the storm unfolded.

All of that Sunday was consumed by the gale, which blew right through Monday before expiring in the first hours of Tuesday. The crew of the *Oswegatchie* used the wind-bound hours to make temporary repairs to their boat and pump her free of the water that had seeped in. Then, when the winds had eased, Captain Currie got up steam and headed out. Interestingly, when the *Oswegatchie* departed Sand Beach in the early hours of Tuesday, October 25, 1887, Currie did not set out onto the open lake in search of his lost barges. Such a search would have been the normal course of action for a steamer that had lost her consorts. Instead, the steamer turned due south and headed for Port Huron. Considering that Currie was one-third owner of the *Norris* and that the barge carried no insurance, his dash for Port Huron says more about the condition of the *Oswegatchie* than his concern over the missing barge. The thrashing that Lake Huron had given the boat must have put her in a very critical condition, otherwise it is certain that a search for the wayward barges would have been conducted. As the steamer neared Port Huron, Currie could not help but look back across the lake, perhaps in search of the lamps of his lost tow. In the storm-tossed distance, there were many schooners afloat, but the *Norris* was not among them.

As soon as the *Oswegatchie's* lines were secured along the Port Huron waterfront, Currie hastened down the gangplank and onto the wharf. Seeking out as many of his fellow mariners as he could find, the concerned skipper was in search of information as to the *Norris* and *Dolphin*. All that he found were a few shrugs and a large amount of scuttlebutt concerning other aspects of the storm. The *Oswegatchie* and her consorts had not been the only lakeboats caught out in the tempest. The rabbitboat *Rhoda Stewart* had also lost her tow of schooner-barges which were said now to be adrift. The schooner *C.O.D.* was reported ashore and wrecked at Port Burwell, Ontario. Up the Michigan coast, the propeller *Delaware* had missed out on the rain and sleet and instead been swallowed by a blizzard. Lost in the snow, she had run aground near Hammond's Bay. The tug *Anna Moiles* had departed Bay City with a dredge in tow and had not been seen since. Reports were that the steam-barge *Maurice B. Grover* was tossed on the beach at Cross Village on northern Lake Michigan, and was rapidly going to pieces. Up on Lake Superior, the schooner-barge *Alva Bradley* had been reportedly shoved onto Shot Point near Marquette and wrecked. Meanwhile, down on Lake Erie the schooner *Zack Chandler* was blown into the shallows four miles east of the lifesaving station and was being mauled by the waves.

Just as Captain Currie was about to consider the *Norris* and her crew lost, the schooner *Breck* came sliding into the St. Clair River. As she passed the *Oswegatchie* a number of people aboard the *Breck* began to wave and shout. When the schooner docked, it was revealed that aboard was the entire crew of the *Norris*—as well as the story of the *Dolphin*.

What had happened when the towline to the *Oswegatchie* parted was that both schooner-barges went adrift at the mercy of the storm. Blowing from nearly due west, the gale pushed the powerless barges out into the open lake. Aboard both schooner-barges, even the most inexperienced crewmembers knew that the they were in real trouble. Hours passed as the helpless lumber barges wallowed in the massive seas and gale-force winds. The *Dolphin*, being in a waterlogged condition, was putting a great deal of strain on the towline. Soon that stress became more than the thick, rotting hemp hawser could tolerate, and it parted. This simple separation of those careworn fibers spelled the fate of all of the souls aboard the *Dolphin*. At that time, members of the crew of the *Norris* watched in horror as the dim amber oil lamps that made up the lights of the *Dolphin* rolled in a slow arc and were snuffed out by the stormy waters of Lake Huron. The waterlogged schooner-barge had capsized. All that was visible from the *Norris* was blackness where the *Dolphin* had once been. Everyone on the *Norris*, knew that the *Dolphin's* people were out there, struggling to remain alive in the churning mountains of ice water and sharp-edged lumber. The crew of the *Norris* was completely powerless and could do nothing to help. Fortunately, the roar of the gale winds smothered the cries for help and the crew of the *Norris* was spared the torment of hearing their fellow mariners plea for help they could never provide. Now the *Norris* was left alone in the gale and giving every sign that she, too, would soon founder. Down in the base of the boat's hull her keel timbers, the very backbone of the boat, had snapped and now she was tearing herself apart in the waves. When the hull timbers of the *Norris* started to separate, she waterlogged just like the *Dolphin*. It appeared certain that the horror the crew of the *Norris* had just witnessed in the fate of the *Dolphin's* crew was a preview of their own fate.

Through the long night of Sunday and the storm-raked Monday that followed, the six mariners aboard the *Norris* waited to meet the same end as those aboard the *Dolphin*. In the blackness of the night the hull humped, sagged, and twisted like a slithering sea monster with a load of lumber on its back. Daylight revealed a frightful sight as the crew saw each wave causing the hull to contort. Her back was broken and any wave at any moment could spell the end. Fortunately, somewhere in her construction, some of the timbers had been fastened with a few iron bolts and bars that had just a bit of extra strength. Three decades earlier the shipwrights had given a little more care and used a little more pride in their work, and now it was enough to hold her together in her last hours. When the darkness of Monday night set in, the crew of the *Norris* were certain that the end was at hand and that they would not see another sunrise. Only then did Lake Huron release the crew from its vengeance. With Captain James Green in command, from out of the gale came the schooner *W. L. Breck*, bringing hope for the *Norris'* crew. There are no written details as to the exact rescue of the *Norris'* people, except that it took place at five o'clock Monday evening somewhere between Sand Beach, Michigan, and Goderich, Ontario. The *Breck* was downbound out of Goderich and stumbled upon the distressed *Norris*. A half a day later, the *Breck* hauled the crew into Port Huron and safely out of Lake Huron's reach.

Interestingly, the *Norris* did make it to the Canadian shore. Washing onto the beach just out of Goderich, the boat was visited by the local volunteer lifesavers and found to be abandoned. Three days later, the hulk was turned over to Captain Sheehan who was in Goderich representing the owners. The boat had, by that time, been "libeled" for $1,287. Apparently, after the boat fetched up, the local lifesavers had come out followed by the tug *Onaping* which had managed to pull the wreck off of the beach and into Goderich harbor. For that service the tug's owner placed a lien on the wreck for $1,200. William Babb, a member of the lifesaving crew, had placed a bill against the boat for $87. No reason for Babb's charge was given but, to the owners of the *Norris*, all of these liens mattered little. Captain Sheehan reported to Port Huron that the boat was a complete wreck and not worth her twisted timbers. So, the owners decided to stick it to the libelers rather than hand over any money. They told them to simply keep the boat to settle all claims. This ended the career of the *Norris* and her documentation was surrendered in 1888. The *Dolphin*, however, never came back from Lake Huron. Some of the boat's wreckage, including her stern, reportedly came ashore 12 miles north of Kincardine, Ontario, but that was all. On March 13, 1888 the *Dolphin's* documentation was also surrendered with the notation, "Foundered 10-24-87, total loss." Oddly, there was no mention of the loss of her crew. The local and regional newspapers quickly forgot the *Dolphin* and her crew almost before her wreckage came ashore. The other interests of the maritime industry covered over the boat and her crew as fast as the lake's depths covered the carcass of the wreck.

For Captain Currie and the *Oswegatchie*, the hard luck streak did not end with the loss of the *Dolphin*. Three weeks after the disaster, the *Oswegatchie* was pulling the barges *Edwin Harmon* and *Charles Hinckley* across Lake Erie in yet another autumn gale. Again, Currie had ventured out onto a storm-tossed lake, and once again, the lake was getting the better of the *Oswegatchie*. As before, the barges broke lose, but this time both the *Oswegatchie* and her consorts were blown ashore. All three lakers slammed ashore at Point Abino a dozen miles northwest of Buffalo. After tossing 75,000 feet of lumber over the side the *Oswegatchie* managed to free herself. The *Harmon* and *Hinckley*, however, each being more than three decades old, were not so fortunate. Neither barge could be released and both were broken up by the wind and waves on Point Abino. After having worked herself free, the *Oswegatchie* ended up in dry dock for badly needed repairs. Four seasons later, on November 26, 1891, Lake Huron took its final vengeance on the *Oswegatchie*. In the face of a fierce gale and towing three barges, the tired steamer was overwhelmed and foundered off of Sturgeon Point, Michigan. Two of the three barges were also lost in the event, the entire story of which is detailed in the author's book *Stormy Disasters*.

The schooner-barge *Dolphin* is almost totally forgotten. The vessel as far as this author has been told, has never been found and no one has bothered to look for her wreck on the lake bottom. It is amazing that a 107-foot schooner and a half-dozen lives could be lost in such a tragic event, and then be lost again so casually in the jumble of history. It is important at this time that we remember that when the lamps of the *Dolphin* were snuffed out on that storm-raked October night, so were the lives of a brave crew. Captain Garrett Johnson would not be reunited with his wife and daughter, but probably died thankful that he had sent them safely ashore for this trip. Joseph Schoen would never again take a seat in his brother-in law's restaurant, and no doubt regretted letting Captain Johnson talk him into returning aboard the *Dolphin*. Joseph Lindlau never finished his first trip as a lake mariner. Instead, he met his fate in the face of Lake Huron's vengeance. Adolph Wirtz, (or Mertz) was swallowed by Lake Huron, and no one ever has figured out his proper name. Strangely, William Bannister survived the *Dolphin* wreck, but that was only because he was never aboard the boat in the first place! Apparently, whoever had taken the job as cook was mistaken for Bannister by the witnesses on the docks in Saginaw. This was revealed when Dr. Hawkins, a friend of the supposedly lost mariner, received a postcard from the dead man dated the second day of November and postmarked "Saginaw." If Bannister had been aboard the *Dolphin*, he would never have been able to write and send that postcard! No doubt that friends and relatives of the real William Bannister were relieved to discover that he was aboard a totally different lakeboat when the *Dolphin* had been lost. As a result, at least one of the *Dolphin's* crewmen went down with his identity known only to those lost with him.

As if the sorrow of losing their son was not enough, Fred Perry's family suffered another loss nearly a year later. On August 8, 1888, at 3:35 in the afternoon, a summer squall line's gust-front swept across the Saginaw River. The winds hit the Charles Lee Saw Mill and when the winds blew back through the mill's tall smokestacks, sparks were blown into the boiler room and set afire tons of wood shavings. In minutes the sawmill, which had been doing business since the 1860s, was a mass of flame. In less than five hours, the mill where Fred Perry had worked when the sailing season was closed had been obliterated—and so had the residence at 608 South Water Street where his family resided. In another twist of history which seems to push the Perry family into additional obscurity, the newspaper accounts which detailed the fire and the destroyed residences listed the Perry home as, "House-owner not known." It was the only property out of the two dozen published to be listed in that manner. In later years the lot where the Perry home had been became a junk yard and today is little more than a vacant lot with rubble strewn on it. The site of the Lee Saw Mill is a riverwalk park. Its location, however, is in a place where few people go for walks.

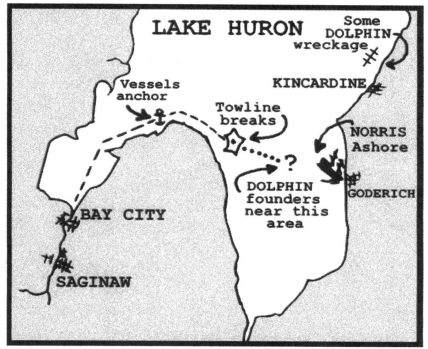

Map of the Dolphin's *wreckage.*

Little Joe's Saloon, where Captain Johnson talked his wayward first mate into taking one last trip, was soon abandoned by Joseph Lindlau. He moved up Lapeer Street a few blocks and opened a cigar manufacturing shop. Later the saloon gave shelter to a number of different businesses including a few barber shops. In a quirk of fate, the author discovered that his paternal grandmother had rented an apartment in the same building in the late 1930s, and had once lived just down the hall from where Joseph Lindlau had resided 40 years before. The site of Little Joe's Saloon is nothing more than a parking lot. The city of Saginaw also fits well into this story. It is a place that has forgotten its history and neglected its past.

Fred Perry's mother had her worst fears become reality. Her proud mariner son met his end out in the wilds of one of the vengeful lakes. To make matters worse, Fred's body was never given up by Lake Huron and so could not be returned home. He had always assured his mother this would be done because of the instructions he carried in his pocket. At this moment, while you read this story, his remains rest buried in the sands of Lake Huron somewhere off of Goderich, Ontario, with a small book in his vest pocket. On the flyleaf is written: "Alfred Perry, 608 South Water Street, Saginaw, Michigan." If found, please return.

INMAN'S DREAM

S ometimes the difference between one's destiny and the course that a life could have taken is as little as the pursuit of a dream. When the troubles and pressures of everyday existence cause us to abandon our wild ideas and creative brainstorms in order to meet the obligations of our life, our dreams may simply die. We can then easily find ourselves set on a track taking us toward a destiny that otherwise would have been successful and rich beyond our wildest imagination—but instead ends in mediocrity. History may later show that, had we taken the time and energy or perhaps been afforded the opportunity to develop that brainstorm, we may just have found ourselves in a far different position at the end. A case in point is that of Byron Bonaparte Inman. On February 15, 1903, Mr. Inman, who was an assistant superintendent in charge of repairs to vessels of the Pittsburgh Steamship Company, died of pneumonia. A financially-strapped former tug line owner from Duluth, Inman had just gotten the position as supervisor of repairs to the company's vessels laid up at Milwaukee. Although the position paid well, Inman's previous dealings as the owner of a whole fleet of tugs had left him deeply in debt, so he was throwing every ounce of his hard work into this new job. To the massive "steel trust" of management and owners of the Pittsburgh Steamship Company, Inman was little more than an obscure name in a distant port. The barons of the company had assembled an armada of 101 lakeboats in 1901 by buying nearly every large laker afloat, and their interests now blanketed the lakes. Within this company Inman was less than a pawn, no matter how hard he worked.

Starting as a simple cold, Mr. Inman's condition had rapidly developed and he truly needed bed rest, but his job of supervising the winter maintenance of the vessels kept him out doors and in the cold most of the time. His residence at the Republican Boarding House in Milwaukee did not do much toward his health, either. The winter had been very cold and the rooms at the boarding house were far from being warm. Soon the 53-year-old Inman was overwhelmed by his illness and passed away in the confines of his spartan rented room after taking only one day off for being sick. At the time of his death, he possessed a pocket watch, three sets of clothes, $700 worth of land near Duluth, and a single patent. Oddly, had Inman chased after his dream, he could very well have been a shareholder and on the executive board of the Pittsburgh Steamship Company, and wealthy and comfortable beyond his wildest imagination instead of an obscure supervisor of repairs. Using the clear vision of hindsight we can tie future events to Inman, and see that although he expired, his dream would later be reborn. The Great Lakes maritime industry would one day stand on Inman's shoulders, and almost no one would know it.

Thursday, October 26, 1967, was indeed a big day at the executive offices of the American Ship Building Company. Its new President, George M. Steinbrenner III, was a happy fellow and every "yes-man" in the office was smiling. The company had just been officially awarded the contract to build the first in a series of a totally new class of lakeboats for the United States Steel Corporation. To the American Ship Building Company, that award was worth a whopping 20 million dollars!

When such a lucrative deal is given to any firm, the future seems truly bright and secure for as long as the human mind can imagine. The deal was for the construction of a monster class of oreboat with dimensions and horsepower never before seen on the Great Lakes. Overall lengths of these giants would stretch beyond 850 feet and their beams would be wider than 100 feet. Best of all, these new lakers would be designed to be strong enough and powerful enough to sail right through the winter ice. American Ship Building Company would, in fact, construct the first year-around Great Lakes bulk carrier. Or so they thought at the time. What no one knew then, and what no one has really put together until right now, was that the American Ship Building Company had in a way already endorsed a scheme for a radical, powerful and gigantic year-around Great Lakes bulk carrier. The twist is that this had all happened in 1897, 70 years earlier, and the guy who designed and patented the boat was a forgotten vesselman named Byron Bonaparte Inman.

Following the 1967 contract award, work on the new monster freighter proceeded at a dizzying pace. Design plans were drawn and parts manufactured, while the steel plates and beams were sent to the shipyard. The big freighter would have to be constructed in the dry dock because she would be too huge to be built on the ways. Over the months the monster began to take shape and grow. The schedule was to have the boat completed by July of 1971, but on June 24th of that year, a fire broke out in the engine area of the nearly-completed boat—with disastrous results! Her engines were nearly destroyed and four of the shipyard's workmen were killed in the event. As a result, the completion of the boat was delayed for a full year and she was launched on June 13, 1972. Despite the delay in her christening, which allowed two larger boats to be launched first, the American Ship Building Company's colossal lakeboat was still a true marvel. Named the *Roger Blough* in honor of the president of U.S. Steel, the boat stretched 858 feet in length and was 105 feet in beam, with a depth of just over 41 feet. Her hull was able to hold an astounding 45,000 tons of taconite pellets. And to add to her efficiency, she was constructed as a self-unloader.

Although the delay in the *Blough's* launch had permitted two 1,000-footers, the *Stewart J. Cort* and *Presque Isle*, to come out ahead of her and thus claim title to being the largest boats on the Great Lakes, the *Blough* remains one of the biggest vessels running. Having two gigantic diesel engines, the *Blough* is rated at 14,000 horsepower. This is more than a match for all but the most heavy of the winter ice found on the Great Lakes. When this year-around lakeboat started her career on the lakes, the folks at the American Ship Building Company were certain that they had, in fact, invented the bulk carrier that could navigate through the winter months. As they slapped one another on the back and boasted over their big steel monster, they had no idea that B.B. Inman could have beaten them to it by seven decades.

According to the amazingly detailed biography of Inman, written by Al Miller and published in 1995 in the journal of the Lake Superior Museum Association, the *Deckhand*, the idea for the year-around lakeboat started in 1884. While sailing aboard the steamer *Kasota* and attempting a late season grain run down the Saint Marys River, the boat was blocked by ice in Mud Lake. Gathering as much steam and speed as she was able the boat charged ahead and began crashing her way through. There is, however another account, Inman's ice-choked passage aboard the steamer *Hiawatha* on May 17, 1883. His boat had to plow through 40 miles of heavy ice inbound to Duluth, and this is when he may have found his inspiration. Inman reportedly stood at the bow and watched as the ice was lifted and broken ahead of the boat. At that moment it occurred to him that a bow that was designed to move beneath the ice and lift it would be an efficient icebreaker, as long as the boat had a very powerful engine. From that time until 1897, the idea of an ice-breaking bulk freighter was always in his dreams. Meanwhile, he continued with his maritime career. For a time he had worked as a captain of freighters, but most prominently, he was a tugboat man. At the port of Duluth, he helped to build up and manage a fleet of tugboats, and soon was known by the title "Commodore," which was probably self-imposed.

Then came the financial panic of 1893. This year-long recession devastated the nation by trashing thousands of small businesses. Many men like Commodore Inman were choked out of business and suddenly found themselves deeply in debt. The captains of industry and the robber barons alike scrambled to cancel contracts and call in their markers. Inman's fortunes began to slowly spiral down hill, as did his tug business. Soon it came to his thoughts that his idea for a year-around vessel could become his financial salvation. He took his dream to the drawing board and began to work on the Inman icebreaker in earnest.

Tug boating at the head of the lakes was an extremely competitive business, and Inman often found himself heavily leveraged in order to stay in business, using the tugs that he owned. Because he ran a large fleet of tugs in Duluth he became very popular with his local peers. Among them was fellow vesselman Augustus Wolvin. When financial pressures fell upon the "commodore" and it appeared that Inman's fleet was going to be sold at auction, Wolvin and George Tomlinson dished out enough cash to keep their friend in business. In exchange, they got a substantial share in the operation.

By 1897, Inman had the plans for his year-around vessel ready for the patent office. The boat he proposed was a great departure from the lakeboats of the day. The design was for the biggest, most powerful vessel ever seen on the Great Lakes. Most unusual in the design was the bow, which had a bulbous shape. This "ram bow" would push deep below the ice causing the frozen surface to lift and break before the boat ever got to it. With the exception of all but one of the whaleback vessels, most lakers of the day had a bluff bow that allowed better maneuvering at the docks. The shape of the hull itself was also different, being 48 feet wide at the bow, but only 45 feet wide at the stern. This tapered hull would, Inman speculated, reduce the friction between the hull and the path that the bow had just cut in the ice. The length of the boat was also an extreme departure from the standards of 1897. Inman's all-season lakeboats were going to be 530 feet long. As a comparison, the longest boat on the lakes in that same period was the steel steamer *Sir William Fairbairn*, launched in 1896, which measured only 445 feet. On the drawing board was the steamer *Samuel F.B. Morse* which was to be launched in 1898, and would measure 475 feet. Interestingly, lakeboats in excess of 500 feet would not be constructed until 1904, more than a year after Inman's death. Lastly, the year-around bulk freighter was proposed to have 30 percent more horsepower than any boat on the drawing board in 1897. The *Morse* was launched with an engine that would give her 2700 horsepower, and an increase of that rating by 30 percent would bring that figure up to a whopping 3510 horsepower. The first boat on the lakes to come out with a horsepower rating anywhere near that figure was the carferry *Grand Haven* which used two engines to give her 3320 horsepower in 1903. Bulk freighters did not approach that horsepower rating until a decade later. So the Inman design was, indeed, a great departure from the normal designs of the time.

Entering the Soo Locks, the Paterson's *Inman style bow is visible.*
(D.J. Story Photo)

As Inman saw his financial and business troubles grow, he was compelled to patent his all-season bulk freighter concept. Once successfully patented, the new boat was marketed around the lakes, and actually began to draw interest. Events of the industry, as they evolved between 1884 and 1897, favored the building of this boat. Hull construction had changed from using oak planking to steel plate, the locks at the Soo had grown from a maximum of 515 feet in length to a maximum of 800 feet. The availability of bulk cargoes from the upper lakes had increased greatly. The value of having a fleet of boats that would continue to operate during the winter months, while others were laid up would easily grow into the millions of dollars. Certainly the time was right for the year-around bulk freighter, and Inman's dream filled the bill.

As he spread his idea of the year-around bulk freighter around the lakes, Inman began to get endorsements from some very respectable

Modern lakeboat Algowood *showing her Inman style bow. (D.J. Story Photo)*

sources. Most promising came from marine architect Frank Kirby. Kirby represented the Detroit Dry Dock Company, and was a living legend in Great Lakes maritime circles. Detroit Dry Dock was willing to build the new boats if Inman could find investors who would underwrite the cost of construction. This could be just what Inman needed. If he could find underwriters to cover the $300,000 price of each boat he would get 10 percent of that amount as a royalty on his patent. When the entire fleet was constructed he would realize a grand total of $180,000, which could easily be reinvested in a part-ownership of the fleet. Inman continued to market his all-season lakeboats until early 1901, and early that year wrote that he was "closing a deal with American Shipbuilding Company" for the building of three of the boats and paying him $10,000 for each. The Detroit Dry Dock Company had been absorbed into the American Ship Building Company in 1899, so this deal makes sense.

It is at this time that Inman somehow came to that invisible fork in the road of his life that we can only see with the hindsight afforded by history. For some unknown reason, Inman dropped his plans to have his lakeboat constructed. Had he gotten just one of these boats constructed that year or at anytime prior to that date, he would have lived far differently, and probably a much longer life. Instead of continuing with his all-season lakeboat, he had, instead, concentrated on the operation of two excursion freighters he owned. Apparently this had started in 1900 when he had been improperly terminated from his job with a tug line when an attempt was made to soothe the ruffled feathers of Captain James Davidson. Davidson had a tantrum over the treatment of one of his barges by a tug crew that worked under the indirect control of Inman. Davidson demanded that a head be lopped off over this relatively minor incident, and decided that he wanted Inman's. The tug company complied, and fired Inman—effectively wrecking his career in the tug business. By the following year Inman had a choice, he could either chase his dream of the year-around lakeboat, or he could chip out a small living on his excursion boats. Perhaps it was the pressures of debt, or the security of at least having some money flowing in, or some other influence that we can not know, that made the decision for him. For whatever reason, Inman elected to work his excursion boats, and the year-around freighter of which he had long dreamed was left in obscurity. By the end of 1901, the excursion steamers were slapped with a lien against their value in consideration for a back debt that had followed Inman from his tug days. He was forced to sell both steamers to cover the expense. He was left unemployed but managed to find work with the new Pittsburgh Steamship Company as a relief captain. Later he would assume duties ashore, where he would serve in the final job of his life.

We will never know the real reason why Inman dropped his idea for the construction of his icebreakers. In his biography of Inman, Miller states that Inman's daughter, Mary, claimed in later years that the effects of the 1893 financial panic had "lingered" and resulted in the dropping of the project. Although it is certain that this was Mary Inman's thoughts, the logic behind this reasoning does not add up. The American economy in the 1890s was highly dynamic and moved rapidly over events. Any effects of the 1893 panic on Inman's assets would have been laid to rest by 1901, or even by 1897 for that matter. Additionally, reading the biography shows that there is really nothing that occurred to Inman during the 1893 panic that should have stopped his icebreaker project eight years later. Apparently, for a reason that we do not know, Inman simply put aside the project that he had worked on for his entire adult life, patented, marketed, and on which he had "closed" a $10,000 deal. It was a minor and obscure event, but had he not dropped the idea, Great Lakes maritime history may have been very different, indeed.

We can see in these events what Inman could not—that the Rockefeller interests had become nervous over their essential iron ore shipments being dependent on several fleets of lakeboats Rockefeller did not control. As a result, the Pittsburgh Steamship Company was formed by these interests in 1901, and the company immediately began buying every large steel laker it could get its hands on. In the acquisition, fleet owners were paid handsomely and many were given positions of power within the company. If Inman had found a way to build any of his giant lakers, they would certainly have been scooped up first. Inman, with a small bit of maneuvering, could have set himself up in an executive office with an income that would have rivaled the richest of Duluth's elite. A prime example of this could be seen in Inman's longtime peer, Augustus Wolvin. When the Pittsburgh Steamship Company was forming, Wolvin's fleet was acquired and he was named vice president and general manager of the Pittsburgh fleet. At the time of the acquisition, Wolvin's Zenith Transit Company owned just five lakeboats, the largest of which was only 450 feet. Had Inman owned part of a fleet—six of his 530-foot icebreakers— his place in the Pittsburgh Steamship Company would have been assured. He could have easily maneuvered himself into the lap of the Steel Trust, and may have become one of the most powerful men in Great Lakes maritime history.

What if Mr. Inman had constructed his big all-season lakers, what then? Out of practicality we have to ask how sound was his concept, and how would have the American Ship Building Company altered the design in order to make it functional? To start, there are some inherent flaws in the design, the first being in the basic length to horsepower ratio. Although it was not known in Inman's day, the ability of an icebreaking vessel can be measured in a comparison of the boat's horsepower to its overall length. The higher this number is, the better the boat's ability to break ice. For example, the *Roger Blough* has a horsepower of 14,000, which, when divided by its 858-foot length, gives it a rating of just over 16.3. Considering that the minimum for an icebreaking vessel is 6.5, we can say that she is an efficient icebreaker. At 3,510 horsepower, and a length of 530 feet, Inman's design would have only had a rating of slightly above 6.62. This is right on the lower end of the icebreaking scale! If, however, the boat's hull was reduced to the size of the largest boat of that era, 475 feet, the rating would have been increased to 7.39.

And what about the horsepower itself? In 1897 a horsepower rating of the value that Inman had in mind could not be reached with any single engine in existence on the Great Lakes. Thus, the Inman icebreakers would require at least two of the big quadruple-expansion steam engines. Two engines of the same kind as installed in the *Morse* would give the Inman winter lakeboat 5,400 horsepower! If the boat was sized down to equate with the *Morse*, its length-to-horsepower rating would be boosted to more

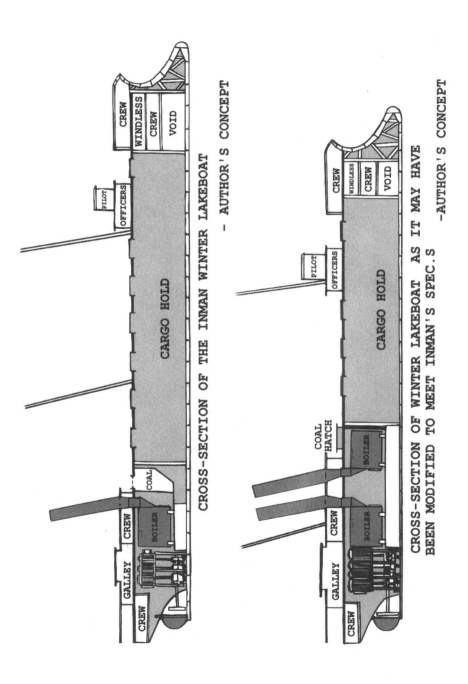

CROSS-SECTION OF THE INMAN WINTER LAKEBOAT
– AUTHOR'S CONCEPT

CROSS-SECTION OF WINTER LAKEBOAT AS IT MAY HAVE
BEEN MODIFIED TO MEET INMAN'S SPEC.S
–AUTHOR'S CONCEPT

than 11.36 with these engines. Having two engines to feed, the boat would also require at least four boilers to provide the necessary steam. Both of these requirements would cut into the available cargo space. Lastly, as a matter of practicality, it should be considered that this type of vessel may require long periods in the ice fields when the ice was thick, and progress through it would become slowed. For that reason, the boats would be unable to simply stop off at any port and refuel. The coal bunkers would, therefore, have to be large enough to not only feed four boilers, but to sustain the boats for long periods out on the frozen lake. This, too, would deduct from the cargo capacity unless the coal was side-bunkered, which would have been an easy solution. So, if the shipyard modified the Inman winter lakeboat to make it practical, the vessel would likely have come out as a 475-footer with two quadruple-expansion steam engines, four boilers, and twin smokestacks, and having a cargo capacity of about 3,800 tons. With these few modifications, the boat would be the ultimate winter freighter, and again would be a ripe target for acquisition by the Pittsburgh Steamship Company.

Looking back the question becomes, could Inman's dream actually have been constructed? The answer is yes. Although the plans were for a type of vessel that was larger and more powerful than anything ever constructed on the lakes at that time, with a few modifications it could have been done. All of the needed technology was in place at that moment in history, and Inman's dream could certainly have become a reality. If it had come into being, the repercussions may have been interesting. Considering the girth of the proposed vessels, they would have probably sailed into the mid-1960s. If equipped with a self-unloading rig in their later years, the boats would have been the traditional season openers in the coal trade in their later years. Should one of the boats have been converted into a cement carrier, it would likely still be in operation today. In fact, the design would be a perfect candidate for the role of self-unloading cement carrier.

As for Inman's unique "ram" bow shape, it was rediscovered and reinvented in modern times. As of this writing, the 730-foot-long Canadian bulk laker *Gordon C. Leitch*, which was originally named *Ralph Misener*, is sailing the lakes wearing a near-duplicate of the Inman ram bow. When the boat was launched in 1968, it was equipped with this "bulbous bow" to achieve greater hydrodynamic efficiency, and the better icebreaking ability was considered a bonus. The boat was designed to be innovative in many ways, and part of that ideal was a consideration for the new thinking toward all season navigation. When the boat's plans were penned out at the Canadian Vickers shipyard, it is highly unlikely that anyone on the design team gave a thought to B.B. Inman. At that time, Inman's dream was less than an obscure footnote in Great Lakes maritime history. In the 1980s, a new breed of lake carrier emerged from the Canadian shipyards, and again

Long after Inman's death, his bow is reborn on the Gordon C. Leitch.
(D.J. Story Photo)

Inman's dream re-appeared. These new "stem-winders" had all of their accommodations placed aft and were designed to operate both on the Great Lakes and on saltwater if needed. The bow of each is shaped with an angular, but recognizable version of the Inman ram bow design.

The basis for Inman's dream of an icebreaking boat was firmly rooted in the needs of a growing industrial revolution to be fed with bulk products. It was thought that year-around navigation could extract profits from an untapped season, and thus was a truly viable concept. During two world wars, the Inman ice-breakers would have been considered a national asset as they fed the blast furnaces of victory. By the 1970s the push toward year-around navigation returned, and in the winter of 1974-75 the bulk carriers succeeded in running uninterrupted. Inman's boats had never been constructed, but modern giants such as *Roger Blough* crushed through the ice as the spirit of B.B. Inman hovered overhead. The hunger for iron ore was so great that the economics of winter navigation again made the operation profitable. Just five years later, however, the dumping of foreign steel and iron ore on an unprotected United States market, coupled with a deep recession (the likes of which had haunted Inman in 1893), spelled the end for navigation on the Great Lakes as it had been known. The industry would never fully recover, and winter navigation would only be conducted by a few vessels stretching the traditional season at one end or another.

Inman's dream lives on. The powerful, and massive oreboat *Roger Blough* reflects his concept of designing a vessel that is far beyond the size and power of anything previously conceived. His ram bow can be found in nearly its exact form on the *Gordon C. Leitch*. Lastly, the concept of the Inman ram bow has been refined and used as a standard design feature on the most recent of lake carriers to come into service.

In the vortex of Great Lakes marine events, we find that some who do not give up on their dreams and ideas leave marks that changed the industry. We can ponder several questions. What if these people had let go of their ideas? Suppose that George Hulett had dropped his idea of the steam unloader, or that Leathem D. Smith had set aside his dream of the self-unloader? What would Great Lakes maritime history look like then? Both of these men were contemporaries of Inman, and the dreams of both were widely implemented and exist today. Oddly, Inman's concept of huge and powerful vessels for year-around navigation were reborn at the same shipbuilding company that had originally endorsed the concept twice before—yet forgot about the entire concept. That reborn idea later went to work for the same company that had employed Inman, and could have made him rich and powerful. The fate that had passed Inman by, returned and became reality seven decades after he had patented his dream. Today, the *Roger Blough*, *Gordon C. Leitch*, and others sail as confirmation of Inman's dream.

Even Inman himself, although long-dead, has a lesson to teach us. When the experts find your concept worth endorsement, you are probably on the right track. Thus, the lesson is to never accept mediocrity and never give up on your dream. Although it may seem far-fetched, you can go far if you believe in yourself. Defy the trappings and pressures of everyday life as they press upon your dreams. Break from the crowd and charge ahead with your creations and dreams. In the eyes of history, you have nothing to lose and everything to gain. Inman could not see the future, but we can do well by looking at his past. The results of bold innovation and leadership can be great, while the results of mediocrity will be dire. Chase your dreams, as we wish Inman had chased his dream.

A LEAK, LARGER THAN ORDINARY, WAS NOTICED

Within the world of Great Lakes maritime history, names of certain individuals always seem to relate to specific regions and specific vessels. Say the name Alexander McDougall, and the ports of Superior, Wisconsin, and Duluth, Minnesota, and his whaleback vessels will spring into the mind of any lakeboat buff. Likewise, James Davidson's name brings to mind Bay City, Michigan, and the largest wooden vessels to ever sail the lakes. Utter Frank Kirby's name and the city of Detroit, as well as the strongest steel vessels to sail the lakes, will come to the historian's thoughts. Talk of George Hulett and there come the thoughts of Cleveland and those powerful unloading machines. Leathem D. Smith's name calls up memories of Sturgeon Bay, Wisconsin, and the self-unloading freighter. Speak the name Augustus Hinckley and the thoughts of Oswego, New York, and leaky wooden lakeboats that tended to sink right out from under their crews will come to mind.

Captain Hinckley's reputation—famed Lake Ontario Historian Richard Palmer called him, "The little old man with the leaky boats"—was not ill-deserved. In fact, Gus Hinckley worked long and hard at driving wooden lakeboats to their finish. His idea of a good operation was to go out and find the "junkers" of the Great Lakes maritime industry and then, after application of a minimum of dollars in refit and repairs, he would work them until they would no longer float. In the modern world of automobiles, the saying is that anyone can operate a new car, but it takes a true "motor-head" to drive a junker. Such may be applied to Captain Hinckley. After all, any mariner can sail a new boat, but it takes a true sailor to run a junker. So it was that Hinckley would find the vessels that no one else wanted and press them into service once again. Hinckley would haul anything that could be crammed aboard his boats. Cargoes would be dumped into the rotting wooden hulls and piled high above the hatch combings. Hull timbers would twist and groan, seams would open and leak and, with a little luck, the boat would deliver its load. When the boats could sail no longer, and their timbers just gave up, the old man would simply abandon them and return to the lakeboat boneyard to resurrect another junker. His profit margins were slim, but his expenses were slimmer. One after another, Hinckley robbed the once proud lakers of their well deserved retirement, and at times it seemed that the boats were set on revenge for this final insult. As a result, the eastern end of Lake Ontario is littered with Hinckley's junkers.

On the steamy Saturday of August 15, 1931, the Great Lakes Dredge & Dock Company was busy preparing the way for construction of the new west breakwater outside the port of Oswego, New York. The project involved dredging the sand and mud from the lake bottom in order to reach bedrock. This was necessary because the riprap stone of the new breakwater would be unstable if placed upon the muddy bottom. Additionally, a large wooden crib was due in on the canal barge *Jane R.* within 48 hours. It would also have to be placed on the bedrock and stabilized. The crib would then be filled with stone and form the foundation for a new lighthouse on the end of the breakwater. Aboard the Dredge *B-7*, the crew worked feverishly but happily. This was one of the darkest years of the Great Depression, and the men of Great Lakes Dredge & Dock were happy to get the work. Likewise, the management of GLD&D was happy to get the contract. If they performed the job smoothly and finished on time, they could be a prime choice for the next job, and Superintendent R. J. Walsh would again have work for his crews.

As the dredge neared the area where the crib and later the lighthouse was to be placed, the clamshell bucket was dropped time and time again to the mud below. Each time it returned with a swill of sand and muck it had bitten from the lake's bottom. But then something odd happened. The clamshell plunged toward the soft bottom and clunked to a sharp stop. A moment later it was hoisted up, but clearly contained no muck from the lakebed. Again it was dropped, and again stopped short and returned empty. Repeatedly the bucket was dropped but was dredging nothing. Likewise, the other components of the dredge *D-7's* bottom-scraping equipment suddenly ran out of muck to bring to the surface. Soon it was apparent that the equipment had run into some sort of obstruction. After many days of smooth operation, the project had now been stopped cold. Superintendent Walsh was sent for and soon came putting out to the dredge by boat. For a protracted period everyone scratched their heads and pondered this obstruction that rested some 20 feet below the surface. Could it be a boulder, or some pre-ice age rock outcrop, or part of some long-forgotten former breakwater? Suddenly, among the crowd of the dredging crew it was remembered! This must be one of Hinckley's junkers—the *Isabella H.* that sank right here in 1925!

Sometime in late 1914 or perhaps early 1915, Gus Hinckley ventured to the lakeboat boneyard at Chaumont Bay, New York, on the southern shore of Lake Ontario. Hinckley was on a shopping expedition for lakeboat junkers. Abandoned, condemned, half-sunken and rotting in the shallows of the bay rested exactly what Captain Hinckley was seeking. It was the 106-foot wooden steamer *McCormick*, and it had been sent to the bay to rot away after being removed from enrollment as "No longer fit for service." Built in Grand Haven, Michigan, in 1887, the *McCormick* had been in the package and passenger trade on the western lakes. After 18 years of service, the old propeller had been retired. Just how the old steamer found her way to Chaumont Bay's lakeboat graveyard is not recorded, but such is normally the case for vessels that are abandoned. Once a vessel is dropped from service, no one cares where they go or how they get there. Now the *McCormick* was just the ticket for Hinckley's junker operations. Where other folks would see only rotting timber, rusty fixtures, and peeling paint, Hinckley saw a workhorse waiting to be reborn.

In short order, Hinckley had the old hulk of the *McCormick* pumped out and hauled to the Chaumont shipyard of Frank Phelps. The cabins were stripped and her fo'c'sle was built up, while a steel A-frame was mounted at her bow to assist a boom for a poor man's version of self-unloading. Sometime prior to June 30, 1915, the vessel was returned to active service as the steamer *Isabella H.* and now in the service of Captain Gus Hinckley. In the 1915 listing, the *Isabella H.* was shown as having official number 213102 with a gross tonnage of 248 and a net tonnage of 141. Her new dimensions were given as 100.8 feet in length, 25.9 feet in beam, and 11.1 feet in depth. The registration showed that her steam powerplant produced 150 horsepower, which was adequate for a fishing tug of about one-half of the *Isabella H.'s* size. Oddly, the listing for the number of crew aboard the boat is "0." Of all of the thousands of freight steamers in the 1915 listing, the ISABELLA H. is the only one that has a crew listing of zero.

For the next decade, the *Isabella H.* did Captain Hinckley's bidding. Coal, stone, phosphate, pulpwood, and any other bulk cargo that could be heaped into the steamer's hold were carried. Hinckley was well-known for loading his boats to the point where less than 12 inches of freeboard were remaining. Each time she was loaded down, the *Isabella H.'s* 150-horsepower steam plant would chug away in its routine struggle to propel the mass of the vessel and cargo. She was, at 100 feet and only 150-horsepower, underpowered by fivefold, and Hinckley staffed her with just seven crew members. It is clear that the old man was out to squeeze every bit of work out of the *Isabella H.* with a minimum of expenditure.

To put the whole picture into the proper frame, it is worth saying that Hinckley was not a Scrooge, or some sort of robber baron. He was simply a man of very thin means attempting to earn an honest wage as best he could. He did not have sights on becoming a magnate of a huge fleet of modern lakers. Rather, he was working hard at just getting by—one season at a time, and one load at a time. Hinckley never sought to cheat or shortchange anyone, he was simply following his calling to work Lake Ontario.

On Monday morning, September 28, 1925, Captain Fred Baldwin had the *Isabella H.* moored at Cape Vincent. Tumbling into the old hull came boulders of riprap stone. This type of stone is very familiar to anyone who has ever visited a waterfront which has a breakwall. The individual rocks can range in size from about two feet in girth to more than eight feet. Each of these rocks can weigh anywhere from several hundred pounds to more than a ton. The rocks are often discarded pieces of concrete used in construction, or odd pieces of rock that have been cut from a quarry. The name "riprap" comes from the fact that each piece has an irregular shape with jagged edges, but such shapes work well when piled up against the seas. This jagged shape, however, can play havoc with the cargo hold of a vessel. When you dump jagged boulders weighing hundreds of pounds into a wooden cargo hold, it takes a heavy toll on the timbers. Unloading that same cargo can do just as much damage as the pieces shift and the unloading rigs dig them out. This was not the first trip that the *Isabella H.* had made with the evil cargo of riprap stone aboard. Hinckley had entered into another of his famed "underbid, overwork" contracts to haul the stone for the breakwater work at Big Sodus, New York, and both the *Isabella H.* and the *Hinckley* had been working hard at moving the product. The punishment that the hull of the *Isabella H.* had been taking during the operation was now beginning to show. She was constantly leaking and her pumps seemed to always be at work. This vessel was old, worn and had previously been abandoned as unfit for service, so it is possible to speculate that she probably leaked most of the time anyway. Now Hinckley had her pressed into a toil that was far beyond her abilities.

While the *Isabella H.* was being loaded, her sister ship the *Hinckley* was tied nearby. Like the *Isabella H.*, the *Hinckley* would be crammed with riprap stone for Big Sodus. In command of his namesake was Captain Gus Hinckley himself. During the loading, apparently some concern had developed over the *Isabella H.* This is apparent by the report that the boat was loaded with only half of her capacity. For a Hinckley boat to be loaded light was surprising, so whatever was the trouble, it was probably quite apparent. The odds are that the boat was leaking more than usual, and the load was reduced to allow the pumps to keep up. Considering that the boat, herself, was powered by only a 150-horsepower steam engine, we can only imagine what kind of power was provided for her pumps. It is a safe bet to say that her pumps were capable to handle modest seepage, and nothing more.

There is no known unobstructed photo of the Isabella H. that exists. This drawing of the vessel is the author's concept of the vessel.

Aboard the *Isabella H.* on that blustery September morning were a total of seven souls including Captain Fred Baldwin. Supervising the loading and clad in his large rubber hip boots was First Mate Hiram Bush. With the vessel in a constant state of seepage, Bush found it to his liking to wear his boots all the time. Often he would find himself wading around in filthy water that seemed always to be sloshing around in the vessel's hull. Also working the deck were Charles Thompson and Moses Bradshaw. One of the other able-bodied crew has had his identity twisted a bit through the passage of time. Sources report his name as being James "Serviss" and "Service." All three of these men were probably required to do double-duty as deckhands and as coal-passers down in the engine room beside Chief Engineer Henry Lovely. The last member of the crew was the wife of Charles Thompson, whose identity has been even more obscured than that of James Service. She is recorded in the reports simply as the wife of Charles Thompson, and nothing more. So, among the thunder of the riprap stone's loading, the groaning of the *Isabella H.'s* tortured timbers and the general clatter of the dockside labor, it was just another autumn morning on eastern Lake Ontario.

At just about nine o'clock that morning the loading of the *Isabella H.* was completed and her lines were cast off. The distance to Big Sodus Bay from Cape Vincent is 66 miles, and using all of her 150 horsepower, it was going to take most of the day for the ship to reach her destination. In the wake of the *Isabella H.*, the *Hinckley* came hissing along. Although constructed specifically for Gus Hinckley in 1901, and not being a resurrection boat like the *Isabella H.*, the *Hinckley* was equipped with an engine of only 150 horsepower. For that reason, the two boats were well-matched to sail together down the lake. After a three-and-one-half mile shove from the confines of the St. Lawrence River, the Hinckley twosome entered the open waters of Lake Ontario. A bluster was blowing, and the surface of the lake was choppy, but the conditions were far from stormy. The two boats were able to make a speed of about eight miles per hour heading down the lake. On a course of 207 degrees, the pair of boats should have been in Big Sodus Bay just after five o'clock that afternoon.

Shortly after the *Isabella H.* was out on the lake, the first signs that this would be her last trip began to appear. It was later reported in the *Oswego Palladium* that "a leak, larger than ordinary" was discovered. At the time, the pumps were hard at work and appeared able to handle the flooding. Still, this gives us cause to wonder—just what was considered an "ordinary" leak aboard the *Isabella H.*? With this in mind, there is little wonder why the first mate wore rubber boots. Until noon, the pair of boats huffed along toward the southern coast of Lake Ontario. At that point the boats were two dozen miles into the lake and about four miles south of Galoo Island. For some reason the water from that larger than

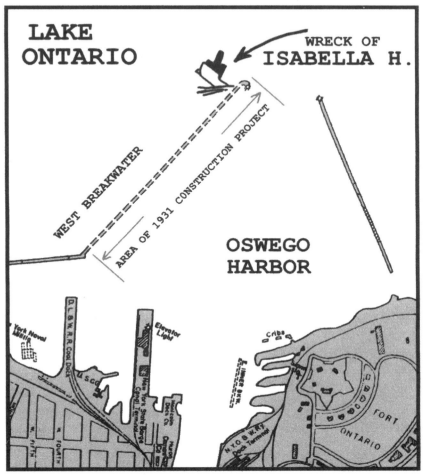

Map of the Oswego Harbor on Lake Ontario, where the Isabella H. *sunk.*

ordinary leak began to rise within the hull of the *Isabella H.* Aboard the nearby *Hinckley*, Captain Gus was signaled, and he drew his vessel into a close formation with the *Isabella H.* Captain Baldwin was concerned that his boat was taking water too fast and was sure that she would never make Big Sodus. Soon it was discovered that something had clogged the *Isabella H.'s* pumps, and that the big leak was now filling the hull. It was then decided to turn due south and make a dash for Oswego. There were 18 fewer miles to run in order to reach Oswego, and once there the pumps could be repaired. Both boats turned and started their snail's sprint for safety.

Each minute seemed as long as each mile while the *Isabella H.* slogged toward Oswego. Crew members scurried around the boat making eyeball measurements on the encroaching water, and estimating the time that she had remaining. Wading around in sloshing ice water the crew did what little they could to stem the flooding. There was little that could really be accomplished, but the effort would help pass the time. Down in the cramped engine room, the incoming water grew deeper as it mixed with coal, ash, mold, rust and any other nasty things that could be picked up. Water splashed against the steam pipes and boilers creating an ugly steam. Most of the crew were veterans of the Hinckley fleet and had been acquainted with leaking conditions before. For that reason, there was little concern and most of the crew were sure that the boat would make Oswego.

By three o'clock that afternoon, both vessels were off the south breakwall of Oswego and approaching the port. Apparently, the sinking condition of the *Isabella H.* was quite visible from shore because, as the two steamers neared Oswego, the Coast Guard had been alerted. The lookout at the station had been watching the two boats for quite some time and through his binoculars it was evident that the *Isabella H.* was in a sinking condition. The lookout's opinion as to whether or not the leaking boat would make the harbor was quite different from those her crew. He knew that this boat was sinking, and he alerted Captain George R. Jackson, the station's commander. Captain Jackson agreed that the little steamer would not remain on the surface of the lake much longer and ordered the station's motor lifeboat to be manned and launched.

Captain Hinckley had run his boat to within 100 feet of the wallowing *Isabella H.* as Oswego appeared to be within reach. But just as it appeared that another of Gus Hinckley's leaky tubs was about to cheat Lake Ontario again, the old man's bad luck took over. Only 1,700 feet off of the Oswego harbor outer light, and rolling heavily in nothing more than a modest sea, the tired old ship decided that it was time to enjoy that retirement that she had been robbed of a decade earlier. Like driving a truck with a bald tire, Hinckley had been driving his fleet in the rip-rap stone trade with the worn hull of the *Isabella H.* As with a worn tire, there are only so many miles that you can force upon a vessel before it gives out. The *Isabella H.* had just reached her point of failure. The weight of the cargo, the working of the seas, the wear of loading and unloading, the working of the water within the hull—and just plain old age—had now all added up to more than the tired lakeboat could stand. At that moment, she decided that she would go no farther.

Aboard the steamer, everyone sensed her begin to give up. First Mate Hiram Bush casually seated himself on a hatch combing and began to remove his big rubber boots.

"Can't swim well with hip boots on," he remarked to some of his shipmates who were standing nearby.

It was at that moment the *Isabella H.* took a sudden long roll and, as she rolled back, sank like an old shoe. The Coast Guardsmen were nearly at the boat's side when she gave out a large puff of white steam and dropped to the bottom. It was half past three o'clock in the afternoon. A heartbeat later the *Isabella H.* had left her crew thrashing on the surface of Lake Ontario, and everyone else stunned that any vessel could sink so fast. Then came the call that so many have heard before. It was that whisper within the soul to set fear aside and help those in need. From the motor lifeboat, Boatswains Mate McCune spotted Mrs. Thompson struggling against the lake. With no hesitation, McCune jumped out of the lifeboat and swam to her. Taking hold of the floundering cook, McCune dragged her back to the lifeboat and safety. Likewise, Machinist Mate First Class Moss saw James Service flailing in the choppy lake and shouting for help. Unfortunately, Service had never learned to swim, and now was not the proper time to take his first lesson. The lake was frigid and the spot where the panicked deckhand now found himself was 20 feet deeper than he was tall. Looking back, it was probably not the best idea for someone who could not swim to sign aboard one of Gus Hinckley's boats. Lucky for Service, Machinist Mate Moss was there to keep the valor. The instant that he spotted the stricken deckhand, Moss found himself diving into Lake Ontario. Within minutes, Moss had reached Service and gotten him to the lifeboat. From the deck of the *Hinckley*, Fireman Joseph Greeney launched the steamer's yawl and aided in the rescue. Nearly as fast as they had been dumped into the lake, the crew of the *Isabella H.* were rescued by the Coast Guard—except for one man.

When a head count was taken, Hiram Bush was found to be missing. Apparently he had been sucked down with the *Isabella H.* or he had not been able to get those hip boots completely removed. Either way, the boat's first mate had been taken away with Gus Hinckley's leaky steamer, and Lake Ontario would not give him back. All that remained above water of the *Isabella H.* was the top of her A-frame and a hint of her smokestack.

An inquiry was held at the office of the steamboat inspectors in the Oswego Federal Building on the day following the sinking. Albert C. Brockner, Inspector of Boilers, and Captain J.H. Dobson, Inspector of Hulls, called everyone involved in the loss of the boat to give statements. The hearing was closed to the public, but when it was finished Captain Hinckley casually returned to his remaining steamer and went on with hauling his rip rap stone. As the *Hinckley* steamed past the sunken *Isabella H.*, all that marked her grave was her A-frame with a bright white lantern attached. The hulk was considered to be a hazard to navigation and the Coast Guard had mounted the lantern to mark it. Earlier that morning a heavy sea from the north had washed away the boat's deckhouse roof, pilothouse, and smokestack. Amazingly, however, there was still talk of salvaging the boat. Although Hinckley was known as a salvage wizard, the talk of saving the *Isabella H.* seemed to come from everyone but him. He certainly knew that she was finished. The following year, the Army Corps of Engineers dynamited the vessel to clear the waters of her obstruction to navigation, and the boat was quickly forgotten.

By the time the crew constructing the breakwall stumbled onto the remains of the *Isabella H.*, Captain Hinckley had been retired from the maritime business for nearly a year. Following the loss of that ship, Hinckley had also lost the *Pentland*, *Hinckley* and *Harvey J. Kendall* to leaks "larger than ordinary." The 1930s were not a time that was well-suited to running a fleet of junkers on the fringes of the Great Lakes maritime industry. With the gloom of the Great Depression came the end of Captain Hinckley's maritime exploits.

Just what was done with the wreck of the *Isabella H.* after it was rediscovered has not been recorded. There was speculation that some of the riprap stone that remained aboard the wreck would be salvaged and used in the last few yards of the breakwater prior to the lighthouse's placement. With the scrap prices being greatly depressed, it is doubtful that the boiler and engine, which were said to be laying near the wreck, were ever recovered. These items were either buried within the breakwall or are still lying there on the bottom. Perhaps on a day when the weather is not suitable for diving out on the lake, some bored scuba diver may venture out and rediscover parts of the *Isabella H.* Then again, anyone with a stout heart can journey out to the end of the west breakwater and look for the riprap stones that appear somewhat different from the rest. Perhaps they are from the last cargo of the long-forgotten vessel.

446,500 REVOLUTIONS

Considering its status as the very first lighthouse established on Lake Huron, one would imagine that the Fort Gratiot Lighthouse would have a large tourist following, a gift shop, and daily guided tours. Such is not the case as the Fort Gratiot Lightstation is an active aid to navigation and a United States Coast Guard Station. Throughout the navigation season on the Great Lakes, the Fort Gratiot Light marks the Lake Huron entrance to the St. Clair River and the port cities of Sarnia, Ontario, and Port Huron, Michigan, and has often represented safety to many a lakes mariner. Constructed of brick, the present tower was placed into service in 1829 and originally stood 66 feet tall. A Michigan history buff would quickly point out that the lighthouse was placed in operation eight years before Michigan became a state! Thus the Fort Gratiot light is not only the oldest light in Michigan, but is older than the state itself.

In 1861 the top of the tower was raised by addition of a 20-foot-tall cylinder of brick and thus the light was placed at 86 feet tall. By 1875 a keeper's quarters and dwelling had been constructed on the site and today serves the Coast Guard crews who occupy the station.

Visiting the Fort Gratiot Lighthouse on a hot July day in 1999, you would be lucky to find a place to park your car. Rare are the times that the public is granted access to the lighthouse and its grounds because it is, after all, an active Coast Guard facility and is not open to the public. Still, the view through the fence is normally enough. The sand beach of the adjacent park is packed with local folks and tourists in good weather. Out on the water, giant modern oreboats steam past, seeming to be so close that you think that they can be touched with an outstretched hand. On the south end of the beach the Fort Gratiot Lighthouse stands like a monolithic reminder of foul weather gone by and gales to come. Indeed, there have been many times when this was a place of salvation rather than a place of recreation.

From Sunday evening, May 20th, until Monday evening, May 21st, 1883, the cups that were used to measure the wind at the Signal Service station in Port Huron, Michigan, rotated a total of 446,500 times. Nearby, the lamp of the Fort Gratiot Lighthouse flashed at a much more relaxed pace. Keepers J.T. Palmer and Samuel Palmer saw to it that the light was maintained throughout that storm, and along with the keeping of this light, the Palmers had also become somewhat of a hero in an act of what they thought was nothing more than simple hospitality.

The reason for the rapid rotation of the wind measuring cups was a nasty spring gale that had swept across all of the Great Lakes. Although somewhat less powerful than its autumn kin, this spring time storm was nearly as rude. Through Sunday evening, the storm began to shape itself into a classic Great Lakes gale, so much so that it got the attention of the ship reporter for the *Port Huron Daily Times*. He grabbed his reporter's pad and a few sharp pencils and headed down to city hall and the Signal Service station located there. At half past 10 o'clock Monday morning, the reporter and Sergeant Perry, the Signal Service officer, climbed the narrow and dark stairway leading to the roof of city hall. Once there they found the winds seeming to scream from out of the north. It was the kind of wind that rips the doorknob from your hand and attempts to take your breath away. Looking out over Lake Huron they saw her to be in an ice water rage. Using the roof telescope, the two men could see an imperiled steambarge and six schooner-barges being tossed by the waves out on the open lake. All appeared to be at anchor, or at least attempting to anchor. They watched in fascinated horror as the waves rolled completely across the vessels. It was the conclusion of the observers that at least three of the schooner-barges had been abandoned by their crews. For at least one of these vessels, that conclusion would be correct. The barge *Clematis* was missing her crew, and would soon sink.

It is not surprising that the *Clematis* is missing from every shipwreck chart, every history book, and every diver's list of targets. This little lakeboat was the most likely to be forgotten when that spring gale came sweeping across the lakes in 1883. Not large and not much of a "looker," the *Clematis* was sort of an odd duck among the Great Lakes fleet. Her career on the lakes started out as a large tugboat when launched by Ira Lafrinier in 1863. Often she towed log rafts or lumber barges across Lake Huron. By 1883, however, her days as a steam-powered tugboat were over. She had her engine and boiler removed, her cabins cut down, and her decks cleared to facilitate the hauling of lumber. Her hull could carry upwards of just over 100,000 board feet of "king pine lumber," and, considering that her operating costs were little more than the feeding of her crew, her profits must have been sweet.

This old postcard photo shows the Fort Gratiot Lighthouse as it appeared in the Clematis *era. (Author's Collection)*

Being towed behind the steam-barge *Lowell*, the *Clematis* was reported to have been keeping company with the barges *Waverly*, *Kate Kelly* and *Smith & Post*. With one lumber barge tied to her bow and another to her stern, the *Clematis* was pulled along in a familiar game of follow the leader. Tows of four barges were actually moderate in size, as steamers such as the *Lowell* at times pulled six or more barges all stacked high with lumber. The entire group had put into the port of Sand Beach, known today as Harbor Beach, prior to their departure for Port Huron. Then, early Sunday morning the *Lowell* pulled her string of barges out of the harbor of refuge and toward the reassuring sight of the Fort Gratiot Lighthouse and the St. Clair River.

Just a few hours out of Sand Beach, the winds began to shift and the storm pounced upon the tiny armada. Officially, the record at Port Huron shows that the winds shifted from a southerly spring breeze to a building northern gale at ten minutes past noon on Sunday. For the next 28 hours the temperature would drop steadily from a balmy 68 degrees down to the freezing point of 32 degrees. Winds would build to a sustained velocity of 40 miles per hour, and that is what set the wind cups at the reporting

The Fort Gratiot Light as it looks today. (Author's Collection)

176

station spinning up toward 446,500 revolutions. In the middle of this meteorological maelstrom was Lake Huron, and, like Lake Michigan just a few hours earlier, Huron was about to be whipped into a tantrum. On her surface, and seemingly within reach of safety, were the *Lowell* and her barges, including the *Clematis*.

In short order, large rolling waves began to take the *Lowell* and her consorts from astern. Soon the rollers turned into combers and their whitecapped crests began to assault the vessels at their heels and attack their weakest point—their rudders. The night had not stretched long before the barge that was in tow ahead of the *Clematis* had her rudder smashed by the waves, and control was lost. The captain of the *Lowell* had no choice but to cut lose his tow and let the barges scatter with the storm. In order to stabilize his boat, Captain J.E. Lockhart, the master of the *Clematis* also let go his hawsers and freed his vessel from the others. With huge waves of ice water billowing over the deck and a house-sized pile of lumber towering overhead. Crewmen Ernest Crispain, Delbert and Lockhart, the sons of the captain, wrestled with the thick towlines under the direction of Mate August Wilson, while the captain tended to the wheel. Then the crew attempted to raise the *Clematis'* meager and moldy storm sail. The entire event was about to become moot, because Lake Huron had set her desires on the barge's steering equipment. With a "crack" that resounded like a cannon shot, the four-inch-diameter iron rudder shaft snapped. In a wink, the entire rudder assembly simply dropped into the lake and Captain Lockhart stood with the boat's wheel in his hand, useless. To make matters worse, the hole through which the rudder post dropped was now left open and the lake came gushing in through the four-inch-wide opening.

Water from the hole entered the *Clematis'* hull and quickly found its way into the cargo hold as the barge began to rapidly fill. Now her crew took to the pumps which were little more than hand-pumped syphons. Hours passed as the *Clematis* wallowed in the lake and her crew worked at the pumps. Soon, however, the water was within a foot of the tops of the pumps and it was determined that the craft must surely waterlog. All that remained in question was if the lumber in her hold would be enough to keep her buoyed up. The pumps were abandoned and the boat's anchor was dropped in the hope of bringing her bow around to the seas. On occasion the winds got their hold on the boat and tossed her into the sea trough, and with that the waves came aboard and began to sweep her deck cargo overboard. In the barge's shack-like deckhouse, the water was nearly as high as it was out on deck. Each roll of the boat caused a tiny series of whitecapped waves—mixed with the crew's possessions—to slosh around in the cabin. In an effort that only lake mariners can muster, the crew actually tried to cook some potatoes while the *Clematis* tossed at the end of her anchor. Lake Huron would have none of that, and sent water to put out their fire and soak their bread. They were left with nothing more to eat than a 10-pound can of Lake Erie apples.

From the Fort Gratiot Lighthouse, all that Keeper Palmer could see of the dilemma out on the lake was a series of amber-masthead lanterns and a few dim cabin lamps rocking in the distance. It must have been a helpless feeling as he could hear the winds howl past the lighthouse tower. Yet all he could do was keep the light operating and wait to see what the storm delivered. So he fed the lamp and tended his light, and hoped that whatever carnage the gale created would not be delivered to his doorstep. By the time daylight began to brighten the low gray sky, the images of the vessels being ravaged out on the open lake became more distinct. From the Fort Gratiot lighthouse it was clear that at least one of the distant boats was sinking and several of the others were in bad shape. Countless planks of fresh cut lumber were being scattered along the beach where, 100 years later, summer sunbathers would lounge.

At eight o'clock that morning, the keepers of the Fort Gratiot Light saw five beleaguered figures stumbling along the lumber-strewn beach toward the lighthouse. The lightkeepers did not know it at first sight, but this was the crew of the *Clematis*. Crispan and Wilson staggered ahead as if seeking good footing, while Nelson and Delbert Lockhart moved along with their father, Captain Lockhart, who was being held up as he was too weak to walk on his own. Immediately, the lighthouse keepers rushed to help the five castaways into the shelter of their quarters. Here, warm and dry clothing, as well as hot food and coffee, was doled out to the starving and soaked mariners. Eventually, all five recovered sufficiently to tell their story. They had stuck with the *Clematis* until the first hints of dawn. Then, at about five a.m., they decided to abandon her. The lifeboat, however, was only a 13-footer and the captain was fearful the high seas would swamp her. Fortunately, the yawlboat was the one thing aboard the old barge that actually worked properly in the storm. All five men piled into it and for nearly three hours rowed for the safety of the Fort Gratiot Lighthouse. This time its beacon truly did represent salvation for mariners in distress.

As Monday stretched on, the storm blew with greater power. By that afternoon the winds had reached their peak, and by nightfall the gale was beginning to blow itself out. Captain Lockhart held out the hope that the waterlogged *Clematis* could ride out the storm in her semi-sunken condition, and then be towed into Port Huron, pumped out and placed back into service. Lockhart's hopes were dashed at five o'clock on Tuesday afternoon. It was then that part of the deck and the spar of the vessel came floating into the St. Clair River, right past the Fort Gratiot Lighthouse. This was the tell tale sign that the careworn little barge, which had once been his command, had surely broken up and was sunk where she had been anchored.

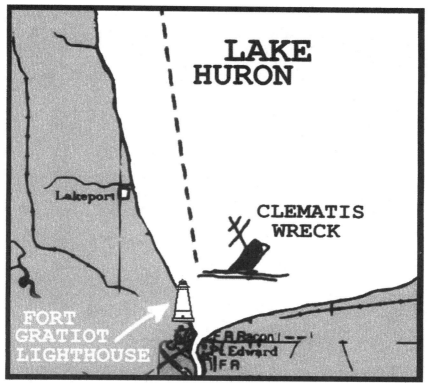

A map of Lake Huron showing the Fort Gratiot Lighthouse and the wreck site of the Clematis.

Such is the end of the story of the *Clematis*. Until now she has been overlooked, ignored, and simply forgotten—as have her crew. The wreck has never been located. Frankly, no one ever thought to go looking for her because no one ever remembered that she existed. Unfortunately, the shelter and kindness offered by the keepers of the Fort Gratiot Lighthouse has also been forgotten. Perhaps that was just the way of the lighthouse itself—to be ever-present and always alert, and to always be the beacon that represents salvation and safety. Maybe the next time the reader visits the sandy beach near the light, its weather-worn and whitewashed bricks will be seen in a new perspective. It will, however, take quite a bit of imagination to see the Fort Gratiot Lighthouse from the same point of view as the crew of the *Clematis*.

VOICES FROM THE NIGHT

here are some cases when every aspect of how and when someone kept the valor is lost. There are no medals issued, no reports entered into official records, and no evidence remaining for research historians to find years after the event. Sometimes all that remains is the rumor of the event, and a few lines written in the local papers. Such was the case for E.A. Foster of Put-In-Bay on south Bass Island in Ohio waters of western Lake Erie. In fact, his story was so buried in the sands of time that even his full name has been misplaced. Fortunately for us, shortly after his adventure, Foster sat down and recorded his little adventure in a letter to the *Sandusky Daily Register*. Also fortunately for us, research diver and shipwreck buff Mark McClain dug into the spools of microfilm 11 decades later and extracted the story. Although there are some areas where the facts are confused or simply missing, the tale of this forgotten hero can be published here with the forewarning that research and discovery is ongoing where this event is concerned.

It was just after 11 o'clock on a balmy midsummer evening in 1884 when Foster noticed something odd out on Lake Erie. The glow in the darkness beyond was the all too familiar and telltale signature of a vessel ablaze on the open water. The day was July 18th, and Foster knew immediately that there were souls in peril in the distance. Certain that he could do nothing alone, he enlisted the help of George Clauson, and the two quickly devised a plan to take Foster's 14-foot flat-bottomed rowboat out to render assistance. The night was still and the seas were calm as the two men launched the boat and began to row to the scene. What two men in a 14-foot rowboat thought they could do at the site of a lakeboat on fire, only they knew. Odds are that they had no idea what they would do once they got to the distressed vessel, but they were compelled by that urge to do something, anything, to help.

For nearly two miles they pulled at the oars until they had gotten close enough to hear and smell the combusting vessel. Foster could see the Green Island Range Lights and calculated that they were near where he had first spotted the distressed lakeboat. All around was as black as ink and only the orange flames of the burning boat provided any illumination. Foster cupped his hands to his mouth and shouted out across the blackness in the hope that anyone in the water might hear, and know that their rescue rowboat had arrived. From out of the night the voice of a woman replied to Foster's shout. Then came the voices of men echoing through the night. Guided through the blackness by the voices, the two rescuers rowed their boat forward.

First to be pulled from the clutches of Lake Erie was Amanda Hamilton. Both men in the rowboat reached for her in an effort to pull her into the boat.

"Wait a minute," She demanded coolly, refusing their help in exiting the water.

She perhaps thought that there were others in the water who were in greater need to be taken from the lake, and she also could be of help boosting them aboard the row boat. Foster and Clauson soon persuaded her that she needed to come out of the water, and shortly after another castaway was located. This individual came swimming up, dressed in what appeared to be his Sunday best, and dragging along his sailor's bag and valise. He wanted his possessions put aboard the little boat!

"Pard," Foster cautioned the dandy fellow, "I would let them things go to the devil in this case."

He would hear none of it, and insisted that his possessions be placed into the boat. Rather than let him upset the tiny craft, Foster gave in and heaved the soaked bags into the rowboat.

Soon there was a third survivor, and then another and another, until there were almost a dozen people clinging to the rail of Foster's rowboat. Somehow during rescue, one of the two oars needed to propel the rowboat was lost to Lake Erie, yet the rescuers went on with the job of robbing the lake of its victims. The boat did well to keep them all afloat, but there was no chance that it could be rowed back to Put-In-Bay while all of these people were holding on. As luck would have it, the lights of a tug appeared heading toward the group. Apparently it, too, had been attracted by the glow of the vessel ablaze. In conversation, Foster and Clauson discovered that Amanda had been the cook aboard the burning vessel, and the rest of the souls who were now clinging to life at the side of the rowboat were the remainder of the crew.

Going about her business and running at full speed, the "tug," which would soon become engulfed in flames, was earning her money that

There are no photos of the tug Relief known to exist, but she was quite likely a large wooden tug which appeared much like this. (Author's Concept)

Friday evening. Suddenly, Engineer James W. Baker heard a loud explosion from deep within the vessel. It appeared as if the blast had come from the boat's crank room where the shaft had been known to run hot and was in need of constant oiling. It was perhaps the residual gas from those lubricants that was the fuel for the explosion. Before Baker could think of calling Captain Chilston, the flames were all around the boat. Baker's concern was unwarranted, because the captain had heard the blast as had the rest of the crew. He hurried to get his people off of the vessel, and knowing that the ship's cook, Amanda Hamilton, was asleep in her cabin, he dashed there to wake her. By the time that he got the befuddled cook to her doorway, the entire boat outside to the door was a mass of flames. The captain and the cook had no choice other than to throw a blanket over their heads and leap through the fire into the lake. Elsewhere on the boat, members of the crew were grabbing life jackets and jumping overboard. Only one of the crew, firemen Peter Shields, was badly burned. Shields had "gone below" in order to find a life preserver, and while below deck had lost his way in the smoke and darkness. In the water, Captain Chilston and Engineer Baker managed to link up and between them kept Amanda afloat until Foster arrived with his rowboat. In the background, the distressed vessel incinerated herself and would continue to do so until she burned down to the water line.

Having spotted the flames, the tug *Cal. Davis* made haste to the scene. By the time she reached the wreck, survivors had been in the water for more than an hour. Still, this was Lake Erie in late July, and not November or April, so the castaways were able to make their way aboard the *Cal. Davis* under their own power. Alarmed by the burns of Peter Shields as well as some of the minor burns of others in the group, the captain of the *Cal. Davis* decided to make haste for Sandusky as soon as all of the crew had come aboard.

That rapid departure left Foster and Clauson in a rather awkward position. They were left behind in a rowboat, some two miles from the nearest dry land, in the middle of the night and in possession of only one oar! To make matters worse, the boat was half-filled with water. Both Foster and Clauson suddenly realized that, in all of the commotion, neither of them had thought to ask the name of the vessel whose crew they had just rescued. Left behind in the rowboat, however, was a single, soggy life jacket and on it the name "*Relief*" was stenciled. Soon after the *Cal. Davis* had left the scene of the *Relief's* burning, several local boaters reached the area, only to find no one but Foster and Clauson there. Now, the rescuers needed a rescue!

Once home, Foster wrote of his and Clauson's efforts and sent the document off to the Sandusky newspaper where it was later published. Oddly, little else was ever heard of the event. Later, one of the crew members was reported to have gone to the offices of Glicher & Schuck, the owners of the *Relief*, and demanded that they supply him with a new suit of clothing because his was ruined in the loss of the vessel. The specific crew member is not identified in the report, but the odds are that he was the same "dandy" who insisted that his clothing go aboard Foster's rowboat. Glicher & Schuck refused to compensate the fellow and he "swore all kinds of vengeance against them." The remains of the *Relief* were reportedly towed to the west end of Kellys Island where they were sunk. The *Cal. Davis* was supposed to claim rights of salvage, but no resolution was ever documented. The exact nature of the *Relief* is even in doubt. Although she is said to have been a "tug," a crew of 10 to 14 is nearly three times that which would be used to man such a vessel. It is worth noting that in the late 1800s the term "tug" was often used to denote vessels much larger than would be normally considered to be a vessel of tug class. Vessels once used for cargo carrying or carferrys were sometimes relegated to a career of pulling at a towing hawser and thus called tugs. The *Relief* could have been such a vessel and so been known as a tug, while having to be staffed as a cargo boat. Her exact history remains an enigma.

Foster had put aside all thought of his own personal safety and, along with Clauson, rowed out onto the open lake and given aid to every member of the *Relief's* crew. Often such an effort would result in recognition of some sort, but in this case there was none. There was no medal, no certificate, no reward from the vessel's owners or from the local residents. Until his story was rooted out by Mark McClain, the entire event had been completely lost. Indeed, Foster and Clauson were heroes, it is just that no one remembered their efforts.

THE GALE THAT STOLE CHRISTMAS

The day before Christmas of 1979 started with gusty winds and a indifferent sky across all of the Great Lakes region. Along with the sullen sky, a world of concerns–from the holding of American hostages in Iran, to the Soviet invasion of Afghanistan, to the rapidly declining U.S. economy–seemed to hang over the holiday season on the lakes. Leaders in Washington D.C. seemed to stumble at every twitch of the globe, and now most of U.S. industry stood on the brink of paying the price. Soon, the Great Lakes maritime industry would find itself at the leading edge of the coming economic recession as the auto, steel, and construction industries would all crash together. Interestingly, the shipping season of 1979 was one that saw record profits and enormous tonnage totals across all of the Great Lakes, but 1980 would be one of the worst since the Great Depression of the 1930s. By Christmas Eve of 1979, nearly the entire lakes fleet had gone into the traditional winter lay up, unaware of the hard times ahead.

Most of the boats that went into winter hibernation would never return to service. It was not uncommon in the 1970s to find lakeboats dating back to the turn-of-the-century, going about the toil of maritime commerce. By the end of the 1980s, however, the number of lakers constructed prior to 1925 remaining in regular service could be counted on one hand, and the overall Great Lakes fleet was cut by nearly two-thirds. Entire fleets, such as the famed Paterson line, as well as the Hindman and Scott Misener lines, found themselves in an economic death spiral from which there would be no recovery. The renowned Cleveland-Cliffs fleet, as well as the Ford fleet, dissolved completely in the wake of the recession of the 1980s. Even some of the icon fleets—Bethlehem and Kinsman for example— shrank to running just a boat or two. Vessels seemed to parade toward the scrapyard in a seemingly endless flotilla of despair. Relatively new boats, born in the late 1950s and early 1960s, were towed to the ship-breakers yard to be cut up along with their turn-of-the-century kin. The one-time "steel-trust" fleet of United States Steel had nearly 50 lakeboats on its roster in 1979, but a decade later had withered to less than a dozen bottoms, now managed as a sideline of a saltwater firm. A good demonstration of the scrapping madness came when the 767-footer *Arthur B. Homer*, constructed in 1960, was laid up and later scrapped. Any boat that was in any way considered to burden its owners would find itself on the end of a towing hawser on the way to the scrapyard. As the mournful boat-nuts watched from the shore, history was butchered before their eyes. Among these saddened boat-watchers was Andy LaBorde of Milwaukee.

At one time, the lakers had passed in regular procession in and out of the port of Milwaukee, and these vessels had been ready material for LaBorde's admiring camera. By 1982, however, the passages in and out of Andy's favorite ports would die to a trickle. Indeed, it was a gray future that lurked beyond the morning of December 24, 1979. With the dawning of that morning before Christmas, the amber lights of the second oldest boat on the Great Lakes, the cement-carrier *E.M. Ford*, were overpowered by the coming daylight as she paused at Milwaukee. At that moment, no one knew of the stormy times that were coming, not only in the years that lay ahead, but in the next few hours. The *Ford* had seen many a hard day, but this would be one of the worst in her long career. Still, the old boat had many a story that her soul could tell, if only the humans would take the time to listen.

On April 25, 1898, President William McKinley proclaimed that the United States was at war with Spain and the nation was abuzz with the news. Exactly one month later, hull number 30 splashed into the water at the Cleveland Shipbuilding Company's yard at Lorain, Ohio. Amid the excitement of the war news it would have been easy to overlook the birth of this rather average-size steel-hulled lakeboat. Measuring an ordinary 428 feet in overall length, the new steamer was somewhat smaller than the new leviathans. Launched less than a month prior to hull number 30 was the *Superior City,* which stretched the limits of the shipbuilder's art at an astonishing 450 feet in length when she hit the water—right next to the building ways where the finishing touches were being applied to hull number 30. Tremendous fanfare accompanied the *Superior City's* birth because she was the first boat launched from Cleveland Shipbuilding's Lorain facility. This hull broke the record held for two years by the twin steamers *Sir William Fairbairn* and *Robert Fulton* of the Bessemer Steamship Company. These two monsters measured in at 445 feet. Yet, when the *Superior City* found the water, everyone knew that her successor was soon to be launched at F.W. Wheeler's yard in Bay City, Michigan. Wheeler's *Samuel F.B. Morse* would slide into the Saginaw River at a whopping 475 feet in length on the last day of July, 1898. Along with her twin sister, the *Douglass Houghton,* which was launched a year later, the *Morse* would hold the title of "the longest boat on the lakes," until the turn-of-the-century. Considering all of this building of vessels, hull number 30 was, indeed, a rather ordinary vessel in the midst of extraordinary times.

Upon her launch, hull number 30 was christened *Presque Isle* and slid into the waters of the Black River with far less celebration than was given the *Superior City.* Constructed to order for her namesake, the Presque Isle Transportation Company, the new boat was assigned official number 150786. Cabins were arranged in the popular manner of the 1890s. The forward deckhouse and pilothouse was placed on the spardeck, and set back between the number one and two hatches. Eleven hatches stretched between the forward quarters and the aft deck houses. There were two elegantly raked masts rigged to the boat, one just aft of the pilothouse, and a second between hatches number 10 and 11. The forward mast was raked at one inch aft tilt per foot, and the aft was slightly more raked at one and one-half inches per foot. As with most lakers of this era, these tall sailing masts served no purpose other than holding her running lights aloft. No sails were aboard to aid her power plant, because by this time steam engines had evolved to the point where things such as sails were no longer needed. Down in the *Presque Isle's* engine room a 1,500 horsepower, quadruple-expansion, joy valve-equipped steam engine provided her propulsion. By 1898 standards she was a very powerful vessel. The hull of the *Presque Isle* was painted black, but her cabins were a unique pea green. These colors would later become the trademark of the Cleveland-Cliffs fleet which would long remain a close cousin to the Presque Isle Transportation Company. Departing Lorain after her outfittings, the *Presque Isle* took her place in the clamor of the ore trade in the midst of the industrial revolution.

In 1915 the cabins of the *Presque Isle* were moved from between hatches one and two and placed atop the fo'c'sle. Reconstructed, the more modern pilothouse and an enlarged Texas house provided a bit more room for the boat's crew. The boat was reboilered seven years later and given new tank tops in 1946. By 1955, however, it was found that she was just too small to compete in the iron ore trade and she went on the selling block. The following year the vessel was towed to the Christy Corporation's yard at Sturgeon Bay, Wisconsin, and a dramatic transformation took place. Deep in her cargo compartment, two long screw-like augers were placed along her keel, running the length of the hold. Her cargo area was reshaped into a hopper configuration and pneumatic unloading pumps were installed at the forward cargo bulkhead. All of this was a special arrangement to facilitate the unloading of cement powder, which from then on would be the vessel's cargo. The Huron Cement Company had found the *Presque Isle's* size to be just right for the

Seen here on July 22, 1961, the E.M. Ford is sporting her green paint scheme for Huron Cement. This photo of her was taken at the 6th Street Dock in Zilwaukee, Michigan. (Author's Collection)

cement trade, and they had wasted little time purchasing the obsolete ore carrier. Once her cargo hold had been modified, the boat's hatch covers were welded shut and four small cylindrical openings made across each hatch, as well as across the deck between each hatch. The powdered cement was transferred aboard by hoses through these loading "scuttles." At the destination port, the powder was funneled down the hopper to the screws where it was augured forward and literally blown overboard into the unloading facility. When the conversion work to the boat was finished, she was given one final touch, a new name—*E.M. Ford.*

After more than half a century of work in the iron ore business, it appeared as if the old *Presque Isle*, had a new lease on life. All that was lacking was the official christening ceremony. That was being put off until May 17, and the City of Detroit's observation of National Maritime Day. The *Ford* was to be the guest of honor at Detroit's prestigious Propeller Club for her official christening. Unfortunately, the ways of the Great Lakes would flow differently for the *Ford*, and the christening event would have to be canceled. Headed upbound in the St. Clair River and sporting her new paint scheme with white cabins and green hull, the *Ford* was running without cargo in clear weather. It was Thursday evening, April 19, 1956, and, as the newly converted cement carrier came abeam of Harsens Island, her 58-year-old steering equipment suddenly broke. Drunkenly, the *Ford* swerved with the current before plowing head-on into the downbound steamer *A.M. Byers*. The *Byers*, bound from Drummond Island, Michigan, to Buffalo with a bellyful of dolomite, decided to sink right on the spot. In the span of just 17 minutes, the *Byers* was resting up to her spar deck in the swift blue water of the St.Clair River. On the other hand, the *Ford* staggered another 200 yards up the river with a massive V-shaped dent in her nose. The collision had mashed the boat's starboard anchor into the wreckage, but her port side anchor was untouched, and the crew was able to drop it and stop the boat. A massive traffic jam resulted in Lake Huron and the Detroit River, as well as a trip back to the shipyard for a nose-job for the *E.M. Ford.*

During the winter lay up of 1956, the winter following the collision, the *Ford* was given a significant enlargement of her forward deckhouse, and in the 1960 lay up her after quarters were rebuilt. She ran for another 15 seasons without any significant work being done. In 1975, the *Ford's* engine was automated and she was converted from coal to oil, yet retained her original engine. Through most of those years, her engine was attended by Assistant Engineer Joe Solnierek. The steam engine that had been constructed back in 1898 became Joe's career and her engine room became his home. By Christmas eve of 1979, Joe Solnierek was the unquestioned expert on every moving part of the *Ford's* power plant. Every employee of the Huron Cement Company swore that the single reason the *Ford's* engine ran better than ever after 80 years of service was strictly due to Joe Solnierek's loving care!

As the day before Christmas, 1979, unfolded, Ship's Steward Phil Simpson found himself part of the "skeleton crew" left aboard the *Ford* over the holiday. Also assigned to spend their Christmas tending ship were the boat's oiler, third engineer, and porter. An additional "relief" sailor was dawdling with the intent of leaving after lunch. For Simpson the task of fulfilling the traditional Christmas Day dinner menu was now at hand. Great Lakes vessels in operation during the holiday had always laid out a feast, without regard to how many members of the crew were aboard. With a pantry stock that would make a corner grocery store envious, this was Simpson's chance to construct a banquet the likes of which his fellow skeleton crewmembers had never seen. Making multiple trips to the refrigerator, and reconnoiters of the pantry with paper and pencil, the diligent steward had the planning for a terrific Christmas dinner well in mind. Over the next 24 hours, chopping, mixing, measuring, sifting, stirring, simmering, roasting and frosting would take place that would surely have every member of the *Ford's* skeleton crew holding their full bellies and moaning with contentment by the end of Phil Simpson's holiday feast. Around the vessel itself, the normal din of activity was missing, but in the galley the atmosphere of intense planning was beginning to grow. Simpson and his porter were going to uphold the tradition, and there seemed that nothing could rob them of the satisfaction of laying out a memorable holiday spread. The only detail that the galley crew had not counted on was that, even while safely tied up in port, the vengeance of the lake can strike out at a boat and such ire knows no holiday.

When the *Ford* arrived at Milwaukee, she had aboard 5,850 tons of powdered cement consigned to remain aboard the boat as a lay-up storage cargo. Captain Gallager was informed that another Huron Cement boat, the *S.T. Crapo*, was at the dock and still unloading. Considering that the *Ford* was carrying nothing more than a winter lay-up cargo, it was decided to dock her in one of the municipal slips and let most of the crew go home for the holiday. Some of them could return after Christmas and manage her to the Huron Cement dock for lay-up. Simpson had watched as the deckhands put out the boat's lines. Then they went about putting out extra lines to make doubly certain that the boat would stay firmly at the dock.

"You've got her tied up like we're gonna be here all winter," the steward quipped to the *Ford's* bos'n.

Such precautions were well-founded, considering the lateness of the season. The lakes in December can explode in frozen wickedness at a moment's notice and with only a skeleton crew left behind, Captain Gallager wanted to make sure that the boat was secure. If a sudden blow should come up, the few men left aboard would be unable to tend parting lines and could be easily outmatched by the lake. Even with the extra

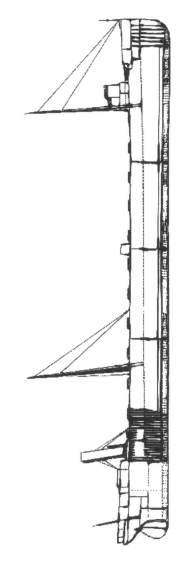

PRESQUE ISLE, AT THE TIME OF HER LAUNCHING.

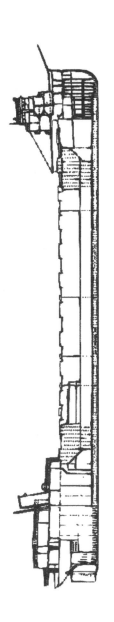

E.M. FORD, AFTER HER 1980 RE-BUILD.

precautions, the power of the lakes in winter could not be properly estimated. Winter navigation was something relatively new for most of the lakers. Certainly, the big carferrys and break-bulkers had been working Lake Michigan year-around since the 1880s, but for the most part the other carriers traditionally laid up in early December. The 1979 season, however, was the fifth year of "Extended Navigation" on the Great Lakes. This combined government and industry effort used every kind of ice-thwarting device that could be imagined to eliminate the annual winter stoppage of raw materials to the lower lakes factories. Although hard on vessels and crews, the extended season did work and tonnages grew—until the coming of the economic crash of the last year of the Carter Administration. The depressed market for ore, coal and other materials would spell the end of year-around navigation. For the moment, however, it appeared as if the *Ford* was snugly secured for any December day. Christmas Eve of 1979, however, was not going to be an average December day.

Through the day of December 24th, the weather went from unsettled to just plain frightful. By lunch time, a wind off of Lake Michigan came ripping across the Milwaukee Harbor and churned the waters within the breakwater into sharp whitecaps. The sky came down gray and irritable and snow streaked horizontally across the coast. In Municipal Slip Number 1, the *E.M. Ford* responded to every gust of wind by groaning and straining at her lines. Having hung around through lunch, the relief crewman stepped outside, got a good look at the weather and promptly decided that it was time to start his Christmas break.

"Well, I'd better get goin'," he told Simpson, "It's lookin' pretty rough out there."

It was shortly after the relief sailor took his leave of the boat the storm began to have its way with the *Ford*. At a local restaurant, Andy LaBorde had been having lunch with a friend. As the two attempted to exit the restaurant, they found that the doors, which faced to the east, were nearly held shut by the strength of the wind blowing in off of Lake Michigan. The motto of every good lakeboat-nut is, "Never go near the water without your camera, and if you live near the water, never go *anyplace* without your camera." Like all good boat-nuts, Andy also knew that bad weather equates to good photo opportunities. With that in mind, LaBorde headed toward the harbor with the hope of getting some good shots of the lake breaking over the seawall. What he would find instead, would be a boat-nut's dream and nightmare all in one, a shipwreck plus the loss of a beloved lakeboat.

Screaming, the wind found the hull of the *Ford* and the boat began to pound against the pier with the oncoming waves. Coincidentally, the gale was blowing directly through the east entrance of the Milwaukee breakwater and straight up the slip containing the *Ford*. Feeling as if he were out on the open lake, Phil Simpson continued to tend to his galley while the deck moved beneath his feet. Sensing that this movement of the boat ment trouble, he ventured out on deck to check the situation. At this same time, Andy LaBorde, having spotted the masts of the *Ford* above the warehouse next to the slip, pulled his car onto the scene. It was half past one o'clock in the afternoon, and the sight that both men cast eyes upon was awesome. The steel lines from the boat were doubled up on the dock's cleat, and as the boat tossed and rolled the wires rubbed together and created sparks. LaBorde got out of his car and strolled up the wind-swept dock. Steel lines snapped against one another, and aboard the boat the winches were attempting to compensate with the movement of the *Ford*. Looking up at the boat, Andy spotted Phil and gave a "Hello" shout. Not being able to understand Andy over the howling wind, Phil answered back, "Yeah, we could use some help." Minutes later, the beginning of the end started. Under the strain of the *Ford's* lines, one of the giant steel dock cleats was ripped from the pier like a staple from a cardboard box. Then came the sound of a cannon shot—a "boom" that echoed through the storm. Before long there was another report as a second "boom" echoed. There could be only one cause for these noises—the mooring lines were parting. Acting as a 400-foot-long steel sail, the *Ford's* hull caught the wind and put the mass of the boat, plus her hold full of cement, against her lines. Somewhere along one of the lines, the strands had been previously stressed just a bit too much, or rust had eaten just enough of the strands to weaken it. Soon the force of the wind, applied to the mass of the boat and cargo, added up to more than the tensile strength of that particular cable. In terms of physics it was much akin to holding up an ironing board with sewing thread. The only difference being that when one of these threads pops, it sounds like gunfire. Once the first lines let go the boat was blown up the slip, and the lines leading forward simply slipped the cleat. Soon the *Ford* would break free and the winds of Lake Michigan would have her.

According to the witnesses, it was the aft lines that began to let go first; the rest were lost in chaos. From Gill & Company, a local marine concern, line handlers arrived at the slip, sensing trouble. Spotting the *Ford's* dilemma, the Gill crew left and soon returned with five-inch braided nylon hawser. Timing the roll of the boat they went aboard and attempted to get her under control. In spite of their best efforts, it was too late.

Now the hull of the ship was being slammed into the pier by the onslaught of waves. Again, it was the mass of the vessel, itself, that did the damage. Hull plates twisted and bent as if made of clay. Rivets that had been skillfully fastened in 1898 were snapped at the head and sheared off. As each hull plate twisted, Lake Michigan found the openings and came aboard. The crew found they were now in charge of a situation against which not even a fully-manned boat with a tug at its disposal would have stood much of a chance. Flooding in the bilge was the first sign of trouble, but when the water entered the tunnel that ran along the steamer's keel, the concern turned to near panic. First in mind was to start the pumps and free the boat from the flooding, and perhaps get up steam and work the engine. But, when the skeleton crew got into the engine room, they discovered they only had access to the workings necessary to keep the donkey boiler up to heat the boat. Every other place the crew needed to get into was locked, and the third engineer did not have the keys! Venturing out on deck the crew saw that a small crowd had formed on the pier, and that the ladder to the dock was useless. Scribbling Engineer Joe Solnierek's phone number on a piece of paper, Phil Simpson managed to pass it to one of the people ashore as the hull of the *Ford* rolled close and made one of the countless strikes against the dock. Shouting for the person ashore to call the engineer, Simpson hoped that he could be reached in time to keep the vessel afloat. Ashore, Andy LaBorde had his camera working full time. He was photographing an actual shipwreck as it happened. Too bad it was the wreck of the *E.M. Ford!*

Flooding from her stern, the *Ford* was well on her way to the bottom of the slip by nine o'clock that night. There was nothing that her crew could do now, other than abandon her. As he came on deck, Simpson was met with the terrifying reality of nature's power. The lake was playfully tossing the boat's giant hull against the pier, and then pulling it back for another smash. All along her beam, the hull plates were bent and twisted in a rude distortion. There was no ladder or gangway to lead to the pier, Simpson would have to jump for it. He knew too well that there was the very real possibility that if he mis-timed his leap he would be caught between the dock and the boat and be squashed like a bug. Sometime between 9:30 and 10:00 p.m., Simpson teetered on the fence of the 428-foot *Ford* and timed the roll of the boat with his instinct to jump. Taking his best shot, he stepped out into the thin air and left his plans for Christmas dinner to the ravages of Lake Michigan.

Landing like a sack of potatoes, Simpson hit the surface of the pier at the same time as the rampaging hull of the ship came smashing into the dock. The crew realized their boat was rapidly sinking. The first order of business was to contact Captain Gallager and give him the bad news. Having gone home for the Christmas holiday, Gallager, in turn phoned a local lake pilot who had once worked the *Ford* and now lived near the boat's slip.

"Just go aboard and keep the coffee hot and make some sandwiches," Gallager asked of the pilot, "there's not much you can do now."

While the storm churned the night, every line holding the *Ford* to the pier had parted with the exception of a single five-inch nylon hawser which held on to the last. As the boat was pulled away by the wind, the hawser was stretched to the point where its five-inch diameter was reduced to an inch and a half! At that point, no human force could keep the *Ford*

Huron Cement Photo

from her fate. The hawser parted with the final "boom" of the night and the big cement-carrier was on her own, adrift in the slip.

By the time Assistant Engineer Joe Solnierek came screeching up to the pier, it was too late. The *Ford* was on the bottom and blown crossways in the slip. It was a sad sight, indeed, with the only fortune being that the boat was sitting upright with only a slight list to her port side. Daylight the following morning revealed the whole of the damage. The boat's entire port beam had been stove in, her stern was holed and sunk all of the way down to the poop deck, and her bow was smashed in nearly as badly as it

197

had been in the *Byers* collision. Worst of all, the lake had gotten into her cargo hold and mixed with the cement powder cargo. It would not be long before the *Ford* would probably have a 5,850-ton solid block of cement in her hold. As Joe Solnierek and Phil Simpson surveyed the damage, a wave of sadness swept over the engineer.

"That's been my home for nearly 30 years," Joe bemoaned in a deep sorrow. "That engine was my baby."

Andy La Borde returned with his camera and dutifully recorded the sad scene of what appeared to be the stormy end of an historic lakeboat. Joe and Phil were sent to company headquarters in Alpena and, after making their reports, were sent on their winter break. To everyone who knew anything about the lakes maritime industry, it appeared that the *E.M. Ford* was finished.

In the months that followed the water was pumped from the *Ford* and she was raised from the bottom. On March 2, 1980, the boat was pulled from Milwaukee by the tugs *Lauren Castle* and *John M. Selvick* and headed north to the Bay Shipbuilding Corporation at Sturgeon Bay, Wisconsin. Three days later, she was in dry dock being surveyed to determine the economics of repair. Repairs would require 435,000 pounds of new steel plating to make her dented hull watertight once more. More than 6,500 rivets would have to be replaced in an era when such riveting had not been used for nearly 40 years. Worst of all, the cement powder had hardened in her augers, drive machinery, air compressors and every other imaginable nook of cargo handling. In her dust collectors alone, three tons of cement had hardened. The cargo hold had a four-foot-thick shell of hardened cement over the entire cargo. With the vessel's redesign as a powder carrier, her hatches had been welded to the deck, so there was no way to get the hardened cargo out other that cutting the deck off and removing the cargo by hand using picks and jackhammers. The job and the cost was staggering.

While the *Ford* was languishing in dry dock, the Great Lakes maritime industry, and the U.S. economy as a whole slid into recession. Around the lakes many an historic lakeboat was tied to the wall, never to be refit. At Duluth, it appeared as if the whole U.S. Steel Corporation's fleet was in permanent lay up. The Toledo waterfront was lined with lakers, as was Cleveland, Lorain, Buffalo and Toronto. Not since the Great Depression had the industry suffered such a blow to its very existence. Under this kind of pressure, what hope was there for the wrecked *E.M. Ford*? The answer was in the heart of the management of the Huron Cement Company. For decades this company had been like a family, and its managers had been true "steamboat men." Economics mattered not—their historic steamboat would live again!

Hull plates were manufactured, rivets machined, torches used to cut decking, and, a chunk at a time, the hardened cement was removed as the ship was brought back to life. From the hold alone, 32 dump trucks-full of hardened cement were removed. The hull was repaired and the engine room and its workings restored to very near their 1898 appearance. By the last day of July, 1980, the *Ford* was ready to be "rededicated." As guests and dignitaries gathered at Bay Shipbuilding, the boat was given a cheering send-off. Later, Huron Cement printed a commemorative booklet to honor the occasion. The last paragraph on the history of the boat stated:

> On July 31, 1980 Huron Cement Division of National Gypsum Company held a ship's blessing ceremony aboard the *E.M. Ford* and she was rededicated to continue her service in the Great Lakes cement trade. On August 7, 1980 the Str. *E.M. Ford* departed the yards of Bay Shipbuilding Corp. to add yet another chapter to maritime history. In a few short years this venerable matriarch of the Great Lakes will set a record which may never be broken when she celebrates her 100th birthday in July of 1998.

Optimistic words, but in the economic times that followed, such was not to be. In the turmoil of the next decade, foreign interests found their

Rusting as a "transfer and storage barge" the E.M. Ford *spent her 100th birthday at the Zilwaukee Dock. (D.J. Story Photo)*

199

way into many aspects of the U.S. economy. Desperate for cash infusions, many depressed American corporations merged with offshore companies or sold out completely. Huron Cement was sold. The vessels of the fleet retained their off-white paint scheme, but the name on the holdings was soon changed to "LaFarge." By the mid-1990s the *E.M. Ford* was placed in lay-up status, and with the more cost-efficient tug and barge trend on the lakes, she had been moored in the upper Saginaw River as a "dead boat." The long arm of foreign management has no feel for the romance or history of the Great Lakes; they are rightly concerned only with their investment. In their ledger, there is absolutely no economic advantage in reactivating the *E.M. Ford*. As of this writing her future appears dim, and the predicted record-setting season that was described in her dedication booklet will probably not happen. It is not likely that any community will find the funds to display her, or that local politicians will find a place to moor her. It is doubtful that anyone at LaFarge will be able to justify her return to service. It is far more likely that this "venerable matriarch of the Great Lakes" will spend her 100th birthday as a dead-boat/transfer barge in the backwaters of Carrollton, Michigan, or will be cut down to a push barge—or worse yet be cut into scrap. When it comes to historic vessels, there are few who appreciate the true value of a vessel like the *E.M. Ford*. The sprit of the venerable matriarch of the lakes will more likely be remembered by people such as Phil Simpson and Andy La Borde, and you, the readers of this story—now that the *E.M. Ford* has reached her 100th birthday.

A CLOSER LOOK
WILL FIND...

O n the evening prior to the hottest day of the summer of 1996, the motor vessel *San Laud* finished loading at Port Gypsum and pushed silently across the mouth of Tawas Bay and onto Lake Huron. Ashore at the city of East Tawas, Michigan, few of the vacationers took more than a casual notice as the lights of the big American Steamship Company self-unloader shrunk toward the distance. The lights of the *Laud* were little more than a momentary distraction from the campfires, cold drinks and general repose of the vacation folk. With the lapping waves providing a rhythmic backdrop, another August day passed from the calendar and Tawas prepared for the coming of another day in the tourist industry. From the peaceful isolation of the state park, which takes up nearly half of Tawas Point, to the shops, first class marina, and hotel that make up the downtown, tourism is the business of the Tawas area. At the heart of town, the city campground serves as the nerve center of the summer season. With its trailers and campers clustered together as closely as the people who occupy them, the same folks stake out the same spots, season after season. Day-trippers and perpetual campers mingle together on the sidewalks, visiting the shops and restaurants as local residents market everything from blue moon ice cream to cedar trinket boxes.

There are so many hidden treasures of Great Lakes history located along this vacation coast that the area practically radiates with maritime heritage. A closer look will find museums such as the Sturgeon Point Lighthouse and the East Tawas Museum. A drive along U.S. 23 just north of Oscoda will take you to the Great Lakes Marine Art Gallery owned and operated by Dave and Jo Allen. The gallery is the repository of the best collection of original lakeboat and lighthouse artwork that ever stunned the viewer. Without a closer look, however, the tourist may simply drive right past this remarkable place and its treasure of paintings and photos.

Likewise, while zooming along the highway, the casual vacationer may also miss the Nor' East Shore Resort located just south of the Au Sable River. There, too, is located a fascinating piece of maritime history. This piece, however, is so easy to overlook that for many years the owners of the resort did not even know what it was. Visiting Tawas, some folks take the time to venture out onto "the point" and hike the nature trail to its sandy tip. Along the way, various markers show points of interest such as assorted plants, critters, and the fictitious wreck of the schooner *Kitty Reeves*—a vessel which never really existed. While stepping onto the very end of Tawas Point, and using just a bit of snooping and a closer look, the alert tourist may discover a wayward plank or two. In fact, the locals tell tales of how, after a big storm, one can wade into the shallows off of the point and walk on oak decking rather than the sandy bottom. Suddenly, there in the shadow of the gleaming white lighthouse, the realization sets in that this was not always a peaceful place of tourism and summer vacation fun.

In this same steamy summer of 1996, a mid-Michigan couple, Mildred and Ray, while cabin-sitting for their son-in-law, were surprised to find some giant wooden objects in the surf outside of their front window. Located about a mile south of the Au Sable River, the beach side house has a startling view of Lake Huron's beauty. But now the lake had apparently seen fit to deposit immense hunks of old wood right in Mildred's front yard. Too massive to move, the pieces appeared from the lake and then were covered again by the sand. Still, as time passed, thoughts of the big oak pieces haunted the residents, especially Mildred. During the winter, sand drifted over the biggest hunks of wood. No one really had any idea what the pieces were. Perhaps they were left from an old dock that broke up long ago, or maybe were the remains of some dramatic, long-forgotten shipwreck. In the summer of 1997, Mildred happened to be visiting the gift shop at the Sturgeon Point Lighthouse when she met a Great Lakes historian. On a whim she mentioned the big hunks of wood on her beach. A few days later, shovels chewed at the sand that blanketed one of the objects, and the piece was again uncovered to the point where the historian was able to identify the object.

"Do you know what you've got here?" the historian excitedly quizzed Ray. "It's a rudder!"

Looking at the rudder, the taper of the leading edge was clearly visible, but the shattered end of the upper post showed signs of many decades of ice wear. It appeared as if the rudder had spent a number of decades stuck upright in the sand in shallow water. After photographing the rudder and the subsequent re-burying of the artifact in the preserving sands, Larry and Becky Schneider, the owners and operators of the Nor' East Shore Resort, happened upon the scene. Larry commented that they may just have

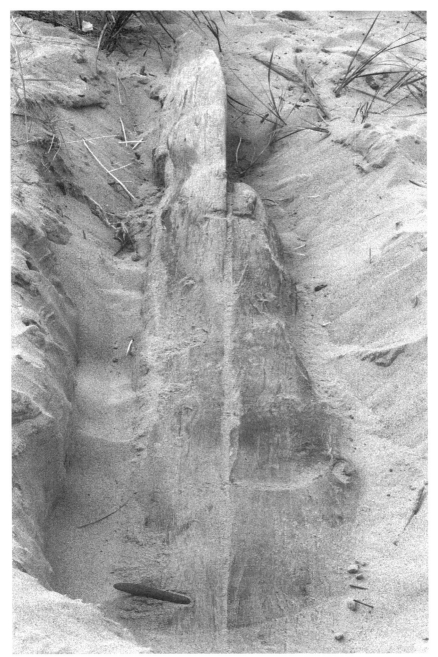

Seen here freshly uncovered, the rudder of the Abraham Lincoln *rests in a sandy grave. (Author's Photo)*

another piece of "something" at their resort a few miles down the road. The Schneiders had taken ownership of the resort in February of 1997, and with it had come the logs, rocks, stumps and other fixtures that create the "up-north" atmosphere. It was said that one particular fixture had been found on the beach a couple of decades earlier. The piece was a large wooden beam about a foot square and several feet tall, with neatly spaced holes drilled through it. For quite some time, both Becky and Larry had pondered the nature of this big piece of wood that had long ago been planted in their yard as a decoration. Often when watching the power of the lake, Becky had given thoughts to shipwrecks—but of course there couldn't be anything near her home. When the historian arrived at the deckhand Shore Resort, however, a different story came to light. Sure enough, there in front of the office that overlooks the cozy and tidy cottages of the resort is planted the centerboard lift of a big wooden sailing vessel, and it has the same story to tell as the rudder in Mildred's yard. It, too, shows the signs of many decades of ice wear while resting upright in the shallows. A closer look into the story of these objects and this area will find a spectacle of disaster and valor, played out on these now-peaceful beaches, that is of a magnitude far beyond anything that Becky and Larry Schneider, Mildred and Ray, or any of the local residents or visitors, could ever imagine.

Summer of 1872 had expired nearly a month before the schooner *Table Rock* tied her lines to Whittemores' lumber dock at Tawas City. In command of the lumber barge, Captain McCauley made sure all of the lines were made secure. The autumn was growing late and the weather was likely to turn foul without warning. For the better part of a week, the diminutive schooner-barge loitered at the dock in the duty of loading and waiting. Each plank of lumber was put aboard by hand, one at a time, and once the lumber-shovers were finished loading the boat, she would have to wait her turn to be towed with the other lumber barges that were also loading. Tawas was a very different place in 1872 than it is in the modern tourist era. More than two and one-half billion feet of Michigan pine would be cut and shipped that season and much of it would be shipped through Tawas. While the *Table Rock* was moored to the dock, her crew would find very little to do ashore. Tawas was not much more than a lumber town garnished with a bit of commercial fishing, and the pleasant distractions of the 1990s were beyond imagination. Making their way from the dock, the *Table Rock's* crew would see not a hint of the tourist industry of the late 1900s. Even the lighthouse, which sits near the end of Tawas Point, was not in existence in 1872; it would not be constructed for another four years. The light which existed in 1872 had been erected in 1852, and within the next 20 years had become almost useless. Located on the inside of the point, where the modern day park ranger's quarters now exist, the light was simply established in a poor location. Soon after the light's activation, the shifting sands of the point would grow to the extent that the 1852 structure would be too far inland to adequately guide vessel traffic. In fact, the point was nearly a mile shorter in 1872 than in 1996, and was then known by the name "Ottawa Point." So, in that autumn of 1872, the only navigational aid for one of the most active ports on the lakes flashed every night in a useless position. It would take a good bit of outcry before the new light would be constructed in 1876. Certainly, Tawas was indeed a different place from the modern tourist town, but the *Table Rock* and her crew were not there on vacation.

Like most of the boats of her class, the *Table Rock* was able to turn a profit by hauling just about anything to just about any place on the Great Lakes. A good example of this can be found in the summer of 1871. Spinning our time machine back to that date, we would not find the *Table Rock* sailing across the lakes with a fragrant cargo of fresh-cut lumber, or poised at a dock while coal is shoveled from her hold, or even scurrying empty across the lake in a hurry to pick up the next paying load. In fact, from July 18th to July 30th of 1871 the *Table Rock* was earning a handy living by doing absolutely nothing at all—and in the service of the United States Government. That summer, the United States Lighthouse Board had commissioned a number of vessels to aid in the initial phase of construction of the Spectacle Reef Lighthouse in northern Lake Huron. As a part of the operation, the *Table Rock* was chartered to hold 310 tons of stone intended for the foundation of the lighthouse. This was scheduled as "reserve stone," and so the schooner-barge was left tied to the dock at Scammon Harbor on Drummond Island, Michigan for 12 days. For this service she was well-paid, and never had to log a single mile to earn some easy money. Apparently, even in 1871, the easiest way to get money from the government was to do nothing at all. A year and two months later, however, the *Table Rock* was right back to work and lumber was the job.

Waiting her turn to load behind the *Table Rock* was the 75-foot scow-schooner *Abraham Lincoln*. The scow-schooner was a fairly unique type of vessel on the Great Lakes. With squared sides and rounded bow and stern, they were able to take aboard a maximum amount of cargo while drawing a minimum of water. The downside of this design, however was the fact that the bow, which gave the appearance of a quarter of a wooden barrel laid on its side, presented a great deal of resistance to the seas. Thus, these scow-schooners were difficult to tow and tended to pound when in rough weather. Normally, these were smaller vessels with just two masts, although some were three-masters. The *Lincoln* was taking aboard a cargo of 300,000 board feet of lath. This was a clear demonstration of the capacity of these sailing scows. Even though lath is a cut of lumber similar to the pickets used in fences, 300,000 board feet of anything is a hefty load to be placed aboard a 75-foot vessel. In spite of the heavy load, Captain Charles Green did little more than wink at his boat's load line. The *Lincoln* was going to turn a tidy profit on this trip, and that was what mattered the most.

Constructed at New Baltimore, Michigan, in 1860 and given an official number of 1122, the little scow-schooner carried a tiny yet fascinating oddity in her name. The boat was launched in July of 1860, and officially christened as the *"Abraham Lincoln,"* but Lincoln, himself, was not yet the President. In fact, Lincoln was nominated at the Republican Convention in May of 1860 at Chicago. He would be elected in November of 1860, and sworn into office in March 1861. He was also the second choice of those in his party, and almost did not get the nomination. So, when Charles Desha dedicated his new scow-schooner and named it *Abraham Lincoln*, he had actually christened the boat in honor of a person who was nothing more than the Republican candidate for president—and an underdog at that! Just why Desha did this is one of the little unanswered oddities in Great Lakes history. There is the chance that the enrollment research or the actual records are in error by one year, but that is highly unlikely. This was also an era when most sailing vessels on the lakes did not carry the names of persons, but were more likely to carry the names of places or things. No doubt, for her first season, the *Lincoln* was a bit of a standout on the lakes, but Desha had the best laugh come the following season. By the time our story finds her loading at Tawas, the *Lincoln* was only a dozen seasons old and, although her namesake was famed and gone, she was still a fairly youthful boat. It appeared that she could handle anything that Captain Green saw fit to load aboard her. So he loaded her to the hilt.

It is likely that conversation around the galley of the *Table Rock* and *Lincoln* often turned to the hottest subject of the time—the upcoming presidential election of 1872. Republican incumbent, Ulysses S. Grant, was in a race against Democrat Horace Greeley. That is, if it could be called a race at all. Grant refused to go out and campaign on his own behalf, forcing his supporters to go out and drum up support. Greeley, on the other hand, hit every state fair and public gathering that he could attend. Under the banner of a "Republican Liberal," Greeley found few supporters. In this era a century before CNN sound bites and assorted media blitzes, the promises and propositions were dispensed by soapbox-standing supporters called "blowers," who would pick a busy street corner and shout their pitch to whatever crowd may gather. As an example of candidate Greeley's popularity, his blower shouted on the corner of Water and Third Streets in Bay City, but the crowd he drew was smaller than that of the blower huckstering "Hamlin's Wizard Oil." This cough balsam and tooth medicine was said to cure rheumatism, lame back, neuralgia, toothache and deafness—for just 50 cents! How could Horace Greeley top that?

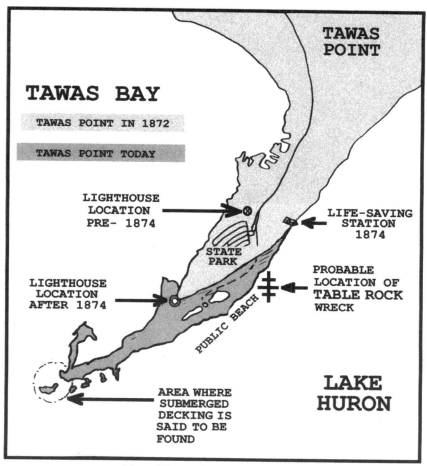

Map of Tawas Bay on Lake Huron.

By Saturday, September 27th, the *Table Rock* had taken aboard her fair share of those billions of feet of pine, and found herself in among a six-barge tow headed across Tawas Bay and down the lake. Although this was a generation when long strings of lumber barges were towed behind tugs and steamers, numbers such as four or five barges in a tow were considered to be large. A string of six barges was going to be an effort to say the least. Along with the *Table Rock*, the barges *Ontario* and *Lincoln* were among the armada attached to the stern of the tug *Zouave*. Fueled by the same felled Michigan timber that was otherwise shipped as cargo, the tug was using every ounce of her steam to haul the string of barges across the lake. Progress for the *Table Rock*, *Lincoln* and their sisters on the towline

207

would be slow, but the profit margin would surely be great. Much like the 104 years later when the *Laud* departed across Tawas and Saginaw Bays, no one ashore paid much attention to the *Lincoln's* and *Table Rock's* departure. In less than 24 hours, however, they would command the full attention of everyone along the Tawas and Au Sable shore. But for now the scene was simply that of the lumber business as usual. Taking the place of the *Zouave's* lumber-barge tow, the steamer *Benton* eased up to the same mooring and the lumber-shovers went to work loading her. As the long string of the *Lincoln* and her companions inched toward the horizon, the sky overhead was turning sullen, and one of the most violent storms ever to hit Lake Huron drew near.

Some 31 miles out of Tawas Bay, the *Zouave* and the six barges in her tow found themselves pounding across an angry Lake Huron and approaching the tip of Michigan's thumb. Just before nine o'clock on that ugly evening, the blustery autumn wind turned suddenly into a violent gale from a direction that no one expected. From due east the winds erupted, and the seas began to build. In short order the tug found herself wallowing in mountainous waves of ice water and completely overburdened by her extraordinarily long tail of barges. A single steamer would labor with a string of six loaded barges in the calm seas of a midsummer's day. Setting out with such a tow in the autumn sailing season was foolhardy at best. Nearly as soon as the winds came up the string of lumber vessels ceased its forward progress and struggled just to keep a heading into the wind. Waves began to climb aboard Captain McCauley's *Table Rock* and pluck at her deck cargo, while Captain Green's *Lincoln* butted her scow chin against the combers. This was real trouble for the little lakeboats, and it was rapidly getting worse.

The *Table Rock's* mate busied himself between attending to the deck load and attending to his spouse, who was in the schooner-barge's cabin nearly overwhelmed by the spectacle of Lake Huron gone mad. She had often heard her husband spin yarns of terrible nights on the lakes, but what was happening now was far beyond anything that she had ever imagined. There was no way for her to know that this tempest was also far beyond anything that her spouse had seen as well. Some who had sailed the lakes for more than four decades were heard to say that they had never before seen a storm, the likes of which Lake Huron had created that night. Outside of the cabin windows of the *Table Rock*, the lake's surface boiled up in heaving gray mounds that seemed as tall as the tops of the masts. The roaring wind ripped the water from the waves and cast it against the cabin in hissing lashes as the boat tossed. Water found every crack and doorjamb and came pouring in in frightening quantities. Outside, the commands of the captain and shouts of response from the crew were muffled by the roaring of the wind in the rigging and the foreboding groans of the hull timbers. The feeling of helplessness experienced by the guest aboard the *Table*

Rock must have been nearly as great as that of her fear. She was a guest in this gale, and Lake Huron was showing no signs of hospitality.

This freakish storm sent the normal driving rain, but it was the wind that was unusual. It blasted from due east with incredible strength. Sails were blasted into rags, and the most powerful of steam engines were quickly outmatched. A thick cloud cover blotted out the sky and everyone on the lake found themselves isolated in the terrible darkness. Normally this time of the year brings storms from directions other than due east. This storm, however, sprang up from the east and seemed to simply explode across the entire lake at the same moment. The whole ordeal was cooked up by a cyclonic storm that formed in Missouri, and whose center passed well south of the lakes region. Normally in the autumn, such systems take a far more northerly track and carry an east-west slope that sends winds angling from the northern quarters of the compass. This storm, however, while skirting to the south, gave its full counterclockwise circulation to Lake Huron, and that meant wind from due east with velocities over 50 miles per hour. Apparently, following directly behind this storm, a second and somewhat weaker storm center developed, which rode up behind the first storm and shifted the winds to out of the south-southwest. This was a very odd and nasty system in a time when nationwide weather services were less than two years old.

A long string of barges is easy prey for any type of storm on the lakes, but the one that swept the *Lincoln* and *Table Rock* and their compatriots that Saturday night was so violent that it took only a short time before the towlines connecting them gave up. There was no sound of the parting of the towlines, the gale effectively masked that. When the hulls of the schooner-barges fell off into the trough of the billowing seas and rolled as if to go completely over, all of their crew knew exactly what had happened. Swinging insanely, the masts of the *Table Rock* looked like they would touch the tops of the waves and her deck load began to cascade into the lake. With the sliding and shifting lumber, pieces of the boat began to go over the side as well. All that those aboard could do was to keep from being tossed overboard with each roll. The waves now began to explode over the hull and swirl about the deck seeking to take the vessel and her crew to their doom. It appeared to Captain McCauley that his boat was surely going to come apart at the next moment right beneath his feet. There were nearly 40 miles for the boat to be blown before it would reach the Michigan shore, and McCauley was certain that the lake would claim them all long before the ship could be flung ashore. Aboard the *Lincoln*, it is a sure bet that Captain Green was now having regrets over that big load his little boat had aboard. Like the *Table Rock*, the *Lincoln* was also taking a considerable beating.

Downbound from Mackinaw City, the sidewheel passenger steamer *Marine City* was headed for Bay City with a load of night patrons. The ride

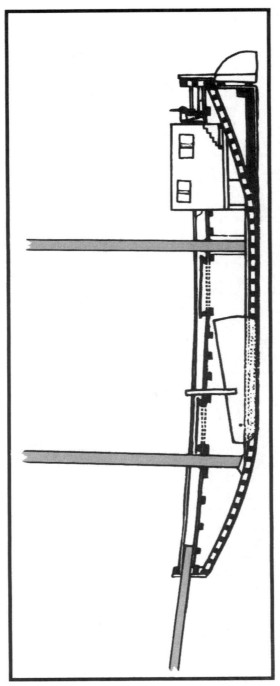

A profile view of a scow-schooner similar to the Abraham Lincoln. (Author's Adaptation)

that Lake Huron was giving the *Marine City's* folks was hardly fit for any kind of sleeping, and most of the passengers were gathered together in a semi-frightened pajama party-like group. By four o'clock Sunday morning, the steamer's master found that seeking shelter was not an option, rather it was pure survival. False Presque Isle was the nearest refuge, and the hook of land that made up the port would offer a perfect lee against the gale. The only problem was that the passage inbound would mean turning the sidewheeler's beam to the sea trough. It was risky, but it was the best bet to keep the vessel afloat. After several attempts, however, it was clear that the effort would only put the boat on the bottom. The wind and waves on her beam were simply too strong. Another shelter would have to be found, and the only choice was Presque Isle. The problem was that the *Marine City* had drawn close into the channel by the time her captain decided to retreat. Maneuvering out of the approach to False Presque Isle would now require backing the boat. Between the loss of way and the time needed for the engineer to shift into reverse, the storm got a hold on the sidewheeler. Her big paddlewheels thumped hard, but she continued to lose her struggle with the storm. Drifting at what her master estimated to be about six miles per hour, the steamer would be on the rocks in minutes. Some of her crew gathered lifebelts figuring on soon being in the water. When the boat was within two boat lengths of the shallows her rudder regained its effectiveness and her stern finally started to swing. Slowly, the *Marine City* put her heels to the wind and pulled herself from danger. Heading north-northwest, the steamer made for Presque Isle harbor some eight miles up the coast. Once again she turned and headed for shelter, and once again the lake set her to rolling insanely. This time the boat's engineer bottled her steam and worked her safety cutoff valves by hand as the boat began drifting. It was a clever tactic and it probably saved the boat. The *Marine City* hissed her way onto sheltered waters and her captain breathed a silent sigh of relief.

Lake Huron was robbed of the 64 passengers and the crew of the *Marine City*, and the boat settled quietly into the protected harbor of Presque Isle. Soon the boat's syphons were working full time expelling streams of the water that had found its way into the hull while dishwear, ashtrays, spittoons, and every other loose item aboard, was located by the crew and restowed. The storm had given the boat quite a tossing, and even her crewmembers had been rattled by the events. In an effort to calm the shaken passengers, the cabin crew decided to hold an informal presidential straw vote of all of the boat's passengers. At this point any such diversion would be a welcome event. While the wind screamed through every wire outside, the mock election took place in the snug confines of the *Marine City's* quarters. The vote tally, as would be expected in 1872, was divided into the men's vote and the lady's vote. Of the men, 37 voted for Grant and 18 for Greeley. Of the ladies, eight voted for Grant and only one voted for

Greeley. As the purser loudly proclaimed the results, there were some cheers and belly laughs toward the lopsided ladies vote. Just what the ladies felt about the election mattered little at the time, because females were not allowed to vote! In fact, ladies would not be granted their right to vote until 1920, forty-eight years after the *Marine City's* straw vote. So, as the mood aboard the *Marine City* started to lighten, the ladies could only wish for the same privilege, responsibility, and patriotic duty so many of us today take for granted.

There is no record as to how long the *Table Rock* drifted that storm-raked night, or exactly when she broke loose from the tow. What is known is that at six o'clock on Sunday morning, the 162-foot steamer *City Of Sandusky* departed her Tawas dock. In command was the heroic master of vessels, Captain Stewart. Besides being one of the well-known "heavy weather" skippers, Stewart had a reputation as a keeper of the valor. Often he was found dashing to the rescue of his fellow mariners, both ashore and on the seas, no matter what their dilemma. Using his normal disregard for the foul weather, Stewart ordered the lines of the *City Of Sandusky* cast off and the hefty side-wheeler departed Tawas on schedule, and churned right into the teeth of the gale. No sooner had the boat cleared the point than Stewart became aware that the winds were far beyond what he had expected. The seas rolled like towering hills of watery doom and it was clear that there was no way that he could turn his boat on an Alpena course. The act of turning any vessel into the trough of the seas resulted in violent rolling, but turning a sidewheeler into the trough was near to suicide. With a paddlewheel on each side of the boat providing the only source of propulsion, the rolling action of the boat causes one wheel to come out of the water as each roll occurs. When one wheel is out of the water and one in, the boat's power is effectively cut in half and the odds are that she will never pull out of the sea trough. Stewart had gotten into a situation where he would have to steam nearly due east until either the winds decided to shift or Canada got in his way.

After heading into the storm for a protracted distance, Stewart and the *City Of Sandusky* stumbled upon the wallowing barge *Table Rock*. Now completely waterlogged, the beleaguered schooner-barge was holding together only through the hand of providence. The lumber trapped beneath her crumbling deck was all that kept the boat from a death plunge to the bottom of Lake Huron. One of the barge's people appeared to have taken refuge up in the rigging, and two others appeared to be seeking relief atop what remained of the boat's deck load of lumber. It took only a glance for Stewart to decide that he had to rescue those poor souls on that beaten schooner-barge. Turning toward the *Table Rock*, the *City Of Sandusky* put her beam to the seas and was almost immediately swamped. Rolling back from the initial assault the steamer lurched and then broached again. This time the wave swept the boat's deck in a violent manner as if to cause her to founder right on the spot. A moment later the boat rolled heavily again and repeated her brutal throws. Before the *City Of Sandusky* could come anywhere close to the *Table Rock*, it became clear that if the steamer persisted in the rescue attempt, Lake Huron would take her vengeance out on the sidewheeler before finishing the schooner-barge. The infuriated lake gave Stewart no choice other than to put his bow into the wind and run for his life. The *Table Rock* was left to find her own fate.

No sooner had Captain Stewart been forced to turn away from the *Table Rock* than another floundering schooner-barge came into view. It was the *Lincoln* and it seemed to be in about the same condition as the *Table Rock*. Completely waterlogged with her decks submerged in every sea, the vessel appeared about ready to go to the bottom. All that remained clear of the seas were the boat's masts. The *Lincoln's* crew had taken refuge in the rigging in a desperate attempt to stay out of the lake. What Captain Stewart could not surmise from his position aboard the *City Of Sandusky* was that the *Lincoln* was in far worse shape than the *Table Rock*. The *Lincoln* had sprung her butts and started leaking almost as soon as the seas came up—long before the towline to the *Zouave* had parted. Proof of this was her current position which was considerably upwind of the *Table Rock*. The *Lincoln* had been the last barge in the *Zouave's* tow, but when the lines parted, the schooner-barge was so waterlogged that her companions, *Table Rock* and *Ontario* were easily carried by the wind right past her toward the west. Even now, as the *City Of Sandusky* steamed away into the wind, the *Table Rock* and the *Ontario* were being rapidly drawn away from the *Lincoln*. Truly, each vessel was on its own and Lake Huron wanted to keep it that way.

At Fish Point, now known as Au Sable Point and located about seven miles north of Tawas Point, the schooner *Summit* had been driven aground at five o'clock Sunday morning. This boat had the honor of being the first of a small fleet to be cast upon the Michigan shore by the storm. She was deeply laden with ore from Lake Superior and found the bottom a fair distance from the beach in a location that was only described as "three miles off Fish Point." Speculating, we could say that the wreck went ashore near what is today known as Avalon Beach. The schooner's yawl had been carried away and it was obvious to those aboard that the boat was about to break up. Her crew were left with only one option, and that was to attempt a swim for the beach. When Captain Webb and his crew elected to swim for it, the boat's female cook insisted that she was unable to undertake such a venture. No matter how they tried, the men could not persuade the terrified cook, Mary Goscaw, to make the swim. With time running out, the mariners struck a deal with the reluctant lady. They would make the swim and as soon as they reached shore, they would procure a boat and come back for her. She agreed. Lashing their cook to the rigging for her own safety, the *Summit's* crew struck out in their swim for survival. Of the seven who went over the schooner's rail, six managed to reach shore alive and exhausted. One of the crew, 18-year-old Charles Hazelburg who had just come to the lakes from saltwater sailing, drowned in his attempt to reach land. His strength sapped by the bitter cold water, Hazelburg was simply overcome. By the time those who did make the beach managed to muster assistance to go out to rescue Mary, the *Summit* had gone to pieces and Lake Huron had claimed the luckless lady of the lakes.

Ten miles from the *Summit's* death, the schooner *White Squall* was thrown against the schooner *Libbie Nau* which was in the same tow on the open lake. Apparently the collision was enough to punch a mortal hole in the *White Squall* because she quickly began sinking. Manning the lifeboat, her crew knew that they were not far from the Michigan coast, and with a bit of hard pulling they may just be able to make land. Lake Huron, however, had other ideas. Into the yawlboat went William Swasman, G. Scabranch, Harry Miller, Frank Root, William Nelson, First Mate John Trawlson, Captain David J. Stinson, and a Swedish crewman known only as "John." As soon as the lifeboat was launched the churning seas flipped it over and chewed on its occupants. Of the eight mariners who were aboard the yawl, only Frank Root managed to regain the lifeboat. No sooner had Root dragged himself back aboard than the lake reached out and dumped the yawl again. This time Root grabbed hold on one of the thin lines called a "painter," used to secure the yawl in fair weather. Hand-over-hand he pulled at the painter until he succeeded in tumbling back into the half-submerged lifeboat. Breathless and choking from having swallowed more of Lake Huron than most drowned men, Root took a moment to recover. All around him the lake heaved in giant gray seas as his break was suddenly shattered and the lifeboat was again capsized. Once more he found himself in a tug of war with the mighty lake. Pulling at the painter in the stinging cold water, Root knew that Huron wanted to swallow him. By the time the *White Squall's* lifeboat washed ashore, the shipwrecked mariner was simply holding on to the painter and dragging along behind. In all, the lake had tossed him from the lifeboat eight times, but he never let go, and he alone survived the wreck of the schooner-barge *White Squall*.

Next, Lake Huron used the same sandy hook of land—that would in the future be the strolling paradise of Tawas vacationers—as its death dagger to end the existence of the *Table Rock*. Alerted by the sight of a nearly sunken schooner blowing toward them, crowds of local residents gathered on the wave-beaten beach of Tawas Point as Lake Huron delivered the *Table Rock*. According to the records at the lighthouse, the wreck hit the beach at "8 a.m.," but this should be considered as only the lightkeeper's approximation of the actual time. Wounded, battered, and disabled lakeboats had been drifting into the Tawas area since early

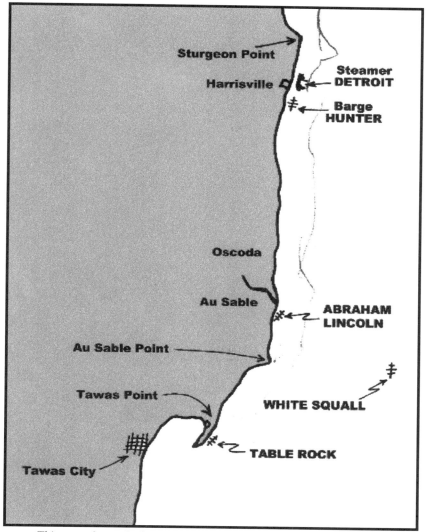

This map shows the locations of the victims of the Table Rock storm.

Saturday night, and most of the local residents had come out in the hopes of not only giving assistance, but also of not missing any of the action. While the crashing surf provided a background, the ill-fated schooner-barge slammed into the shallows and began to crumple like an eggshell. Just to complicate the scene, the winds were now rapidly shifting to the southwest, and soon threatened to blow the wreckage back out onto the lake. She was too far out for those ashore to attempt to make a rescue

215

through the surf, and the lifesaving service would not exist until four years into the future. It was certain that all aboard the *Table Rock* would be taken by the lake, and those ashore could do nothing more than watch helplessly.

From the rail of the steamer *Colin Campbell*, which was safely anchored in Tawas Bay, a handful of courageous mariners set out to the rescue in the predawn darkness of that awful Sunday morning. Lowering the steamer's yawl and manning its oars, they struck out toward the wreck. The pull must have been harrowing. With the winds shifting, the waves were not only crashing around the point, but were now building on the bay itself. One wrong breaker would put them all in the water, and Lake Huron would have them along with the crew of the *Table Rock*. As the amateur lifesavers neared the *Table Rock*, it was clear that it was breaking up rapidly. A series of breaking waves had jarred lose the deckhouse with Captain McCauley, one of the sailors, and the mate and his wife on the roof. The structure floated from the ship's shattered hull and was carried away onto the lake, vanishing into the darkness of the deadly storm.

The men of the *Campbell* pulled onward toward the disintegrating *Table Rock*. A lone crewman remained aboard, struggling to stay alive. The *Campbell's* men skillfully maneuvered their yawl to the wreck and plucked the castaway from certain death. Then, turning their yawl toward Tawas Point, the rescuers pulled toward the beach. Indeed, it was a magnificent display as they overcame the breaking surf, and with the help of a crowd of local residents, landed the tiny boat. Lake Huron had been robbed of another life in her tantrum. His name was not recorded, but surely he was the most grateful visitor who ever set foot on the sands of Tawas Point. Lake Huron spent the rest of the night beating the *Table Rock* into the shifting sand of the point, and setting her sights on other vessels.

A mile and a half below the Au Sable River, the *Abraham Lincoln* came into the shallows and began to rapidly break up. When the wind shifted from out of the south, southeast, the *Lincoln* had been caught a distance out in the lake. As a result of her early waterlogging and slower drift, the *Lincoln* was now carried up the coast and dumped on the beach nearly 10 miles north of the wrecked *Table Rock*. Her deckload of lath had long ago been washed away, and now the luckless schooner began to spill her below-decks load as well. Ashore, Au Sable residents Alex Price, Charles Ceering, Alexander Waddington, James Forrest and Alex Young saw the boat coming and knew in a heartbeat that she was doomed. As quickly as they could, the five men commandeered a local yawlboat and placed it on a cart. Hustling to the very same beach where, 125 years later, Mildred would look from her son-in-law's beach house and ponder over the *Lincoln's* giant rudder washing up in the sand, the five men risked their own lives by launching the yawl and heading to the rescue. Rowing through the surf-tossed mass of lath that was spilling from the *Lincoln*, the local boys burst the breaking waves and pulled to the wreck. They rescued all five of the schooner's crew and rowed them safely to the beach as the scow-schooner broke up in the surf. It is said that Captain Green had "gone crazy" from the cold and the gale. A rough translation of this 1872 vernacular is that the man was simply chilled senseless by the cold vengeance of Lake Huron and the shock of the loss of his command. For the residents of Au Sable, it was a heroic rescue that would be the talk of the town for years to come.

Like the sands of Tawas Point, the sands of time were quick to cover the scars of that fearful gale that exploded in the last days of September, 1872. One by one, the bodies given up by Lake Huron were properly attended to. Some were sent home to sorrowing kin, but most were put in graves near where they were found. Lake Huron kept Captain McCauley of the *Table Rock* until December 10, 1872, when his body was deposited on the beach near Tawas. The remains of the good captain were taken to Tawas and given proper care. He was, as far as research can tell, the last of the storm's human victims to be returned by Lake Huron. Horace Greeley ended up losing the 1872 election to U.S. Grant and in fact did not win a single electoral vote. Captain Stewart continued to keep the valor for many years and shows up often in the adventures of the mariners on Lake Huron.

All of the wrecks of the September, 1872 gale seemed to have either been covered by shifting sands or remain in the depths, forgotten. Lake Huron, however, is not completely stingy with her victims. In that sweltering summer of 1996, the lake, which contains one third of all of the shipwrecks of the freshwater seas, gave back pieces of the *Abraham Lincoln* and Mildred found them. Normally, in writing a story such as this, we can not say precisely that such a thing as a stray piece of a shipwreck belongs to a specific vessel unless a nameplate or other identifying marking is found. But, unlike other pieces of lost wooden boats, the rudders tend to stay close to the wreck site, and the location of the *Lincoln's* wreck is very specifically listed in a number of sources as being almost exactly where Mildred's rudder was washed up. Additionally, there are no records of any other significant wreck within this area. There is very little doubt that this massive rudder belongs to the scow-schooner *Abraham Lincoln*, and is a significant piece of history—considering that little is known about the actual design of scow-schooners on the Great Lakes. It is also a mute testament to the fury of Lake Huron and the valor of the ordinary citizens on that dreadful night in 1872.

There is one remaining example of a scow-schooner that is currently in the registry, and is well-preserved and available to the public. Remarkably, it has nearly the same dimensions as those of the *Lincoln*. Unfortunately, the scow-schooner *Alma* is far from the Great Lakes and is afloat in San Francisco Bay. Walking her decks you can get the scale of the *Lincoln* and a feel for the dilemma of her people as Lake Huron tossed her.

No one knows what other relics Lake Huron may decide to cast upon its beaches, and perhaps the rest of the *Lincoln* will turn up. Then again, maybe the lake will decide to keep its wrecks from the 1872 storm covered up forever, leaving us with only the *Lincoln's* rudder and centerboard lift to view. If, however, the reader should happen to be camped at the state park on Tawas Point, the city campground in East Tawas, vacationing on the Huron shore, or staying at the Nor' East Shore Resort—or even just cruising past enroute to points north—it would be well worth while to venture out to Tawas Point and along the nature trail or wade along the sandy beaches. Always keep in mind that the sands upon which you walk are where terrified mariners perished, brave sailors and residents risked their lives, and broken vessels as well as broken bodies came ashore. It is possible that the vacation sands beneath the blankets of the summer sunbathers hide the bones of the *Table Rock*, or *Abraham Lincoln,* and the discovery of their forgotten shipwrecks is as close as the scoop of a child's sand shovel. Indeed, Tawas Point's beach and the beach near the Au Sable, like most of the Great Lake's beaches, are vacation places with thrilling pasts, and a closer look will find it. Go there and read this story once again, and be on the lookout for that shattered oak hull timber that is half-buried in the sand. Perhaps the tale you have just read is its story.

GIVE WAY!

Beach drills had just been completed in the bitter spring weather as Thursday, April 15, 1880, drew to a close at the Ottawa Point Lifesaving Station near Tawas City, Michigan. The winds across Lake Huron were screaming from the northeast, having just shifted from due west as the surfmen stowed the equipment used in the day's drill. Some folks may say that autumn is the worst season for sailing the lakes, and statistically that would be true, but the spring season is often just as wild. With that in mind, Keeper Freeman Chute was itching to get the evening's beach patrol started as soon as possible. With the sudden shift in wind, his mariner's experience told him that the area was in for a real dandy of a spring gale, and he wanted the patrol out early if feasible. What Keeper Chute and his crew did not know, was that the sudden shift in wind which occurred just after the noonhour was, at that moment, sending them in a test of valor toward a distant beach. Within the next day they would be on the receiving end of the product of Lake Huron's vengeance. It was the moment in history for which they had trained and drilled, and that Chute had prepared for since 1877. It was a moment when fate and the lakes vengeance came together to test the valor of those who would tempt both.

On July 1, 1877, Freeman Chute took the position of keeper of the Ottawa Point Lifesaving Station. In this change of command he was taking over from Keeper George Haskin, who had opened the station the previous season. Although Ottawa Point would later be renamed Tawas Point after the twin cities of Tawas and East Tawas that are established at its base, to those who live, work and regularly visit the area, it is simply known as "the Point." To Captain Chute, what the point was called mattered very little. What was important was his new responsibility as a station-keeper at that place in the newly organized United States Life Saving Service. At age 35, Chute had spent most of his life sailing for the Great Lakes maritime industry, and was very familiar with the treachery of the lakes. He knew too well that many luckless mariners had died in shipwrecks within reach of land, but there was no means by which rescue could be performed. This new lifesaving service was intended to be the answer, and Chute was given the honor of a station command. The intention was that only the bravest and most able mariners would be selected to become a part of the service, and that selection meant becoming an instant legend in the local community. For Captain Chute, this appeared to be the apex of his career. A resident of Bay City, Michigan, he had started his maritime career as a cook aboard assorted lake schooners. While moving from one vessel to the next, he had also moved up the chain of authority from cook to command. The 1870 season found him working the river steamboats between Saginaw and Bay City, Michigan, where he stayed until the offer of keeper of the Ottawa Point station came up. Without hesitation he leaped at that opportunity and headed up north to the point.

Arriving at the station, newly-commissioned Keeper Chute found that the burdens of his command would indeed be heavy. The lumber industry was in its boom times and vessel traffic was extremely heavy in the Tawas area. The point, itself, was the division of the contrast between a calm but vessel-crowded Tawas Bay, and the wild and heavily traveled expanse of Lake Huron. His station was constructed on the outside of the point, and it faced southeast across Saginaw Bay. Within the station was a spanking new 25-foot surf boat along with every tool needed in the operations of lifesaving, from anchors and augers to a speaking trumpet. Every item of equipment was under the keeper's direct accountability, and any damage or loss would be his to explain to the district superintendent. Then there were the eight brave surfmen, each of whom had sworn to risk his life to save mariners in peril. Ranked by number, the surfmen were also the responsibility of the keeper, who was expected to train them and then maintain their skills at an edge so fine that they could easily do battle with the lake and return in victory. Behind all of these tangible responsibilities rested a much larger latent responsibility. By taking charge of the only lifesaving station in the area, Keeper Chute was, in effect, taking responsibility for the safety of every vessel, passenger, and mariner on the whole of Saginaw Bay. In 1877, this was one of the most heavily navigated areas on the Great Lakes, there always seemed to be a vessel on the horizon. Every type of lakeboat, from the smallest pleasure sloops to the giant side-wheeled steamboats crammed with hundreds of passengers, sailed these waters. All would be counting on Chute and his crew should the worst happen. Such awesome responsibility was so far beyond that of wheeling a steamer up and down the Saginaw River that, to Freeman Chute, it must have been unimaginable. As he stood looking across the hypnotic blue of Lake Huron, and feeling the gravity of his command,

The original 1876 Ottawa Point Life Saving Station still stands as of this writing. Notice the "Coastguardville" signs. (Author's Photo)

questions must have echoed in his mind—"When will the time come? Will I be up to the challenge? Will my crew be ready?" Indeed, the duty of station keeper would require a constant watch on everything and everyone without a single blink.

Keeper Chute ran straight away into the birth pains of the Life Saving Service on the Great Lakes. Every soul in the service was new, and almost no one had much practical experience with any of the equipment. The station at Ottawa Point had been through one previous rescue on November 14, 1876, when the 305-ton schooner *William Home* went ashore, and nine of her crew were rescued by the Tawas lifesavers. For Chute, this whole business of lifesaving was completely new. Complex operations, such as the firing of the Lyle gun and the launching of the projectile and line to a distant mast, along with the deployment of the breeches buoy, were incredibly elaborate and required great skill and instinct. A new keeper such as Chute had no experience with such gear, yet it was his sole responsibility to operate the equipment. Operations as simple as the launching of the surf boat held the potential for disaster if improperly performed in an emergency, and embarrassment if clumsily performed in practice. As if to add to the pressure of the establishment of the new Life Saving Service, every move the station crews made was under the scrutiny of the local residents. Rumors and whispers as to the doings of the station were a constant source of gossip and cheap entertainment on the mainland. Word of any bungling on the part of the lifesavers would spread like a wildfire among the populace, and faith in their capabilities would be damaged. In these first days of the service, there were plenty of critics who were just waiting for the opportunity to lash out at the lifesavers with little regard to circumstance. It was also Keeper Chute's job not to provide those critics with their needed ammunition.

Perhaps it was most important that the surfmen and their new keeper at least look like they knew what they were doing. For that reason, the service provided a detailed manual of the step-by-step operation of each piece of equipment. These instructions were amended and clarified in 1878, and improvements in efficiency were always sought. From it, Chute drilled his surfmen in the precise movements and use of their tools. The surfmen all were assigned a number, from one through eight, and each had that number sewn onto their uniform's left sleeve. These numbers ranked each surfman. In any rescue, each man had specified position and action which was laid out in accordance with his number in the drill manual. The only hope for the new keeper was to drill his surfmen over and over until the routine reached perfection. A schedule of training was also specified in the manuals and was followed to the letter at each station. Mondays were used for practice with the beach apparatus, including the firing of the Lyle gun and the rigging of the breeches buoy. This same drill was repeated on

Another view of the Ottawa Point Life Saving Station. (Author's Photo)

Thursdays, but after the first month of station operation for a given season, the Monday beach drill could be eliminated and that day used for other activity as needed. Tuesday was the day to practice launching the surf boat, an operation that included capsizing the boat and then righting it again as soon as possible. Wednesday, the crew worked with the *International Code of Signals* book—as if the average Great Lakes mariner had any idea as to how to read them. Thursday was again beach apparatus day, and Friday was the day to practice the form of artificial respiration called "Method for Restoring the Apparently Drown." No drill was scheduled for the weekend as Saturday was the day for groundskeeping and housekeeping, and Sunday was left open. The station drills were held in all kinds of weather, from April to December.

There is little doubt that Keeper Chute used his open Mondays for doubling up on his drills, especially when it came to the use of the beach equipment and the surf boat. When the keeper first took command, there were only two months before the autumn storm season would be upon him, and he had better become proficient at firing that Lyle gun and directing that surf boat. He had no idea how the first lives would be saved by his station, but it would likely be soon and he must be prepared. Oddly, despite all of the intense drill and with all of the complex equipment, the first lives saved under Chute's command would occur under very ordinary circumstances. None of the equipment would be used and it would be accomplished without the help of a single member of the keeper's crew!

It was nearly a five-mile walk from the lifesaving station to East Tawas, and most of that distance was through heavily wooded and swampy wilderness along roughly defined trails. For that reason, the easiest way to get from the station to town was to launch the station's small sailboat and navigate around the point and across Tawas Bay. When it was time to fetch supplies, the keeper normally took on that task, thus leaving the station in charge of the number one surfman. So on, Tuesday, August 14, 1877, Keeper Chute gave charge to his number one man and launched the sailboat shortly after sunrise. He would head into East Tawas, pick up the needed supplies, and upon his return the rest of the station crew would commence the day's boat drill. Crossing Tawas Bay was no easy matter. The place was crowded with schooners, steamers, tugs, barges and lumber rafts, plus a number of skiffs and sailboats mariners were using to transport themselves around the area. Chute made good progress, however, and once in town went straight to his errands. By half past nine o'clock that morning he had loaded the boat and was headed back to the station. The wind had come up fairly strong, and did well to fill his sail as he tillered his boat through the chop of the bay. Just what caught the keeper's attention is not known, but glancing leeward of his position he happened to see another small sailboat with two men aboard suddenly capsize throwing the occupants into the bay. The two men were the mate and engineer from the tug *Burnside*, and were shuttling between the tug and the shore when the wind outmatched them. Without a moment's hesitation, Chute turned his boat and headed for the two men. Soon he was at their aid and they switched from clinging to their overturned boat to climbing aboard Chute's boat. It was 10:30 a.m. on August 14, 1877, and the first official act of lifesaving under Chute's command had been accomplished, by him alone, and almost as an act of courtesy rather than of bravery. Returning to the station, all of the surfmen—with the exception of the man standing watch atop the station—gathered around as Chute wrote the first report of lives saved under his command, although this was not the station's first action. At the time it was significant. Some of the surfmen probably reminisced about the rescue of the schooner *Home*, while others looked ahead to that next big rescue and wondered when it would happen.

As fate would have it, the sailboat rescue of the two tugmen was the only official action for Chute's station in the 1877 season. The big disaster he had expected, and likely felt so unprepared for, did not occur that year.

In fact, the whole of the season of 1878 passed with no major action. This does not mean that things were relaxed at the lifesaving station. Aside from the daily drills, there were the numerous surprise inspections by the superintendent, the nightly beach patrols and the all-day watches on the lake. Chute kept his crew's attention focused on the lake as if a giant passenger vessel was about to plow in and wreck at any moment. That way the storm-warriors would always be ready. When a season passed quietly, such as 1878, he knew that the station had done its job despite the lack of disaster. For Keeper Chute, like every other station keeper, the pressure was enormous. He never really knew when the next inspection would occur, and every detail of the station was his obligation. Additionally, political pressures were high in this era, and nearly every station keeper had to deal with them as well. Although it was not supposed to happen, there was always the pressure to adopt a favored local fellow into the service. Such a crew member rarely was productive. To make matters worse, his command remained untried and he knew that the only test of his mettle would come with the station's next shipwreck. It is likely that the question of Chute's actual ability hung over him, and seemed to grow on his soul. The weight of the job of station keeper was very heavy and grew greater with each passing day.

Still, the daily schedule of drills was maintained and Keeper Chute felt that his surfmen were as sharp as he could make them. Each time that the boat drill was performed the crew would launch her and ready their oars.

"Give way!" would come the keeper's command, and with that the crew would begin to pull at their oars as if a life depended on their efforts.

Every Tuesday—in rain, wind, snow or blistering heat—the crew would take their positions for the boat drill until the boat became like another member of the crew. Each surfman would pick up his oar, which had the letters "USLSS" engraved in its wood, and then wait for the keeper's order.

"Give way!" Keeper Chute would bellow the familiar cue and each surfman would use the oar like an extension of his body. That was the order, the call to arms, the signal to do battle with the lake over the life of someone that you had never met. For the storm-warriors it was a call to do their duty, perhaps at the expense of their own life.

By the opening of the 1879 season, Keeper Chute must have been wondering if there would ever be a significant rescue in his locality. Then on April 16, 1879, while returning from East Tawas in the station's supply boat, Chute again spotted a capsized sailboat. This time a man and his wife and child were thrashing around in the water. Once again Chute sailed to the rescue, plucking the lady and child from the water. The man elected to remain with his boat or try to bail her out while Chute shuttled the other family members to the nearby lighthouse. He later returned to the swamped boat and helped the man bring her in to safety. Doubtless there was considerable ribbing from the surfmen when the keeper reached the station. After all, why were they doing all of the drills if the keeper was going to do all of the lifesaving?

Later that season there came a summer night that everyone at the station thought was the one they had been waiting for. The beach patrol had just changed watch. The sunset-to-midnight patrol returned to the Ottawa Point Station and the midnight-to-four o'clock patrol took the lantern and struck out along the shore. It was a blustery summer darkness that folded over the first hours of Monday, June 9, 1879, but at least the conditions for conducting the patrol were much more pleasant than they would be in April or November. These all-night beach patrols were considered one of the most important duties of the lifesavers, and they were ordered to be conducted in all weather conditions without fail. As the south patrolman trudged off toward the end of the point, it is doubtless that he was thankful for the warmth of a summer night—blustery winds and all. With the roar of the surf in his ears, the surfman seemed locked in his solitude as he stepped along the sand and driftwood. Ahead in the blackness, the amber lights of a small steamer appeared as he rounded the bend in Tawas Point. Then it struck him that the lights seemed out of place; in fact, they were far too close to the lighthouse. Instinctively, the surfman quickened his pace. For a moment he stopped just to get a clear vision of the lights. They were rolling sharply and it was clear that something was very wrong. Now he broke into a dead run until he was as close to the lights as the shore would allow. There it was, a vessel in distress, a steamer that had run onto the shoal at the end of the point! There is no record of the use of a Coston signal or of any other communication between the lifesaver and the boat, but it is likely that some form of signals was exchanged. Without taking time to catch his breath, the surfman turned and ran as fast as he could toward the station.

The station's late night's silence was shattered as the surfman came running back and started excitedly ringing the alarm bell. Leaping from their bunks the lifesavers were more than ready to dash to the rescue. The patrolman explained between breaths that he had discovered a steamer on the shoal. An atmosphere similar to a coiled spring hung for a moment around the station crew, and it was then that Keeper Chute demonstrated his mettle. He halted the eagerness of the moment and pressed the patrolman for details of where and how the boat was fetched up. Then he weighed the weather conditions and made a cool-headed decision. Rather than launching the station surf boat and his entire crew toward the stranded boat, Chute elected to take a more conservative course of action. He ordered some of his crew to take the station supply boat and go to the steamer to determine her condition, while he stood by ready to launch the surf boat if needed. The crew of the supply boat went to the stranded steamer and found that she was the tugboat *Annie Moiles*. While towing a raft of logs from AuSable to Tawas she had run onto the reef and, although pounding heavily, was not in a life-threatening condition. The lifesavers took the tug's mate aboard the supply boat and sailed him into Tawas

226

A Great Lakes gloom hangs over the Tawas Point Light. It is one of few that lighthouse fans can enter and climb. (Author's Photo)

where he could charter a tug. Later the crew of the Ottawa Point Station aided the mariners in freeing the *Moiles* and saving her raft. Officially, the seven mariners aboard the tug were counted as "persons saved," although Keeper Chute probably felt that the effort was somewhat minimal. In a historical perspective, however, the event said a lot about Chute's ability.

Later in the summer of 1879, the Ottawa Point crew got the chance to launch their surf boat. On August 28th, they launched and went to the assistance of the tug *N.P. Sprague* which was sounding a distress signal with her whistle. As it turned out, the tug was simply having trouble with her raft of logs and needed assistance. The lifesavers went into Tawas and arranged for a tug. Keeper Chute must have been just a bit miffed. After all, his crew was there to save lives, not shuttle messages as a tug service. But, the tug's captain had elected to use a distress signal to get the station crew to come out, and they had to respond appropriately. Launching the surf boat with a full crew seemed a waste under such circumstances. This event, however, was a foreshadowing of a problem that annoys the Coast Guard in modern times. Boaters often radio in distress calls when the problem is as small as being out of gas. Still, Chute must have felt that the big wreck—and his day of judgment—was surely coming.

On October 23rd of that same year, Keeper Chute sailed to the rescue once again using the station's supply boat, but this time there may have been a significant twist in the save. Having sailed the supply boat to the end of the point, he was on the beach, some distance from the station, enjoying a bit of late autumn solitude. The all-weather toil of the service, the constant pressure, and unending responsibilities were beginning to take their toll on him. The load of his job had also started to affect his health, and the thoughts of leaving the service were beginning to enter his mind. No doubt the exceptionally low pay had also taken much of the luster out of the job. In the upcoming season, Keeper Chute would be paid $400 for the entire season. He could earn nearly twice that amount as a simple tug captain if he were to leave the service. As he pondered his future, he spotted a dismasted fishing schooner with two men aboard drifting swiftly out onto the open lake. Launching his supply boat, the keeper sailed out and took the helpless fishing boat in tow. Interestingly, the fishing boat was under the command of a Tawas man whose name is listed in the official records only as "Ocha." The Ocha family of Tawas produced two lifesavers, Albert and Frank, who both went up the ranks to the position of Keeper. Albert Ocha started as a surfman at the Ottawa Point Station in 1882. He went up the ranks at assorted stations to the grade of Keeper, resigned twice, and was reinstated both times, rising again to the keeper's position. He died while serving as the keeper of the Eagle Harbor Station, Michigan, on Lake Superior, in November of 1912 at age 49. The other Ocha brother, Frank, eventually became the keeper of the Ottawa Point Station in 1888. In October of 1896, after a visit to the family home in

Tawas, Keeper Frank Ocha simply vanished, leaving only his rowboat which remained tied to the commercial dock in Tawas, and his hat, which was found floating in the waters of Tawas Bay. No other trace was ever discovered, and to this day his end remains a mystery. We can not help but ponder if one of these two Ochas was aboard that rescued fishing boat and was thereby inspired to seek out a career in the Life Saving Service.

For the remainder of the 1879 season there were no additional recorded actions at the Ottawa Point Station, and the station closed quietly for the year on December 1st. By the first days of April, 1880, when Keeper Chute reopened the station for the upcoming season, the thoughts of leaving the service were probably heavy on his mind. Thus far, his tenure at the station had been one of constant readiness and command with very little action. The boys at Sturgeon Point, just 32 miles up the coast, had made a number of dramatic rescues so far, but Chute's crew seemed always ready—and never used. There were also problems in dealing with the surfmen themselves. It is difficult at best for any group of individuals to walk the beach all night, every night, in all weather, row out into the cold surf and roll their boat over once a week, plus stand watch in a tiny box atop the station all day, every day, and not have personnel problems. Every station had its troubles with drunkenness, sleeping on duty, and simple desertion. At a station which had not seen any significant action in three years, there can be little doubt that Chute had his share of problems. In short, the pay was low, the pressure was high and the rewards few. Although the job was steady, indeed, much of the glamour implied by the position back in 1877 had, by this time, worn off. Then came that gale-raked April afternoon and Keeper Chute's test of valor.

Heeling upbound from Kellys Island on Lake Erie, to the town of Frankfort, Michigan, over on the Lake Michigan coast, the 90-foot clipper-styled schooner *Criss Grover* was pounding her way when the wind shifted. She was the final test of valor that the Great Lakes would send for Keeper Chute. It would be the test of his command and the test of his life.

Some 50 miles above the Ottawa Point Station, off of South Point at the bottom of Thunder Bay, the little sailing boat was taking advantage of the west wind. Unlike many lake sailing vessels, which were of a schooner rig, the *Grover* had a square sail rigging on her three masts. Captain Jones, the *Grover's* master, had aboard a very sizable quantity of stone from the Kellys Island quarry. In fact, the *Grover*, which had a measured depth of her hold of nine feet, was drawing eight feet of water! Clearly not only was the boat loaded, but considering the season, she was well overloaded. Also aboard the little wind-grabber were First Mate Joseph Emmons, and Crewmen Mark Mahr, John Tabor, Leonard Robertson and Gilbert Wiles all of whom were from Lorain, Ohio. The only person aboard the boat not from Lorain was the female cook, Miss McNeil, who was from Detroit. The sudden shift of wind caught the *Grover* off guard, and before her crew could scramble in the rigging to trim and reef for the new wind, the blasts made rags of her canvas and sent her foremast overboard. In a wink the boat was broaching helpless in the seas, driven before a hefty wind. For just under nine hours, the *Grover* wallowed in the sea trough as she drifted the 40 miles to nearly the same spot where the scow-schooner *Abraham Lincoln* had wrecked eight years earlier.

It was just about nine o'clock on that stormy Thursday night when the *Criss Grover* slammed into the shallows 660 feet from where the remains of the *A. Lincoln* would be found 117 years later. The boat had fetched up nine miles north of the Ottawa Point Station. This was well out of range of the beach patrol, and the extension of Au Sable Point blocked the area from any visual cue. Thus, the night passed and there was not so much as a hint that the *Grover* was aground. At dawn on Friday, three of the *Grover's* crew launched her lifeboat and rowed into the village of Au Sable. Although there is no record who was in the boat, it is most likely that Mate Joseph Emmons led the landing party. The seas were heavy, but the three mariners had little trouble getting to the mainland. Marching in a drenched condition past Gram's dock toward town, one of the locals tossed a comment concerning their trip from the *Grover* to the mainland.

"There's a big sea on," was the retort from one of the soaked sailors.

Tramping around the village at six o'clock in the morning, the crewmen were seeking a tug to pull the *Grover* out of the shallows. Finding that no tugs were available in Au Sable, the crew had a telegraph message sent to Detroit to request a tow. With that done, the mariners headed back toward the *Grover* to await their requested tug. Arriving at the *Grover's* side the three crewmen went aboard and simply left the yawl, which doubled as the vessel's lifeboat, moored by its painter to the lakeboat's rail. This, it was thought, would be more convenient than hauling it back up on the davits. The crew would probably want to make a number of trips between the *Grover* and Au Sable, and hoisting and lowering the yawl repeatedly would be a pain. Hoisting it up would, however, protect it from high seas if the lake should get rough. Such thoughts were not on the minds of the crew as they secured the yawl's painter and headed into the warmth of the vessel's cabin.

Down at the Ottawa Point Lifesaving Station the morning chores were under way that same Friday morning when, at just after 10 o'clock, the windows shook. It was the kind of wind gust that gets your attention. Outside, the wind roared and snow squalls appeared in the distance. Out on the lake, the waves did not come up but appeared flattened by the sudden sweeping winds. Keeper Chute checked on the lookout atop the station, and told him to keep a sharp eye out. The lookout was having a hard enough time keeping himself from being blown out of the tower, let alone doubling his watch. This was the type of freak wind that can turn the point from a sandy extension of a lovely coast into a fang of destruction jutting into Lake Huron. The constant vigilance of the surfmen would have to be increased as much as possible just in case that big wreck should occur. What Chute and his surfmen did not know was that their long awaited "big wreck" had been taking place since about the time they had finished the previous afternoon's beach drills.

When the winds came blasting down across Lake Huron, they caught the *Criss Grover* in the worst possible position. She was stuck hard in the sand with a bellyful of stone, her foremast overboard and, worst of all, her only lifeboat dangling out in the open water. The first thing to be plucked from the vessel was the yawl. Almost as soon as the wind came up, the yawl was carried away. It would have been the first item the crew would have dashed to secure when the winds began gusting, but the yawl was carried away in spite of the crew. Odds are that they arrived on deck just in time to see their lifeboat being carried down the coast by the wind. Next, the seas began to build and within minutes they were exploding against the side of the *Grover*. The grounded lakeboat had very little freeboard, and each wave was soon sweeping over the rail and washing across the deck, waist-deep. Ropes, ladders, tarps, buckets—and everything else not nailed down—were swirled up as frigid shipwreck debris and lodged between the boat's rails. In less than an hour it was clear from shore that the *Grover* was done for.

A huge crowd consisting of nearly every resident of the village of Au Sable gathered on Mildred's future beach and watched as the seas burst across the stranded schooner. Soon the crew were seen coming on deck. A moment later they all climbed into the *Grover's* standing rigging and atop her deckhouse to escape the bitter water. Shouts of encouragement were made from the crowd on the beach, but not a word got to the vessel. It was later said that "You could not make a man ten feet to windward of where you stood hear the sound of your voice, save in the momentary lulls of the storm."

Shortly before noon, it seemed apparent that the people of the *Grover* were likely to perish in front of the eyes of the whole town. Something had to be done to save them or there would soon be bodies washing onto the beach. Each sea that exploded over the wreck caused a collective gasp from the crowd, followed by shouted opinions as to how little more the boat could take. Several of the locals, J.C. Gram and a fellow named Quinn, manned a small rowboat and headed out into the lake. Their rescue effort got only a few yards out before the lake spit them back onto the sandy beach. Another group, by the names of Keating, Brown and McCoy, remanned the boat and again headed out toward the *Grover*. They were cast back onto the beach as quickly as the first group. It was then decided that the only chance was to fetch the lifesavers from Ottawa Point. Charlie Dease, one of the local folks, leaped onto a swift horse and galloped off toward Tawas, and the lifesaving station. Behind him three teams of horses, two belonging to George Loud and one belonging to Mr. McCann, were sent toward Tawas. These teams were to be used in helping the surfmen pull their equipment up to Au Sable. The road between Au Sable and the Ottawa Point Station was little more than a trail at that time, and was, in fact, actually called "the Sand Trail." For that reason, a lot of power would be needed to get the lifesavers to the wreck. While two of the horse teams headed to the lifesaving station, one team would wait at what was referred to as "the half way house" to relieve the other teams as needed. With the plan of rescue firmly in place, everything was in motion by noon. But everyone knew too well that it would be many hours before the storm warriors arrived, and some were not content to simply wait.

Sometimes, in the face of a community emergency, the most educated, stable, and intelligent of persons can be drawn into the situation to the point where they cross from being noble to being amazingly inept. The results of such activity are almost always disastrous. Such was the case with John Glennie, J.C. Gram, George Loud, Thomas Wilkin and Frank Fortier—all of whom were respected local businessmen. It was thought that if they could just find a way to get a line out to those poor souls on the *Grover*, perhaps they could save them. Someone recalled having heard that the lifesavers used a small cannon to shoot a projectile out to stranded vessels. Then someone remembered that George Loud had an old condemned cannon on his property, and that just may do the job. As the winds roared and the surf crashed, the small gang of stupidity headed off to obtain the cannon and other elements that could be used in the firing.

Part of the dilemma that allowed these good citizens to be lured into incredible stupidity was an atmosphere of urgency that hid the true circumstances of the *Grover*. The boat, although constantly impacted by breaking waves, was not in any danger of going to pieces. Unlike the - scow-schooner *Abraham Lincoln* eight years earlier, the *Grover* had a hold that was packed with a cargo of stone. Now her hull acted like a crib and stood up solidly against the seas. Had anyone on the beach had experience with shipwrecks, it would have been obvious that the signs of the boat's continuing integrity were clearly present. Her remaining masts and rigging were tight and her hull was firmly settled in the sand and was not pounding or hogging. The only question of urgency was if the crew could hold on in the rigging and atop her deckhouse until help arrived. Persons have been known to hold on in a boat's rigging for more than 24 hours in weather worse than that which now attacked the *Grover*. Although the crowd ashore developed an air of urgency, there was no life-and-death hurry to get to the wreck. But without taking the time to quell the sense of emergency and properly evaluate the entire dilemma, the community leaders hastened into action.

Just what these otherwise rational citizens thought they were going to accomplish by shooting a line over the wreck is highly questionable.

Give Way!

In this excellent photo of a horse-drawn boat-cart, we can see the manner in which the Ottawa Point lifesavers transported their cart to the wreck of the Criss Grover. Those narrow wagon wheels were of little help along the "Sand Trail" between Tawas and Au Sable. Oddly, although this photo of the Grand Marais crew was taken sometime after 1914, as indicated by the words "US Coast Guard" stenciled on the surfboat, it is likely that the boat in the photo is the same class of Beebe surfboat used by the Ottawa Point crew in the 1880 Criss Grover action. (Superior View Photo)

233

Professional lifesavers used a gun and projectile that were designed specifically to carry a line out to a wreck. Additionally, they drilled weekly in not only firing the gun, but in faking the line so that it would unwind while going out and not snap. Also, should the local citizens actually manage to get the line out to the wreck, what then? They had no breeches buoy, and no life car, and certainly no one could hand-over-hand a yawl out to the wreck. Their only result would be that they would now have a rope that was leading out to a shipwreck. The folly of this adventure was lost on the whole crowd as the team of well-meaning amateur lifesavers returned with the 11-pound cannon. Taking a long iron bar and knotting a thick rope around its middle, the make-shift projectile was stuffed into the two-inch bore of the gun preceded by a heavy powder charge. There was no carriage for the gun to be mounted upon, so a log was placed beneath it to elevate the barrel. A second log was hollowed out and placed behind the piece to prevent it from recoiling too far, and another log was placed atop that one. By this time it was two o'clock in the afternoon. John Glennie took charge of lighting off the gun, an act that required three attempts as Gram, Loud, Wilkin and Fortier watched closely. Glennie was the village treasurer and customs collector for the port of Au Sable—until the moment the cannon went off!

At the thundering "boom" of the gun, pieces of unidentified material whizzed past everyone. A massive cloud of white smoke billowed, instantly covering the whole scene, and then was swirled away down the beach by the gale. When the cloud thinned, the cannon was gone—as were the logs and the five amateur lifesavers who were laying flattened on the sand like toy soldiers. The crowd stood for a moment in stunned horror, then with a collective panic rushed toward the downed men. Condemned weapons are exactly that, condemned! For that reason alone, putting a powder charge back into such a piece is pure madness, and the odds that the gun will explode are very high. In this case Loud's gun had indeed exploded, and the results were now apparent. Both Wilkin and Fortier picked themselves up, having only been knocked over by the concussion of the exploding gun. Gram was badly bruised just above his right knee, having been hit by a piece of one of the logs. Likewise, Loud had been hit under his right knee by a piece of one of the logs and was badly cut. Glennie, however did not get off so easily. His right hand was destroyed, and his right leg was shattered by the bursting cannon. For a moment, everyone forgot completely about the shipwreck and went about lending aid to Glennie. He was transported to the home of his sister, Mrs. Keating, where, while under the care of several local doctors, he died at four o'clock that same afternoon.

About 15 minutes after John William Glennie died at the village of Au Sable, Charlie Dease came galloping up to the Ottawa Point Lifesaving

Station shouting "Shipwreck!" Within moments, Keeper Chute had his crew fully mustered, and their equipment ready to go. The surf boat was placed on its cart and the beach equipment was ready to roll. Inside of a quarter of an hour, the teams of horses had arrived and the storm-warriors were on their way toward the wreck of the *Criss Grover*. The winds of the storm were beating through the bare trees, which were still waiting for their spring buds to sprout, and there was a moaning whistle normally heard only in deep winter storms. The trail through the gray forest was littered with fallen trees and stumps. Snow blasted through the branches in a blizzard, and the night's darkness came early. The pace that the lifesavers and their equipment made was no less than a forced march. There was no way to move the rescue equipment along the beach. The breaking surf and narrow beach was completely unpassable. The only route to Au Sable was inland along the sand trail. As they neared the halfway house, the rear axletree of the surf boat cart suddenly broke, and the boat had to be dragged from that point on. Reaching the halfway house, the crew found fresh horses and a change of wheels on the boat cart. As an interesting side note, this same halfway house was, in the 1890s, owned by the parents of the lifesaving Ocha boys. Whether the Ocha's owned the halfway house on this night in 1880 is not recorded.

In all it took just over eight hours for the lifesavers and their companions from Au Sable to reach the area of the shipwreck. Some accounts say that they arrived at exactly midnight, others say that it was 30 minutes later. The Benner House was their first stop. There, the exhausted crew was given food and hot coffee prior to proceeding to the beach. Even at this late hour, it appeared as if the entire population of the village was gathered on the beach to watch the lifesavers. Everyone had heard the legends of what these storm-warriors were able to accomplish, now they would see the action first hand. The official record says that the surf boat was launched at 12:15 on Saturday morning, April 17, 1880. The snow had stopped, but the night was sackcloth-dark and the winds continued to scream insanely. In the entire area, the only illumination was a giant bonfire that had been kept burning on the beach. As the storm-warriors shoved off into the raging surf and inky blackness of night, a single shouted order was heard above the rage of mighty Lake Huron,

"Give wayyyy!" Keeper Chute commanded as his fearless crew of lifesavers took to their oars.

A breaker was split by the bow of the surf boat, and then another, and then the boat was swallowed by the darkness of the night. All that was visible were the incoming graybeards of the rolling surf, and all that could be heard was the roar of the angry lake. On the beach the hundreds of onlookers held their collective breaths as all that could be witnessed was the stormy void of night. The brave surfmen had rowed out into the teeth of the powerful lake without a single moment of hesitation, and whether they would ever return, only Lake Huron knew. Standing by their bonfire the whole town of Au Sable watched and waited.

A little more than 117 years after Freeman Chute and his crew of lifesavers rowed off into that stormy blackness, a stiff wind once again blew across Lake Huron. On the blustery summer morning of August 12, 1997, a United States Coast Guard HH-65 helicopter hovers over the choppy waters of Tawas Bay. Less than 100 feet below a 44-foot Coast Guard motor lifeboat tosses in the waves. Coordinating with the use of VHF marine radio, the modern-day storm-warriors practice the rescue of simulated victims in the grip of Lake Huron. Once every three months, with the same sense of duty as Keeper Chute and his crew of lifesavers, the modern crew of the Tawas Station drills in the art of lifesaving. Numerous times the basket is lowered from the rotorcraft into the lake, and then raised as if plucking a person from the watery danger below. Next, a wetsuited Coast Guard rescue swimmer goes "D.I.W.," or "Diver In Water," and the HH-65 moves in to blow him around in its rotor-wash—"just for practice." Clad in his protective diver's suit, the swimmer can spend long periods in the lake's frigid water and is trained in the skills of pulling benumbed survivors from danger. Surprisingly, the rescue diver is a relatively new position in the Coast Guard, and demands great skill, strength and courage. Not surprising is the fact that the job of a rescue swimmer is one of the most sought after positions in the Coast Guard. There are only about 250 qualified rescue swimmers in the United States. The HH-65 is designed for the job of scrambling off to anyplace where life is in peril, and it can do so at speeds in excess of 160 miles per hour. Like its predecessor the surf boat, the modern 44-foot motor lifeboat is designed to be able to roll over 360 degrees and keep going. The helicopter is based in Detroit and the motor lifeboat, which is simply called "the 44 footer," is from the Tawas Station, which is located on the other side of the point from the original lifesaving station. All of these people and devices are a far cry from the original lifesaving service, but somehow they are still related.

The original building from which Keeper Chute set out on his test of valor still stands, and is owned by the Coast Guard. In visiting it the question comes to mind, if the *Grover* wreck occurred today, how would the modern storm warriors respond? In order to answer that question, the author sent the exact circumstances of the wreck of the *Criss Grover* to the Tawas Point Station, and the present-day storm-warriors used it as a drill to test their response, 118 years after the actual wreck.

A composite report of their modern test would read something like this—

Just after noon, the Tawas Station receives a call by telephone that a 90-foot sailing vessel has gone aground just south of the Au Sable River. Immediately the officer on duty is notified. In Detroit, the Group

Controller is also notified and preparations are made for the launching of the HH-65 rescue helicopter. Additionally, the station coxswain and crew prepare CG44391, the station's 44-foot motor lifeboat, for launching. The weather requires that the crew wear their "dry suits" to protect them from the sting of the ice cold lake. It takes no more than seven minutes for the modern lifesavers to be ready. A general call for assistance is sent out to other vessels in the area who may be able to render assistance, but with the *Grover* in her present position, only the Coast Guard is equipped and trained to reach her.

Launching both of the Tawas Station's motor lifeboats, the storm warriors, under the command of Chief Boatswain's Mate R.E. Smith, do what Keeper Freeman Chute's surfmen could not, they sail out onto the wild lake and head for the wreck by water. At the same time the HH-65 is launched from Detroit. The weather is deplorable for flying, the ceiling being less than 200 feet, and the cloud layer thick and severely turbulent. Such is the weather that often calls the HH-65 to duty, and her crew will fly in spite of the conditions. Even though the HH-65 can autodescend in hover to 50 feet, it is a dangerous procedure under these conditions. For that reason, the HH-65 will fly to the scene and stand by in case the boats can not effect the rescue. Unlike Keeper Chute's crew, the Coast Guard takes only two and one-half hours to reach the scene of the *Grover's* wreck. Once on the scene, two of the Coast Guard crew members strap on heavy weather belts, as the coxswains maneuver the motor lifeboats up close and evaluate the situation to determine the safest approach. It is decided to approach bow-on on the leeward side of the vessel. Ordinarily, a Jacob's Ladder is required to board a vessel of the *Grover's* size, but we will assume that it, like the yawl, has been washed away. For that reason the rescue will have to be performed by the belted Coast Guard crew at the bow of the motor lifeboats. By use of a loud hailer, the coxswain instructs the people in the *Grover's* rigging to come down and prepare to be removed. Maneuvering with the skill of hundreds of hours of practice and drill, the coxswain moves the 44-footer up to the *Grover's* rail as the belted crew readies their lines. One at a time, the shipwrecked crew are removed, as the weather conditions require that each removal be done with a separate approach of the 44-footer. As soon as each survivor is removed, they are treated for hypothermia by means of warm, dry blankets. When all are safe, the motor lifeboats are headed for the Au Sable River and safely placed in the hands of local paramedics. The Coast Guard will then release the HH-65 to return to Detroit. They will also return to the wreck area to evaluate any pollution concerns. When it's all over, they will return to the station, order pizza and discuss the day's work. In the time it took for the word of the *Grover's* wreck to get to Keeper Chute's station in 1880, the crew of that same station in 1998 would have performed the rescue and be back at the station eating pizza.

And what of Keeper Chute and his crew of untried lifesavers, you may ask? What of his final test of valor? What happened after his surf boat and his crew were swallowed into that stormy night? Well, as it turned out, on that storm-raked Saturday morning in April of 1880, the crew of the Ottawa Point Station performed a feat of rescue that is still considered a marvel of efficiency, professionalism, and valor. In the amazing time span of just 15 minutes, they pulled from the beach, rowed through the darkness, found the unlighted shipwreck, removed the entire crew, and then took them safely to the beach!

While the residents of the town of Au Sable waited on the wind-swept beach, the story of the *Criss Grover* continued out in the darkness beyond. Using his mariner's instinct as well as hundreds of hours of practice and drill, Keeper Chute guided the surf boat to the wreck. This in itself was an amazing feat considering that, if the tiller oar had steered the lifeboat off-course by as little as 15 degrees in the darkness, they would have rowed right past the wreck. Much like the modern Coast Guard coxswain, Keeper Chute elected to maneuver up on the leeward side. Once at the rail of the *Grover*, at least two of the lifesavers had to go aboard to help remove the survivors. The seas were sweeping completely over the deck and cascading across the *Grover's* rail like an icy waterfall. Unlike their modern counterparts, the crews of the United States Life Saving Service did not have "dry suits" to protect them from the sting of the ice water, nor did they have heavy weather belts to secure them from being swept away. Chute's crew were clad in oilskins to fend off the cold water, and muscle power alone secured them to the wreck. In the darkness, the seven benumbed survivors were helped into the pitching surf boat, one by one. All were too battered and cold to speak, and some could not walk. As soon as all of the *Grover's* crew were aboard the surf boat, Chute shoved off and headed back toward the flicker of the distant bonfire.

Only a quarter of an hour after the lifesavers had launched to Keeper Chute's command of "Give Way!" a second shout was heard from the lake as the surf boat reappeared from out of the night. Dimly illuminated by the bonfire, the white image of the Ottawa Point Station's surf boat gliding upon the gray beards of the breaking waves came into view—like a ghost riding atop the crests of the seas. Pulling together in perfect coordination, the surfmen rowed as Keeper Chute triumphantly guided the boat with the tiller oar. Huddled aboard the surf boat were the seven shivering crew members of the *Grover*. In moments, the surf boat headed toward the beach as if Lake Huron were surrendering the *Grover's* crew and was now putting them safely ashore. The lifesavers had, indeed, gone out and tamed the angry lake. En masse, nearly the entire population of the village of Au Sable rushed down and helped land the surf boat and its occupants. The unending training, the daily drills, the step-by-step following of the manual, the constant preparedness and Keeper Chute's insistence on being "ever ready"—all had paid off that night in the saving of seven lives from Lake Huron's rage. As if to make matters better yet, the crew of the Ottawa Point Station made it look easy. Word would spread widely of this remarkable feat where Chute's crew of storm-warriors demonstrated the very best of the United States Life Saving Service.

Being helped from the surf boat by the countless hands of the villagers, the *Grover's* master, Captain Jones, lost his strength and collapsed as his feet hit the sand. Likewise, all of the rest of the vessel's crew were in a state of exhaustion and near collapse. In the worst condition of all was Miss McNeil, the boat's cook. She appeared near death and could not even speak. All of the castaways were taken to the bonfire and warmed with hot drinks, then transported to Benner House where they were made comfortable. All but Miss McNeil were quick to recuperate, and she only needed a few days in the care of a doctor to fully recover. The lifesavers remained at Au Sable that night and, although it was not recorded, they probably stayed at Benner House as well. The storm let up at four o'clock that morning, and at first light the Tawas Point storm-warriors set out on their victorious march back to their station. Whatever doubters and critics that must have existed in the neighborhood were well-silenced by the remarkably professional job the lifesavers had accomplished. It is certain that any doubts that the surfmen had about themselves had now also been erased. Oddly, there had been only one fatality involved in the wreck of the *Grover,* and that was the death of John Glennie—which occurred on dry land. Officially, his death did not occur within the activities of the United States Life Saving Service, and thus did not reflect in any way on Keeper Chute or his crew. The narrative report of the rescue within the official United States Life Saving Service record wrongly states that there were 10 crew members aboard the *Grover*. That same report, in its tabulation section, states the number correctly as 7, as do all of the other published accounts written during the time of the wreck.

Salvage was the next step for the *Criss Grover* herself. The boat, although declared a total wreck, was unloaded, raised, and repaired. She soon returned to service on the Great Lakes sailing for many productive seasons. The boat went on to Lake Superior, often shuttling dynamite to the mining camps, a chore that no other boats would take. On October 24, 1899, the *Grover* was cast onto the shoals near Split Rock, Minnesota, by a late season storm. This time she did not survive, and was broken to pieces on the rocks.

Keeper Chute retired from the United States Life Saving Service exactly four months after the *Grover* rescue. Upon leaving the service he returned to captaining tugs on the Saginaw River. Officially, he left his position as keeper of the Ottawa Point Station on August 15, 1880 for "health" reasons. Keeper George Plough took command of the station upon the departure of Chute. Later Captain Chute published his reason for leaving as being "on account of failing health brought on by anxious watchfulness and care for the safety of those exposed to danger in stormy weather on the coast over which he had charge."

Although the modern members of the Coast Guard at Tawas keep an unending watch in the same tradition as the lifesavers of the past, until this story, they had no idea who Keeper Freeman Chute was. The original 1876 lifesaving station still stands in its original location on Tawas Point, but it has had some additions and, for the most part it has been relegated to obscurity. Being the fifth of the first five stations opened on Lake Huron, the Ottawa Point Station was activated October 6, 1876. Of those original stations, only three remain. Currently, the original Ottawa Point Station is used as a part of a group of crew and family dwellings, located in "Coastguardsville" on Tawas Point.

In 1915, the Life Saving Service was merged with the Revenue Cutter Service and thereby became the United States Coast Guard. Much of the old Life Saving Service has been long-forgotten in the passing of time. Gone are the Lyle guns, powder charges, beach carts, surf boats, breeches buoys, beach patrols, Coston signals, faking boxes and lookout towers. These have been replaced by helicopters, self-righting powerboats, diving suits, high-powered radios, and search and rescue jet aircraft. Although the command to action of "Give Way!" has been replaced by proper radio verbiage, the valor is still being kept—every time the anger of the lakes lashes out at souls who venture upon them. The Coast Guard's motto, "Semper Paratus," is translated as "Always Ready," and so they drill and practice and watch the lake. In the sprit of Keeper Chute and all of the other lifesavers, the storm-warriors of today continue to put their lives on the line and charge into often frigid waters to the rescue. Yet, even in modern times, there is an important reason to remember Keeper Chute and his Ottawa Point crew of surfmen. The toil of anxious watchfulness, and care for the safety of those exposed to danger in stormy weather on the coast over which they have charge, may seem pointless at times. But the Great Lakes will forever be vengeful toward those who sail upon them, and so—despite budgets, politics, critics, and tedium—the valor must always be kept.

The next stormy test for the keepers of valor may be developing as you read this book. Perhaps one stormy day when the Tawas Coast Guard crew dashes off to launch their 44-footer, a distant voice will be heard above the howling wind and roaring waves, as if shouting a command across time to a thousand rescues and acts of valor. "Give Wayyyyy!" will come the ghostly command as the storm-warriors prepare to do battle once more against the mighty lake. The tools of the trade may be different, but the anxious watchfulness and care for the safety of those exposed to danger in stormy weather remains the same.

ABOUT THE AUTHOR

Author W. Wes Oleszewski was born and raised in mid-Michigan and spent most of his life with an eye turned toward the Great Lakes. In the past 12 years he has authored 11 books on the subject of Great Lakes maritime history and lighthouses.

Noted for his meticulous research, Oleszewski has a knack for weeding out the greatest of details from the most obscure events and then weaving those facts into the historical narratives which are his stories. His tales of actual events are real enough to thrill any reader while every story is technically correct and highly educational. Oleszewski feels that the only way to teach history in this age of computer and video games is through "narrative." Along the researcher's

W. Wes Oleszewski
Great Lakes Maritime Author
and Research Historian

path, this author has also become acquainted, sometimes first-hand, with the multitude of ghosts and ghost stories that haunt the history of the lakes. The final product of his efforts are captivating books that can be comfortably read and enjoyed by everyone from the eldest grandmother to the grade-school kid and future historian.

Born on the east side of Saginaw, Michigan in 1957, Wes Oleszewski attended public school in that city through grade nine, when his family moved to the town of Freeland, Michigan. In 1976 he graduated from Freeland High School and a year later entered the Embry-Riddle Aeronautical University in Daytona Beach, Florida. Working his way through college by way of his own earned income alone, Oleszewski graduated in 1988 with a commercial pilot's certificate, "multi-engine and instrument airplane" ratings as well as a B.S. Degree in Aeronautical Science. Along with his writing, he has pursued a career as a professional pilot. He holds an A.T.P. certificate and to date has logged more than 5,000 hours of flight time most of which is in airline category and jet aircraft. Samples of his writing can be found on his website at www.lighthouses-lakeboats.com.

BIBLIOGRAPHICAL SOURCES

COURAGE AND REVENGE
Sources:

United States Life-saving Service Annual Report, 1878, 1879, 1880, 1881, 1896

Saginaw Daily Courier, November 10, 14, 1877

Wreck Ashore, Stonehouse

A Pictorial History of the Great Lakes, Hatcher

Shipwreck!, Swayze

Great Lakes Lighthouses, Roberts and Jones

Ships and Men of the Great Lakes, Boyer

Great Lakes Shipwrecks and Survivals, Ratigan

Coast Guard Register, 1935-1938

Personal overflight of Burnt Cabin Shoal, author, 1988

Alcona-the Lake Pioneers, Gauthier

BUT, EDITH MORGAN WAS THE FIRST
Sources:

USLSS Annual Report, 1876, 1877, 1878, 1880

Wreck Ashore, Stonehouse

Wreck & Rescue, Vol.1 No.4, Spring 1997, *African Americans in the U.S. Life-Saving Service*, Peterson

Port Huron Daily Times, April 15, 1883

E-mail from Dave Swayze, August 12, 1999

E-mail from Fred Stonehouse, August 24, 1999

List of Lights of the United States, 1880, 1879

Great American Lighthouses, Holland

ARE WE THERE YET?
Sources:

Phone conversation with Kristi Merren, and Mary McWilliams, Point Iroquois Lighthouse, August 24, 1999

Personal interview with Kay and Joe VanDosen, caretakers Point Iroquois Lighthouse, July 22, 1999

Author's visit to Point Iroquois Lighthouse, July 22, 29, 1999

Author's visit to Whitefish Point, July 22, 29, 1999

List of the Lights of the United States, 1857

List of the Lights of the United States, 1880

GUESTS FROM THE STORM
Sources:

Erie Dispatch-Herald, October 5, 6, 8, 13, 1932

Buffalo Times, October 6, 1932

Lorain Journal, October 6, 7, 1932

Bay City Times, October 5, 6, 7, 1932

The 100 Best Great Lakes Shipwrecks, Vol. I & II, Kohl

Seaway, LesStrang

Lake Carriers, LesStrang

Marine Engineering, August, 1900

Namesakes 1930-1955, Greenwood

Author's visit to the port of Erie, PA, July 21, 1999

Phone conversation with Paul Ehorn, May 21, 1997

A SCIENTIFIC PERSON RESIDING AT MILWAUKEE SAYS...
Sources:

Bay City Tribune, September 7, 8, 9, 10, 11, 12, 13, 15, 19, 23, 25 28, 1883

Bay City Evening-Press, September 8, 1883

Port Huron Daily Times, September 25, 1883

Cleveland Herald, September 18, 1883

Huron Times, September 20, 1883

United States Life-Saving Service Annual Report, 1884

List of Merchant Sailing Vessels of the United States, provided on request by the Institute for Great Lakes Research.

DON M. DICKINSON's Master Sheet, provided on request by the Institute for Great Lakes Research.

Sounds of Disaster, Oleszewski

Namesakes 1900-1910, Greenwood

Shipwrecks of the Straits of Mackinac, Feltner

Dive Ontario Two!, Kohl

Shipwreck Tales: The St. Clair River (to 1900), Kohl

Shipwreck!, Swayze

WHAT BERT HUBBARD FOUND ON THE WAY TO SCHOOL
Sources:

United States Life-Saving Service Annual Report, 1881, 1887, 1896

The Bay of Dead Ships, Reich, and transcripts of *Oswego Daily Palladium* contained in this book.

Oswego Daily Palladium, December 2, 3, 4, 6, 7, 8, 9, 1886

Wreck Ashore, Stonehouse

Port Huron Daily Times, October 22, 1886

The Huron Signal, November 5, 1886

Shipwreck Data Base, Dave Swayze

List of the Lights of the United States, 1880

A BEACH HE'D RATHER FORGET
Sources:

South Haven Sentinel, February 19, 1887; October 15, 22, 1887

South Haven Messenger, October 7, 14, 21, 28, 1887; November 26, 1887

South Haven Daily Tribune, October 9, 1914

United States Life Saving Service Annual Report, 1887, 1888

Shipwreck!, Swayze

Wreck Ashore, Stonehouse

A Pictorial History of the Great Lakes, Hatcher

Lake Michigan, Quaife

Logbook from the South Haven Lighthouse, October 2, 3, 4, 1887

Undated manuscript from the files of the South Haven Maritime Museum-author unknown

OUTSIDE OF THE LEXINGTON WINDOW
Sources:

Bay City Daily Tribune, October 21, 23, 24, 1890

Bay City Times, October 21, 23, 1890

Port Huron Times Herald, April 25, 1998

Marine Review, November 1890

History of the Great Lakes, Mansfield/Beers

United States Life Saving Service Annual Report, 1892, 1893, 1894

Meeting with members of the Great Lakes Shipwreck Exploration Group, August 2, 1997

Phone conversation with Jim and Pat Satyr, August 3, 1997

Vessels Built on the Saginaw, Roberts, Swayze, Comtois

Namesakes 1910-1919, Greenwood

Author's visit to Lexington, August 1, 1999

List of the Lights of the United States, 1880

MARTHA HART'S FIRST COMMAND
Sources:

Oswego Palladium, July 5, 10, 12, 1877

E-mail correspondence with Research Historian Richard Palmer, January 7, 23, 1998

Early American Steamers, Vol. 6, Heyl

Lake Ontario

Annual Report of the Operations of the Lighthouse Board, 1896

List of the Lights of the United States, 1880

IF FOUND, PLEASE RETURN
Sources:

Saginaw Courier, May 6, 11, 14, 1887; October 15, 16, 18, 19, 20, 21, 23, 25, 26, 27, 28, 29, 1887; November 6, 13, 15, 1887; August 9, 1888

Saginaw Evening News, October 4, 5, 6, 12, 13, 14, 15, 17, 25, 26, 27, 28, 1887

Bay City Tribune, August 17, 1887; November 19, 20, 21, 22, 23, 27, 28, 29, 30, 1887; November 1, 1887

Port Huron Daily Times, November 24, 25, 26, 27, 28, 29, 31, 1887; November 4, 12, 1887

Detroit Free Press, May 24, 1856; October 25, 26, 27, 29, 1887; November 5, 1887; June 1, 1888

Huron Signal, (Goderich, Ontario) October 28 1887; November 4,1887

Saginaw & East Saginaw Directory, 1885, 1886, 1887, 1888, 1889, 1933, 1934, 1936, 1939, 1940

E-mail from Dave Swayze, Great Lakes Historian and Author

Correspondence with R.J. Thompson, Goderich Branch Library, April 10, 1997

Shipwreck!, Swayze

USLSS Annual Report, 1888, 1887

Survey map of the city of Saginaw, 1877-1916

Shipwreck data base, collected by Dave Swayze

Saginaw's Changeable Past, Kilar

Sounds of Disaster, Oleszewski

Author's visit to 608 South Water Street, Saginaw Michigan, August 7, 1997; July 26, 1999

INMAN'S DREAM
Sources:

Freshwater Whales, Wright

Steamboats & Sailors of the Great Lakes, Thompson

Queen of the Lakes, Thompson

The Great Lakes Car Ferries, Hilton

The Best of Ships Along The Seaway, Gillham

Great Lakes Shipwrecks & Survivals, Ratigan

Marine Engineering, June, 1897

Port Huron Daily Times, May 21, 1883

Sidelights, August 1957, "The History of Pittsburgh Steamship"

Inland Seas, Winter 1993, "Mr. Mather Buys A Boat or Two", Jones

Nor'Easter, September-October 1995; November-December 1995; "The Life and Times of B.B. Inman", Miller

Correspondence with C. Patrick Labadie, Director, Canal Park Museum, Duluth October 27, 1997

Namesakes II, Greenwood

A LEAK, LARGER THAN ORDINARY, WAS NOTICED
Sources:
Oswego Palladium Times, September 28, 29, 30, 1925; October 1, 3, 1925; August 15, 1931

E-mail from Richard Palmer, December 3, 1997

Inland Seas, Summer 1992, "Gus Hinckley- Lake Ontario Mariner", Palmer

Inland Seas, Winter 1992, "Shipbuilding At Chaumont Bay, New York", Palmer

List of Merchant Vessels of the United States, 1915

Namesakes 1900-1909, Greenwood

Namesakes 1910-1919, Greenwood

Dive Ontario Two!, Kohl

446,500 REVOLUTIONS
Sources:
Port Huron Daily Times, May 21, 22, 23, 24, 26, 1883

Annual Report of the Activities of the Lighthouse Board, 1896

Lake Huron, Landon

Great Lakes Lighthouses, Roberts and Jones

The Northern Lights, Hyde

E-mail from Dave Swayze, August 11, 1998

Author's visit to the Fort Gratiot lighthouse, August 1, 1999

VOICES FROM THE NIGHT
Sources:
Sandusky Daily Register, July 19, 20, 21, 22, 23

Correspondence with Mark McClain, October 17, 1995

Annual Report of the Activities of the Lighthouse Board, 1896

E-mail from Dave Swayze September 3, 1999

The Great Lakes Car Ferries, Hilton

The 100 Best Great Lakes Shipwrecks, Vol. I & II, Kohl

History of the Great Lakes, Mansfield/Beers

Dive Ontario Two!, Kohl

Annual Report of the United States Life Saving Service, 1884, 1885, 1886

THE GALES THAT STOLE CHRISTMAS
Sources:

Queen of the Lakes, Thompson

Freshwater Whales, Wright

The Telescope, November/December 1980 "Looking Fore and Aft", Hoek

The Telescope, September/October 1987 "Great Lakes & Seaway News" section.

The Telescope, March/April 1995 "Wreck, Ice Paralyze Shipping-Huge Loss Expected in Tie-ups", (reprinted from the April 21, 1956 *Detroit Free Press* article) Haseltine

Phone conversation with Phil Simpson September 22, 1996

Lake Carriers, LesStrang

Phone Conversation with Andy LaBorde, May 19, 1997

A CLOSER LOOK WILL FIND...
Sources:

Iosco County Gazette, October 3, 1872

Bay City Daily Journal, October 1, 2, 3, 4, 5, 6, 8, 1872

Port Huron Daily Times, September 30, 1872; October 1, 2, 3, 4, 7, 1872; November 12, 1872

Detroit Free Press, April 28, 1856; September 10, 1857; May 19, 1871; September 28, 29, 1872; October 1, 2, 4, 5, 1872

Abstract of Oscoda area shipwrecks compiled by Patricia Sherman, Oscoda MI

Abstract of reports of shipwrecks at or near light stations, National Archives.

Personal visit to Tawas Point, August 8, 1996; August 15, 1997

Around the Bay, Thornton

Shipwreck!, Swayze

Lake Huron, Landon

American Presidents, Holmes

Correspondence with Dave Swayze, August 4, 1997

The Dave Swayze shipwreck data base

Phone conversation with C. Patrick Labadie, Director, Canal Park Museum, Duluth, August 20, 1997

Author's visit to, and digging up of, the rudder of the *Abraham Lincoln*, August 16, 1997

History of the Huron Shore, Pub. H.R. Page & Co., 1883

Annual Report of the Operations of the Lighthouse Board, 1872

Fact sheet on schooner. *Abraham Lincoln* compiled by C. Patrick Labadie, Director, Canal Park Museum, Duluth, August 25, 1997

Letter from C. Patrick Labadie, Director, Canal Park Museum, Duluth, September 26, 1997

Scow Schooners of San Francisco Bay, Olmsted

Grolier's Encyclopedia

Hutchinson Electronic Encyclopedia

GIVE WAY!
Sources:

History of Bay County, Pub. H.R. Page & Co., 1883

History of the Lake Huron Shore, Pub. H.R. Page & Co., 1883

Bay City Evening Press, April 13, 14, 15, 16, 17, 19, 20, 21, 22, 23, 1880

Iosco County Gazette, April 16, 1880

United States Life Saving Service Annual Report, 1876, 1877, 1878, 1879,1880, 1881

Wreck Ashore, Stonehouse

Around the Bay, Thornton

Lake Superior Shipwrecks, Wolff

Fresh Water Whales, Wright

Phone conversation with Coast Guardsman Oliser Ward, Tawas Station, September 10, 1997

Abstract of Oscoda area shipwrecks compiled by Patricia Sherman, Oscoda, MI

The Dave Swayze shipwreck data base

E-mail correspondence with Fred Stonehouse, Author/Historian, October 2, 1997

Synopsis of action and response to the circumstances of the wreck of the *Criss Grover* as would be conducted by the United States Coast Guard Tawas Station, submitted by that station's crew to the author.

Other Wes Oleszewski titles by Avery Color Studios, Inc.

- *Great Lakes Ghost Stories*
  Haunted Tales Past & Present
- *True Tales of Ghosts & Gales,*
  Mysterious Great Lakes Shipwrecks
- *Stormy Disasters,*
  Great Lakes Shipwrecks
- *Ice Water Museum*
  Forgotten Great Lakes Shipwrecks
- *Ghost Ships, Gales & Forgotten Tales*
  True Adventures On The Great Lakes
- *Mysteries and Histories,*
  Shipwrecks of the Great Lakes
- *Great Lakes Lighthouses,*
  American & Canadian
- *Lighthouse Adventures*
  Heroes, Haunts & Havoc On The Great Lakes

Avery Color Studios, Inc. has a full line of Great Lakes oriented books, puzzles, cookbooks, shipwreck and lighthouse maps, lighthouse posters and Fresnel lens model.

For a free full-color catalog, call **1-800-722-9925**

Avery Color Studios, Inc. products are
available at gift shops and bookstores
throughout the Great Lakes region.